D1104674

BOBCAT

Kevin Hansen

B O B C A T *Master of Survival*

OXFORD
UNIVERSITY PRESS

2007

OXFORD
UNIVERSITY PRESS

Oxford University Press, Inc., publishes works that further
Oxford University's objective of excellence
in research, scholarship, and education.

Oxford   New York
Auckland   Cape Town   Dar es Salaam   Hong Kong   Karachi
Kuala Lumpur   Madrid   Melbourne   Mexico City   Nairobi
New Delhi   Shanghai   Taipei   Toronto

With offices in
Argentina   Austria   Brazil   Chile   Czech Republic   France   Greece
Guatemala   Hungary   Italy   Japan   Poland   Portugal   Singapore
South Korea   Switzerland   Thailand   Turkey   Ukraine   Vietnam

Published by Oxford University Press, Inc.
198 Madison Avenue, New York, New York 10016

www.oup.com

Oxford is a registered trademark of Oxford University Press.

Library of Congress Cataloging-in-Publication Data

Hansen, Kevin.
Bobcat : master of survival / Kevin Hansen.
p. cm.
Includes bibliographical references and index.
ISBN-13 978-0-19-518303-0
ISBN 0-19-518303-7
1. Bobcat   2. Wildlife conservation.   I. Title.
QL737.C23H3546 2006
599.75'36—dc22

2006000071

9 8 7 6 5 4 3 2 1

Printed in the United States of America
on acid-free paper

For Bertle Daniel Hansen, Jr.

1922–2005

I should have written faster.

Foreword

The fall of 1953, the year I acquired a driver's license, I spent most weekends hunting desert rabbits and quail north of Cave Creek, Arizona. Where every two-track left the main Bartlett Dam road I found stacks of skinned fox, coyote, and bobcat carcasses. Some contained the bodies of 15 or 20 animals. These gruesome cairns were constructed by federal trappers to show the public how well they were doing their work. My upbringing was rather uninformed and neutral regarding predator control, and I at times even fantasized about becoming a trapper. Being paid to hunt and trap seemed rather an idyllic life. Nonetheless, I remember feeling, even then, that something wasn't quite right about such indiscriminate killing of these small predators. I also remember being surprised at the number of bobcat carcasses in the piles. In all of my days afield, I never saw a bobcat; I was not yet tuned into their tracks and sign. I had assumed the cats were relatively scarce.

Only after completing college and becoming a wildlife biologist for the Arizona Game and Fish Department did I learn that bobcats were relatively abundant, if somewhat invisible, and that they could be trapped with ease. Even so, once the federal trappers eased off on small predators during the environmental movement of the 1970s, we, as wildlife managers, ceased to worry much about the species. But by the end of the 1970s, fur values had increased to the point that commercial trappers were taking large numbers of foxes, coyotes, and especially bobcats. Prime bobcat pelts were bringing $300 or more, and trapping became a viable occupation for a few years. By this time, federal and international regulations were forcing the state wildlife agencies to monitor bobcat harvests more closely. This need for knowledge led to several field studies of the species, which began to provide new perspectives. Where once the only repository of knowledge on the cat had been trappers, and that mainly limited to methods of catch, a tremendous volume of information began to accumulate. Trapped bobcats no longer necessarily died at the trap site. Instead, they were fitted with radio collars and released to eat, move, reproduce, and provide hundreds of data points for curious biologists. The trap site was no longer the end point of understanding; it became the point where information began to accrue.

As time passed, fur values declined, and trappers became rare for a while in the Southwest. As Arizona became urbanized, citizens passed a ballot initiative that banned use of leghold traps on public lands. Such increased restrictions on harvest of bobcats may well have helped to once again stimulate fur prices. Whatever the cause, as I write this piece, bobcat furs are once again valuable, and trappers are increasingly active.

Just two weeks ago, during my evening walk, my two-year-old boxer let out a yelp. From a distance, I could see something coiled around her right front paw, and my first thought was rattlesnake. I was actually relieved to find that the coiled object was the chain attached to a small leghold trap clamped onto the dog's foot. Having run hounds during the peak of the trapping surge of the 1970s, I had been through this many times. I threw my jacket over her head, sat on her shoulders, and squeezed the trap until it eased off enough for her to extract her foot. She suffered no damage. Nonetheless, I experienced an adrenalin rush and was irked that anyone would trap so close to town. Had this happened to someone inexperienced with traps, the dog and possibly the owner might have suffered more serious damage. Even the gentlest of pets may bite their owners when confused and hurting from a trap. In the heat of such an emotional event, major confrontations with trappers can occur.

Such events, along with continued urbanization of the West and the increased presence of a recreating public unacquainted with trapping, are among the reasons that trapping has fallen into ill repute. As a youth, I could indulge in a bit of hero worship for the independent Mountain Man who lived off the land, and the modern trapper seemed an extension of those wild survivalists. As a professional biologist, I accepted the fact that commercial trapping was a use of the wildlife resource that helped justify our efforts to sustain the species and, more importantly, to protect its habitat. I even trapped a bit myself to better understand what it entailed, but I was soft-hearted and came to sympathize with the animals, waiting unknowingly for death. I definitely understand the feelings of those who seek to ban trapping. Even so, I did not support the initiative that banned trapping in Arizona, and I recently refused to sign a petition that could create a similar initiative in New Mexico, where I now reside. Whatever feelings I may have for the animal, for me to support such a measure would be hypocritical, considering my past. Also, I believe strongly that the greatest threat to all forms of native wildlife in the western United States lies in the loss of habitat that results from commercial land development. To me, excluding any stakeholder group that values wildlife, including trappers, reduces the larger political force available to oppose subdivisions. To put it bluntly, I may not be fond of trapping, but I have a seething hatred for land development and the American consumerist mentality that funds it. We can't afford to disenfranchise anyone who values wildlife, whatever their reason.

So I suffer mixed feelings about bobcats and their management. As with other wild carnivores, the issues involving the species are complex. As our human population increases and spreads over wildlands, the issues multiply and become more complicated. More citizens become concerned and curious but find reliable information difficult to locate. Too often it exists only in technical journals, written in biologists' jargon. A sound synthesis of old and new knowledge, aimed at a general audience, is badly needed. Thus Kevin Hansen's book is especially timely.

Kevin is well suited to write such a book. Kevin grew up in a family of hunters, although he never quite took to the sport himself. He became acquainted with the complexities and uncertainties of carnivore management while writing his earlier book, *Cougar: The American Lion*. He has worked throughout the United States, in many of the habitats where bobcats reside. He has also worked for many of the federal and state land management agencies that are responsible for bobcat habitat. So, while Kevin writes as a critic of bobcat management in the United States, he is not a basher of agencies. He understands well the complexities of politics surrounding management of carnivores. He has dealt with the many publics that consider themselves stakeholders in bobcat management—conservationists, agriculturists, trappers, hunters, naturalists. He has strong feelings about the species but is able to lay such feelings aside in order to objectively report bobcat biology and management.

In compiling this book, Kevin has traveled much of the United States. He has been afield by himself, as well as with researchers studying bobcats. He has corresponded extensively with biologists, and he has immersed himself in the literature. Writing the book has not been a quick and easy process. It has been ten years in the writing, while Kevin has kept himself fed working at various state and federal jobs. Writing over such a long period carries its own special problems, not least which is the need to constantly update the manuscript as new research and new management strategies appear.

At a time when pumas, wolves, and grizzlies monopolize the limelight, and the jaguar has hogged attention along the Mexican border, the bobcat seems to have slipped from view. Perhaps that is its nature. However, I for one am over-joyed that Kevin has had the fortitude to stay with the book. I hope it is widely read and serves to dispel many of the misunderstandings about our most abundant and perhaps most underrated American felid.

Harley G. Shaw
Hillsboro, New Mexico
Author of *Soul Among Lions,*
Mountain Lion Field Guide, and
Stalking the Big Bird

Acknowledgments

Researching and writing *Bobcat: Master of Survival* was a ten-year odyssey. Fortunately, there were many along the way who helped. Melanie Roberts and the Summerlee Foundation provided the initial grant that made writing the book possible. I shall be forever grateful for your trust, faith, and infinite patience. The remarkably dedicated women of Wildlife Damage Review (Clarke Abbey, Marian Baker Gierlach, Lisa Peacock, Julie St. John, Nancy Zierenberg) asked me to write the book in the first place. A special thank you to Nancy Zierenberg for tracking down requested information and for her gentle prodding. May WDR rise again.

Susan Morse showed me around bobcat heaven-on-earth, let me peruse her excellent library, regaled me with wonderful bobcat stories, patiently answered endless questions, and read the manuscript. You were a great host in Vermont and are a good friend. Seth Riley let me tag along in the field, and introduced me to bobcat #12 outside Bolinas, California. He was always generous with his knowledge of these remarkable felids. Clayton Apps answered all my questions about bobcats in British Columbia and reviewed portions of the manuscript. Dawn Simas introduced me to Billy the bobcat and enlightened me about the horrors of the illegal trade in wildlife parts. Kerry Murphy of Yellowstone National Park took time to offer insightful comments on the manuscript and consistent encouragement. Shura Bugreeff, DVM, tracked down many hard-to-find physiology and anatomy articles and offered her unflagging support. Lisa Haynes was always willing to share her enthusiasm for *Lynx rufus* and help me locate technical resources.

Karen Cebra turned me loose in the excellent mammal collection at the California Academy of Sciences in San Francisco. Serge Lariviere was kind enough to provide an early copy of his monograph on *Lynx rufus* and to answer many questions. Tom Gallagher took the time to show me the bobcat through a professional photographer's eyes during a memorable hike in Tennessee Valley. Tom Skeele of the Predator Project provided many requested documents. John Perrine and Bill Snape of Defenders of Wildlife provided information on the bobcat legal battles. Steve Torres at the California Department of Fish and Game was generous with his time and literature resources. Steve Pavlik shared his knowledge of the bobcat in Navajo culture and mythology. Bill Clay and Rick Wadleigh of USDA Wildlife Services were always helpful in providing requested information and answering questions. David Hamilton of the Missouri Department of Conservation, Greg Linscombe of the Louisiana Department of Wildlife and Fisheries, and the helpful folks at the International Association of Fish and Wildlife Agencies (IAFWA) provided many of the bobcat harvest statistics.

George Schaller at the Wildlife Conservation Society, Mel Sunquist at the University of Florida, Clayton Nielsen at Southern Illinois University, and Gary Koehler and Rich Beausoleil with the Washington Department of Fish and Wildlife were kind enough to read the manuscript and offer their insights and helpful suggestions. Drs. Sunquist, Nielsen, and Koehler, as well as Eric Anderson at the University of Wisconsin and Robert Rolley with the Wisconsin Department of Natural Resources, referred me to additional information sources and patiently fielded my frequent e-mail questions regarding their field research on bobcats.

My heartfelt gratitude goes to the reference staffs of Shields Library at the University of California at Davis, Sacramento State University Library, California State Library, and the Main Library in Sacramento, the Burton Barr Central Library in Phoenix, the Daniel E. Noble Science and Engineering Library at Arizona State University, and the Science-Engineering Library at the University of Arizona. A special thank you to Linda Eade, librarian at the Yosemite National Park Research Library, for providing refuge and a good ear.

I am indebted to the many officials at federal, state, and provincial wildlife agencies throughout the United States and Canada who returned telephone calls, answered questions, and filled many requests for facts and figures. A special thank you goes to the staff at the U.S. Fish and Wildlife Service's Office of Management Authority, who were courteous, prompt, and thorough in responding to my requests for bobcat pelt and Canada lynx export data. You folks never get the credit you deserve for the important work you do.

My thanks to Ken and Pat McLatchey in Sacramento, for providing endless encouragement, great meals, and a quiet place to write. (Yes Ken, the book really is done.) To Jan Elliott for her patience, forbearance, excellent listening skills, friendship, and for giving me a quiet sanctuary in which to write. Jeff Trembly prodded, pushed, and prodded some more, but always gently. Thank you. Thanks to Steve and Marilee Flannery, my good friends in Fair Oaks, for opening their new home to me, feeding me, nursing me when I was sick, lending a good ear, and for providing a spare room in which to finish this book. My family was a source of constant support and encouragement. My love and gratitude to Danny, Susan, Lee, Pamela, Christine, and Bill.

Thanks to Gary Ashcavai for my first computer and for providing the preliminary maps and figures for the book. Larry Scott of Kestrel Graphic Design stepped in at the last moment to rescue the graphics. Jim McCain generously donated the illustrations found at the beginning of each chapter. I'm deeply grateful to these three talented gentlemen for augmenting my text with beautiful art.

Romey Keys was always there to remind me how important books are, and to listen. Greg Potter provided a nonbiologist's comments on the manuscript. Peter Hay and Lara Schmit guided me through the bewildering maze of book publishing. Gary Emery kept me focused (most of the time) and kept asking what I wanted. Steve Follett supplied my second computer, steadfast friendship, support, counsel, and infinite patience in answering and/or fixing my myriad computer questions and problems. (You were right Steve, writing is hard.) Walter Welsch pushed me gently but steadily down the final straightaway to completion, constantly chanting the mantra "F-B-B."

Dr. Christine Hass lent her discerning eye and consummate editorial skill to reviewing the manuscript. She patiently explained endless ecological concepts to me, offered frequent critical observations on both text and graphics, and generally tolerated my grousing and whining. As her final contribution, she provided some of the excellent photographs.

Dr. Dave Maehr took time out of his busy research and teaching schedule at the University of Kentucky to perform a thorough and insightful technical review of the final manuscript. Thank you for making me look so good.

Harley Shaw, my mentor and friend, encouraged, cajoled, counseled, critiqued, consoled, commented, listened, admonished, begged, threatened, pleaded, prodded, pushed, proofread, provided sources, listened some more, nudged, suggested, recommended, explained, kicked my butt, reviewed, edited, supported, questioned, made me think, urged, advised, and consistently told me to finish the book. Then he agreed to write the foreword. My appreciation and gratitude are boundless.

Finally, my thanks to those amazing bobcats; may they endure.

Contents

BOBCAT

Introduction

Early one morning, on the southern coast of Everglades National Park, Ranger Jan Kirwan backed her Boston Whaler away from the dock and swung the bow toward the marina access canal. I busied myself in the stern sorting water quality test equipment. Over the next four hours, we would be collecting and testing water samples taken from sites throughout the southern end of Everglades National Park. The half light of dawn hung over the Flamingo Marina. I could just make out the mangrove trees behind the maintenance shops and gas pumps as they receded behind us. It was not until we rounded the small peninsula that marked the entrance to the larger Buttonwood Canal that I saw the bobcat sitting onshore.

Pleased with this rare sighting, Jan idled down the engine so we could get a better look. Our appearance earned us an annoyed glance from the feline, nothing more. Its attention was focused beyond us. This was puzzling, because there was nothing behind us but water. Glancing over my shoulder I was greeted by a spectacular sunrise over Florida Bay. Orange fire framed a small mangrove island in the distance, festooned with herons and egrets. These restless birds would soon leave the safety of their rookery and launch themselves toward their daytime feeding areas in the Everglades. But, for now, the drama on the horizon seemed to suspend all movement.

Back onshore, the bobcat's gaze was unchanged. As we entered the main channel of the canal, our line of sight brought us directly behind the

*bobcat. The pointed ears and distinctive cheek ruffs were perfectly framed
by breathtaking light across the shimmering water. The bobcat wasn't
looking at the birds; it was watching the sunrise.*

■

The story of the bobcat is a generally positive one. Of the 38 species of cats recognized around the world, 16 are in danger of extinction and another 7 have at least one subspecies facing a similar fate (Sunquist 1991). Most wild felines have had their historic ranges substantially reduced due to conflict with humans. Not bobcats. Bobcats retain most of their original range, which extends from southern Canada to central Mexico and from California to Maine. They roam the dense coniferous forests of the Pacific Northwest, the blistering deserts of the Southwest, the cold Northern Forest of New England, and the subtropical wetlands of Florida's Everglades. They eat an impressive assortment of rabbits, rodents, birds, deer, and domestic animals. Most importantly, they live close to humans—and survive. Why bobcats are thriving, when so many other wild felines are in trouble, is the subject of this book.

The bobcat dwells in shadows. Such is the nature of a predator that depends on surprise to ambush and kill its prey. The bobcat also dwells in the shadow of its larger and more majestic cousins, the mountain lion, Bengal tiger, African lion, jaguar, and spotted leopard. Each is more familiar to the public, having been served up in frequent and generous portions via the Disney Corporation, the Discovery Channel, and *National Geographic.* The diminutive bobcat lacks the prestige necessary for its own television special. Perhaps it needs a better publicist. Lastly, the bobcat dwells in the shadow of our ignorance. This is surprising, because it is perhaps the most thoroughly studied wild felid in the world. Having been subjected to the best science and technology that research biologists could throw at it, the bobcat still slips our grasp. We know bobcats are the most widely distributed native feline in North America; we know they are territorial carnivores that coexist with each other through a sophisticated matrix of adjacent and overlapping home ranges; we know they are efficient predators capable of capturing a variety of prey; and we know they have been the most heavily exploited wild cat in the world, millions having been killed for their skins. However, many fundamental questions remain: no reliable way exists to census the elusive cats over a large area; our understanding of their social organization is incomplete; the impact of intense harvest (trapping and hunting) on their population dynamics is poorly understood; and it is still unknown whether they enjoy a beautiful sunrise.

Most North American native cultures pay homage to the bobcat. For instance, the Navajo do not have a word for carnivore or predator. The closest word in their language is *na'azheel*, meaning "the ones who hunt." Bobcats play a prominent role in the Navajo creation myth, as guardians of the house of First Man, repelling attacks from the Wolf People, and later from the Kit Fox People and the Badger People.

In daily life, the bobcat was respected as a skilled hunter but was also killed for food and body parts (Steve Pavlik, ethnozoologist, personal communication).

Early trappers demonstrated a similar duality in their encounters with bobcats. The feline was viewed first as a commodity, albeit not as valuable as beaver—but one member of the Joe Walker party in the Bradshaw Mountains of Arizona in the mid-1800s was impressed enough to name Lynx Creek (near Prescott) after a bobcat that attacked him after he wounded it (Harley Shaw, The Juniper Institute, personal communication). To early settlers, the bobcat was primarily a nuisance. The farm boy who caught one in a trap probably felt he was protecting his chickens and took satisfaction in the extra money he made from the pelt.

To modern urban/suburban denizens, the bobcat is all but invisible. Most imagine the feline far away, roaming wild country, a symbol of the wilderness. Although this is partly true, the bobcat is frequently our neighbor. Haunting the fringes of our towns and cities at twilight, the bobcat dines on squirrels in the city park at night or snatches an occasional housecat. Late-night trips to the store may be rewarded with a glimpse of the apparition silently crossing the road, or a walk in the woods may reveal a wraith sitting quietly near the trail, then gone.

There was little public concern for the status of the bobcat before the early 1970s. The bobcats' nocturnal and stealthy habits made them difficult to study. The felid's pelt rarely brought more than $5.00 from 1950 to 1970, so the bobcat was of little economic importance compared with other furbearers. Attacks on sheep or chickens were rare, so there was little incentive for state or federal wildlife agencies to conduct research or manage the bobcat (Anderson 1987; Anderson and Lovallo 2003). However, in 1973 two events placed the bobcat squarely in the management spotlight and transformed international conservation of wild felines on an unprecedented scale.

The first was passage of the Endangered Species Act (ESA) in late 1973, which prohibited the import of fur of endangered cats into the United States. The second event was the gathering of representatives from 80 nations in Washington, D.C., to negotiate a treaty controlling international trade in wild animals and plants. Two years later, in 1975, the United States and 79 other countries signed the Convention on International Trade in Endangered Species of Wild Fauna and Flora (CITES), which provided international protection for endangered species, such as leopard, ocelot, and cheetah. The bobcat was listed in Appendix II, which required member countries to provide evidence that exporting bobcat skins would "not be detrimental to the survival of that species" (Anderson 1987:23). The ESA and CITES caused European furriers to turn to the nonthreatened bobcat and Canada lynx as replacements. The bobcat's thick and soft fur became a popular substitute, especially the spotted "belly" fur, and harvest levels in the United States rose dramatically (McMahan 1986; Kitchener 1991). From 1970 to 1977, the annual harvest of bobcats in the United States rose from 10,854 to 83,415 (see Figure 5.3 in Chapter 5), while the price for a bobcat pelt increased from $10 to $125, with $250 for an exceptional one (Anderson 1987).

Today, 38 states allow killing of bobcats (Woolf and Hubert 1998), with about half of the pelts entering the international fur trade (Sunquist and Sunquist 2002). Canada allows harvest in seven provinces (International Society for Endangered Cats Canada 2001), and Mexico regulates bobcat hunting in five states (Nowell and Jackson 1996). The pelts are converted into coats, trim, and accessories (Obbard 1987). A short bobcat coat can be bought in the United States for $5,000 to $6,000. Bobcat skins are among the most heavily traded in the world: 118,929 were exported from Canada, Mexico, and the United States between 1998 and 2002 (CITES 2004).

State wildlife agencies, who bear primary responsibility for wildlife management, responded to the requirements of ESA and CITES by launching many new research studies of bobcat natural history to justify the increased harvest levels and to answer concerns about possible overharvest. Studies of all aspects increased dramatically—including food habits, reproduction, home range, social organization, parasites, and disease—but studies of population status received the greatest attention. The published bobcat literature on population status increased by 1000% during the 1970s, indicating the paucity of available information during the previous decade. Unfortunately, many of the studies lacked clear objectives or testable hypotheses. Too frequently, the goal was simply to gather as much information as possible. As a result, there is extensive duplication and redundancy in the scientific literature (Anderson 1987).

The situation was further complicated by a turf war between state and federal wildlife officials. Many state wildlife agencies viewed the new regulations as an attempt by the feds to dictate to the states, and they resented the interference. During several of my interviews with state wildlife managers, the resentment was still palpable. In the end, the states won a partial victory.

In 1982, the U.S. Congress amended the ESA by removing the requirement that states must make population estimates. This negated the CITES requirement that reliable bobcat population estimates were prerequisite to the "no-detriment" finding. Five years later, wild fur markets crashed, as did the rest of the stock market, on October 19, 1987—the now famous "Black Monday." The Dow Jones Industrial Average lost 22.6% of its total value, and hundreds of commercial furriers went out of business in both the United States and Europe (Stock Market Crash 2005).

Today, the bobcat is no longer the lightning rod of controversy it once was, but interest in the wild feline remains high among researchers. During the height of the bobcat debate, three conferences were convened—one in 1979 at Front Royal, Virginia; the second at Reno, Nevada in 1982; and the third in 1984 at the University of Maine in Orono. Most recently, in September 2000, a symposium took place at the Wildlife Society 2000 Conference in Nashville, Tennessee. Research biologists and managers gathered from across the country to present papers and discuss current research on biology and management of the bobcat. The hosts of this symposium, Woolf and Nielsen (2001), believed that the bobcat's future was bright indeed. They pointed out that the bobcat population appeared healthy through-out its North American range and that fears for its survival, professed in the 1970s, were unfounded. They noted that wildlife managers had adapted their manage-ment strategies to changing times, and better data were available on which to implement science-based management. However, they warned that wildlife man-agers would be faced with increasingly difficult issues to resolve, and the need for solid, scientific data on which to base management decisions would increase. "Adverse impacts of humans and their activities on wildlife and their habitats also can only increase. Bobcats seem tolerant of human presence, but exurban devel-opment will intensify pressure on bobcat populations. In spite of increasing human pressure and increasingly contentious debates over management goals and objec-tives, we remain optimistic" (Woolf and Nielsen 2001:3).

Clay Nielsen (Southern Illinois University, personal communication) insists that the only reason bobcats have come back is harvest protection, which was in-stituted by state wildlife management agencies. Most state wildlife officials agree. Critics claim the agency restrictions on bobcats harvests were not instituted will-ingly and that the feline's success has caused it to slip through the conservation cracks. Whether the bobcat's comeback is due to management efforts, or in spite of them, is open to debate. Bobcats are indeed resilient, but they are not invulner-able, and there are storm clouds on the horizon. Loss of habitat continues through-out much of their range, the fur market is resurgent, bobcat pelt prices are rising (North American Fur Auctions 2005), and trappers are oiling up the tools of their trade and venturing afield in increasing numbers (see Figure 5.3 in Chapter 5).

Bobcat: Master of Survival is my attempt to coax the furtive feline out of the shadows, although the cat has proved as elusive on paper as in the wild. What began as an investigation into the bobcat's biology and behavior became a journey that wound through the mythology of native cultures, the commercial fur trade, the history of predator control, animal rights, wildlife management philosophy, and international conservation of wild felines. It is a story as much about economics, politics, and human ego as it is about science. I came away with enormous respect for how the bobcat has endured hostile landscapes, elusive prey, bitter cold, op-pressive heat, hunger, injury, steel-jawed traps, snares, dogs, mountain lions, hunters, and wildlife biologists. Through it all, the bobcat abides, watching from the edge, regarding all with classical feline insouciance, truly a master of survival.

1 Bobcat Basics

Billy the bobcat and Conner the rottweiler are playfully wrestling in Dawn Simas' backyard. The cat and dog are best buddies, but the relationship seems in jeopardy when Conner's jaws clamp too firmly on one of Billy's rear legs. Billy spins with the remarkable speed and dexterity common to cats, and clamps his jaws on Conner's testicles. The dog lets out a yelp, releases his hold, and jumps clear of the fray.

"That always works," laughs Dawn as we stand watching the encounter. The sun is setting over the oak trees that surround her home in the foothills of northern California's Sierra Nevada Mountains. At first glance the 100-pound purebred rottweiler would seem to have the edge over the 35-pound bobcat, but the feline's speed, reflexes, strength, and aggressiveness more than compensate.

Dawn inherited Billy from an airline pilot who purchased the bobcat from a Montana fur farm as a pet. The new owner eventually realized the rambunctious feline was more than he could handle and asked Dawn to take him. Dawn operates a nonprofit organization called Wild About Cats, which rescues injured and unwanted exotic cats and educates the public about their plight. She uses Billy in presentations to local school groups, nature centers, and museums.

"Billy is a freak," explains Dawn as we watch Conner cautiously circle the resting bobcat.

"Why is that?" I ask.

"For one thing he's so big. Adult bobcats in the wild typically weigh around 25 pounds, but they can and do weigh up to 40 pounds, especially in the north. It's not unusual for Billy to weigh over 40 pounds in the winter; in summer he'll drop to 30 pounds. It's because he comes from Montana stock and was raised on a fur farm. He was bred for his size and pelt." (Bobcats from northern climates tend to be larger than those from southern latitudes, and breeding them on fur farms allows them to be fattened up to produce larger pelts.)

His coat is magnificent—tawny brown with a snow-white underbelly, both covered with brownish-black spots. A darker stripe of fur runs down the middle of Billy's back. It's the fur from the spotted white underbelly the furriers are after—to be transformed into expensive coats or used as trim.

As I crouch to take his photograph, Billy rises and trots over to me. Through my camera lens I can make out the distinctive ruff of fur around his face and the tufts of hair at the end of each ear. As he places his front paws on my knees, I lower the camera and begin to stroke his head. The bobcat immediately thrusts his face in mine and begins to "cheek-mark," vigorously rubbing the scent glands near the corners of his mouth against my neck and face. Cheek-marking allows him to mark me with a scent too subtle for humans to detect, whose meaning only another bobcat knows for sure.

"That's the other reason Billy is unusual" nods Dawn, "he is so darned friendly. Bobcats are normally feisty and high strung. They don't make good pets. I worry that Billy's friendly behavior gives audiences the wrong impression during my talks."

Just then Billy interrupts by leaping onto my shoulders, not an easy feat when you have been declawed. He continues to cheek-rub my head and nibbles at my left ear. Bobcat drool runs down my face. Next he jumps down to the ground, climbs back into my lap and thrusts his muzzle into my right armpit.

"He really likes armpits," smiles Dawn, "but be careful."

"Careful of what?" I ask innocently. I'm thoroughly charmed—that is, until Billy sinks his teeth firmly into the flesh of my armpit. Between the pain and my scream, I can still see Dawn smiling.

"Good thing his former owner filed down those fangs."

■

What's in a Name?

Although my first close encounter with a bobcat was at the business end, so to speak, the story of the bobcat actually begins at the other end—the tail. Bobcat is shorthand for "bob-tailed cat" (Lariviere and Walton 1997; Sunquist and Sunquist 2002). It is their short tail, averaging only 14.8 cm (6 inches) in adult males and 13.7 cm (5 inches) in adult females (McCord and Cardoza 1982), that sets them apart from their feline brethren. However, in his classic book, *The Bobcat of North America*, biologist Stanley Young (1978) pointed out that the name may also be related to the bodily motion of the bobcat while running. At full speed, the feline exhibits a bobbing motion similar to that of a rabbit.

Audubon called the bobcat the common American wildcat (Guggisberg 1975). The designation "wildcat" probably was partially influenced by the feline's reported pugnacious reputation. Young recalled that in pioneer days a frequent boast was that a man "could whip his weight in wildcats." One bellicose Missouri River boatman was looking for a fight and claimed, "I'm from the Lightning Forks of Roaring River. I'm all man, save what is wild cat and extra lightning" (Young 1978:4). Although the bobcat's reputation is probably inflated, it is not wholly undeserved. The medium-sized cat is capable of killing deer, turkeys, domestic sheep, and goats.

> After Billy released my armpit, Dawn and I watched as he repeatedly stalked and playfully attacked her full-grown horse, Jericho. Jericho appeared more annoyed than frightened, as he easily shook off each assault with a kick of his leg or a shake of his rump.

Wildcat is the common name that still persists in some parts of North America, although its use is inconsistent. There are those who insist that bobcats inhabit the lower foothills, whereas wildcats prefer the higher mountains. Others use bobcat for males and wildcat for females. In *Wild Cats of the World*, writer C.A.W. Guggisberg stated, "Another piece of 'unnatural history' makes the bobcat out to be a cross between the Canada lynx and the domestic cat!" (Guggisberg 1975:59). Explorer Henry Hudson applied the name Kaatskill (Wildcat Creek) to the Catskill Mountains of New York state, the famous peaks west of the Hudson River (Young 1978). Many high schools and colleges embrace the wildcat as their mascot.

"Wildcatting" is a term commonly applied to oil exploration in unproven oil fields, where such operations involve substantial financial risk. The term originated in the early 1800s, when many western banks issued bank notes with practically no financial backing. Inscribed on the bank notes was a picture of a wildcat, and thus the term became associated with any business venture involving unsound risk (Young 1978).

Early settlers referred to the bobcat as catamount or cat-of-the-mountain, the same name given by New Englanders to its much larger cousin, the puma, *Puma concolor*. The term may have originated from the Spanish *gato monte*, meaning mountain cat. The bobcat's similarity to its more northern relative, the Canada lynx (*Lynx canadensis*), led to the nickname lynx cat or bay lynx (the latter also on account of its color). To colonial Swedes living along the Delaware River, the bobcat was known as katta lo or cat lynx. Other common names include red lynx, barred bobcat, and pallid bobcat. To French Canadians, the diminutive wild cat is *lynx bai, chat sauvage, chat sauvage de la nouvelle cosae,* and *pichou.* In Mexico, the moniker *gato monte* still holds (Young 1978; Sunquist and Sunquist 2002).

There is disagreement among biologists regarding the scientific name of the bobcat. Since 1777, the bobcat's genus and species name has been *Lynx rufus. Lynx* in Latin means lamp, from an original Greek word meaning "to shine." Both refer to the reflective quality of the cat's eyes when struck by light at night. *Rufus* is Latin for red, which refers to the bobcat's pelage. *Lynx rufus* was challenged in 1975 when Texas Technological University in Lubbock published the *Revised Checklist of North American Mammals North of Mexico* (Jones et al. 1975), which changed the genus of the bobcat from *Lynx* to *Felis. Felis* is Latin for cat. Although many authorities believed the change lacked supporting documentation, major North American wildlife journals adopted *Felis rufus* (Anderson 1987). More recent taxonomic research and literature indicates that *Lynx* is the valid genus, although there is still no general consensus (Werdelin 1981; Wozencraft 1993). To avoid confusion and for the sake of consistency, *Lynx rufus* is used throughout this book.

Disagreement surrounds not only the bobcat's scientific name and its classification within the cat family (Felidae), but its relationships with many other living species of Felidae. Classification within the family is difficult, mostly because many species have evolved and split from each other relatively recently (O'Brien 1991; Sunquist and Sunquist 2002). To better understand the confusion, it is necessary to examine feline origins. That requires going back in time 60 million years, to when carnivores first appeared.

Whence Came Cats?

Living in the forests of the northern hemisphere 60 to 39 million years ago were small mammals called miacids. Similar in appearance and size to modern genets, they had long bodies and tails, short flexible limbs, and small brains. They lived in trees and moved about the branches using wide paws and spreading digits with which to grasp. They may even have had retractile claws. The miacids were the first primitive carnivores. An explosion of evolution and diversification approximately 40 million years ago gave us the modern families of the order Carnivora: bears, dogs, raccoons, mongooses, weasels, seals, civets, hyenas, and cats (Neff 1991).

Carnivores are more than simply meat-eaters. Some species, such as pandas, are almost complete vegetarians (Neff 1991). Carnivores share a number of characteristics, but the key feature is the possession of four carnassial teeth. Carnassials are modified molars and premolars with sharp tips, high cusps, and jagged edges that act as shears to cut through tough hide and tissue (MacDonald 1984). Other skeletal traits in carnivores include the fusion of some bones in the foot, which may aid in running, climbing, and grappling with prey; reduction in the size of the collar bone to accentuate the fore-and-aft swing of the legs used primarily for running down prey; and two sets of powerful jaw muscles used in killing and dismembering prey (MacDonald 1984).

Taxonomists generally divide the carnivores into two major groups: a bear-like group (arctoids), consisting of bears, seals, dogs, raccoons, pandas, badgers, skunks, weasels, and their kin; and a cat-like group (aeluroids), a lineage including the cats, hyenas, genets, civets, and mongooses (NeV 1991). Among the carnivores, the cats are the most specialized for a predator lifestyle.

Paleontologists and biologists have traditionally relied primarily on fossils and differences in physical structure (morphology) of modern animals to map the evolution of a particular species. This has proved difficult with cats for two reasons: many ancestral cats occupied tropical forests, where the conditions for preservation of fossils is poor; and most of the physical characteristics of cats are related to the capture of prey, with the result that all felines are very similar in structure. As a result, no less than five different hypotheses have been offered to explain the relationships among the various groups and subgroups of extinct and modern cats (Neff 1991). New tools are needed to explain speciation and resolve the origin of reproductive isolation between feline populations. Dr. John Seidensticker, Curator of Mammals at the National Zoological Park in Washington. D.C., wrote in 1991 that "the taxonomy of the Felidae, based on morphological analysis, has advanced about as far as it can with the specimens now available in museums. Advances in our understanding will come with detailed studies of behavior, ecology, and population genetics" (Seidensticker and Lumpkin 1991:28) His words have proved prophetic.

Just such an approach to the evolutionary and taxonomic puzzle of feline classification has now been taken through the application of the new science of molecular genetics. By examining the rate of change of genes in the DNA molecules of various cat species, biologist Stephen J. O'Brien and his colleagues revealed that the 38 species of modern cats evolved in three distinct lines. The earliest branch appeared 12 million years ago and includes the seven species of small South American cats (ocelot, jaguarundi, margay, and others). The second branching took place 8 to 10 million years ago and produced the domestic cat and five close relatives (Pallas's cat, sand cat, and others). About 4 to 6 million years ago, a third branch split and gave rise to the middle-sized and large cats. This third line gave rise to 24 of the 38 species of living cats, including the cougar, cheetah, and all big cats. The most recent split (1.8 to 3.8 million years ago) divided the lynxes from the large cats (O'Brien 1991).

More recent work has further refined what we know about feline phylogeny. It now appears that the 38 species of modern wild cats evolved through eight major lineages within the past 10 to 15 million years: ocelot, domestic cat, puma, leopard cat, *Panthera*, caracal, bay cat, and lynx (see Figure 1.1). Among the four existing species of *Lynx*, the Eurasian lynx and the Canada lynx are closely related and share an older ancestor with the bobcat. The position of the Spanish lynx (*Lynx pardinus*) within the lineage is still debated (Pecon-Slattery and O'Brien 1998; Sunquist and Sunquist 2002).

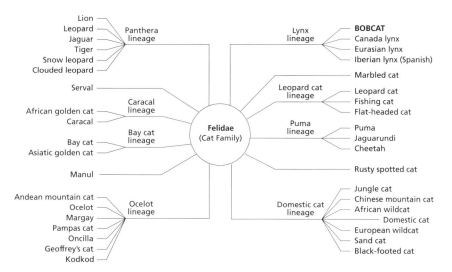

Figure 1.1
Proposed phylogeny of the cat family (Felidae) (Wozencraft 1993; Sunquist and
Sunquist 2002.)

Just as there is disagreement about where cats came from, there is debate over
how to classify the 38 species of cats that exist today. At least ten different classification systems have been suggested, with the number of genera ranging from 2 to
23, and the number of species from 36 to 39. Each classification system has been
based on an assortment of characteristics, including tooth shape and size, tooth
number, vocalizations, hybridization records, foot and nose morphology, shape
of the pupil, cranial dimensions, karyotype, and DNA analysis (Leyhausen 1979;
Neff 1982; Nowak 1991; Sunquist and Sunquist 2002). Again, the confusion is rooted
in the fact that almost all cats share a similar predatory lifestyle. They hunt, stalk,
ambush, pounce, and kill their prey using similar movements, teeth, and claws.
The result is that, despite their enormous range in size, wild felines show little
variation in appearance and behavior (Sunquist and Sunquist 2002).

Some taxonomists using vocalization as a criterion divide the cat family (Felidae) into two groups, or genera: *Panthera*, the large roaring cats, and *Felis*, the
smaller purring cats. They postulate that the ability to roar depends on a carti-
laginous portion of the hyoid bone, to which the muscles of the trachea (wind-
pipe) and larynx (voicebox) are attached. The tiger (*Panthera tigris*), African lion
(*Panthera leo*), leopard (*Panthera pardus*), jaguar (*Panthera onca*), and snow leopard (*Panthera uncia*) represent this group. These cats cannot purr. Members of
Felis possess the ability to purr or make shrill, higher-pitched sounds because
the hyoid is completely bony, but they cannot roar. Of the 38 species of cats, 30
are classified as *Felis*, and 5 are classified as *Panthera*. The clouded leopard (*Neofelis
nebulosa*) and the cheetah (*Acinonyx jubatus*) are classified as separate genera. Of

the seven cat species in North America, only the jaguar (*P. onca*) belongs to *Panthera*. The other six—puma (*Felis concolor*), ocelot (*Felis pardalis*), margay (*Felis wiedii*), jaguarundi (*Felis yagouaroundi*), Canada lynx (*Lynx canadensis*), and bobcat (*Lynx rufus*)—are purring cats and are classified as members of *Felis* by these researchers (MacDonald 1984; Peters 1991).

According to Gustav Peters and his collaborators, who have published extensively on vocal communication in felids, such a criterion is speculative. "Anecdotically, purring has been reported in many species but verifiable evidence has been presented for only a few. Which felid species actually purr? The question cannot be answered definitively; a correlation between the degree of hyoid ossification and the ability to purr is not proven" (Peters 1991:76–77).

Nowak and Paradiso (1983) closely followed the nomenclature just described, but with an even greater degree of consolidation. They did not recognize the domestic cat (*Felis catus*) as a legitimate species, believing it to be most closely related to the wildcat *Felis silvestris*. More importantly, they placed the lynxes in the genus *Felis*. Many other biologists have questioned the scientific justification for lumping the stumpy-tailed, long-legged bobcats and lynxes with the long-tailed wildcats and desert cats belonging to the genus *Felis* and believe that the lynxes belong in their own genus. Nowak and Paradiso (1983) also considered the Eurasian lynx and the Canada lynx to be the same species, *Felis lynx*. The resulting classification system divides the 38 existing species of cats among four genera.

Wozencraft (1993) was a definite splitter when it came to the taxonomy of the Felidae. The same 38 species of cats were divided among 18 genera. For instance, he recognized the puma as a separate genus and renamed it *Puma concolor*. Wozencraft did not recognize the domestic cat as a legitimate species, but he did give the bobcat and lynxes their own genus, *Lynx*. Of course, with 18 genera he had plenty to spare. Wozencraft listed four species in the genus *Lynx*: the Eurasian lynx (*Lynx lynx*), the Spanish lynx (*Lynx pardinus*), the Canada lynx (*Lynx canadensis*), and the bobcat (*Lynx rufus*). A fifth species, the caracal (*Caracal caracal*), of Africa and the Middle East, was once thought to belong to the lynxes because of its long ear tufts, but it was determined not to be closely related to the true lynxes.

For the sake of clarity, this book follows the taxonomy presented by Wozencraft (1993), which is also used by the World Conservation Union, formerly known as the International Union for the Conservation of Nature (IUCN), and by the Convention on International Trade in Endangered Species of Wild Flora and Fauna (CITES).

The Missing Lynx

What makes a lynx a lynx? They are generally medium-sized cats with short tails. Their faces have a prominent ruff of fur around the border, and their ears are tipped with tufts of black hair. Lynxes have long legs relative to their body length and relatively small heads. Probably the most distinguishing characteristic of these cats is the absence of a set of upper premolars, which gives them 28 teeth instead of the usual 30 found in other felines (Anderson 1987; Kitchener 1991; Anderson and Lovallo 2003).

Although the fossil record for most small cat species is poor, lynxes are the exception (Kitchener 1991). The ancestor of the modern lynxes made its first appearance in fossil deposits of South Africa, dated 4 million years ago. This ancestral lynx, known as the Issoire lynx *Lynx issiodorensis*, existed until approximately 500,000 years ago. The Issoire lynx had shorter and more robust legs than modern lynxes. It had a longer neck, and its head was much larger in relation to its body. It more closely resembled cats of the genus *Felis* than the long-legged lynxes of today. However, it did possess the distinctive short tail and 28 teeth (Werdelin 1981; Anderson 1987).

From its African origin, the Issoire lynx spread to Europe and throughout the northern hemisphere 1.25 million years ago. Swedish scientist Lars Werdelin believed that, in Europe, the Spanish lynx *L. pardinus,* is a direct descendant of the Issoire lynx. In China, the Issoire lynx gave rise to the Eurasian lynx *L. lynx,* which spread westward to Europe 100,000 years ago. During the glacial periods of the last 200,000 years, this ancestral lynx crossed eastward to North America and evolved into the Canada lynx *L. canadensis* (Werdelin 1981) (see Figure 1.2).

Figure 1.2
Proposed phylogeny of *Lynx* (Werdelin 1981; Anderson 1987).

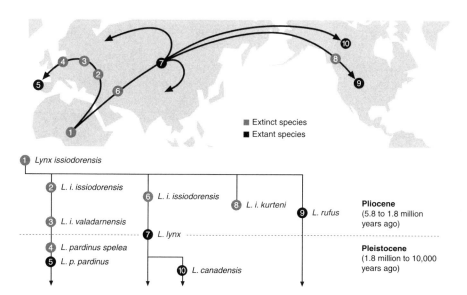

For a long time, it was thought the bobcat was a southern form of the Canada lynx. We now know that the bobcat evolved separately and was present in North America long before the Canada lynx colonized what is now Alaska and Canada. Fossil evidence indicates that the Issoire lynx entered North America during the late Pliocene Epoch (5 to 2 million years ago). The first evidence of the cat's presence was documented from Cita Canyon, Texas, and has been dated to 2.4 to 2.5 million years before the present. After arriving in North America, the species evolved into an intermediate form, *Lynx issiodorensis kurteni*, and then into *L. rufus* (Werdelin 1981; Anderson 1987; Kitchener 1991). The Issoire lynx was therefore also the ancestor of the bobcat.

The bobcat adapted so well that it is one of the most commonly found mammals in Pleistocene fossil deposits (1.8 million to 10,000 years ago). Remains from this period have now been found in Arizona, Arkansas, California, Colorado, Florida, Georgia, Idaho, Kentucky, Mexico, Missouri, Nevada, New Mexico, Pennsylvania, Tennessee, Texas, Virginia, West Virginia, and Wyoming. The reduced size of the modern bobcat was probably a result of competition with the larger ancestral felids. The bobcat's smaller size allowed it to take advantage of smaller prey. Competition between lynx and larger cat species in Europe probably resulted in a similar size reduction (Kurten 1965; Anderson 1987:3; Kitchener 1991:37).

Today, wildlife biologists recognize four extant species of lynxes. The two Old World species are the Eurasian lynx, which has the largest range, extending from Europe through Central Asia and Siberia to East Asia, and the endangered Spanish lynx, which is holding on in small, isolated populations in Spain and Portugal. The Canada lynx and the bobcat are the two New World species (Wozencraft 1993; Sunquist and Sunquist 2002).

Wildcat Turf

"Adaptable" is the word most frequently used to describe the bobcat, both in the biological literature and among the experts interviewed for this book. The wildcats' adaptability manifests itself in the enormous geographic range they occupy, the diversity of habitats in which they exist, and in their ability to live in close proximity to humans—and survive.

Bobcats have been documented in every state except Alaska, Hawaii, and Delaware. They range into Canada as far north as central British Columbia (55 degrees North) in the west and the Gaspé Peninsula in the east, and as far south as central Mexico (17 degrees North), making them the most widely distributed native felid in North America (Anderson and Lovallo 2003) (see Figure 1.3). The diminutive felines roam the dense coniferous forests of the Pacific Northwest, thorn scrub in Mexico, high mountain ranges in the western United States and Canada, the cold Northern Forest of New England and southeastern Canada, and the subtropical wetlands of the southeastern United States. In the west, they have

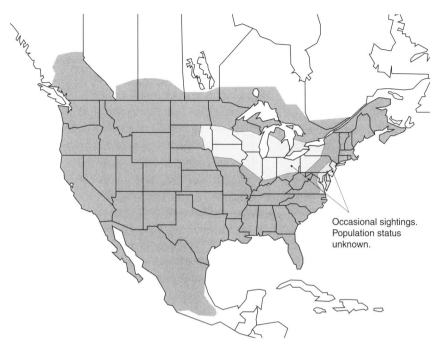

Occasional sightings.
Population status
unknown.

Figure 1.3
Bobcat distribution in North America (McCord and Cardoza 1982; Anderson 1987; Rolley 1987; Lariviere and Walton 1997; Sunquist and Sunquist 2002; Anderson and Lovallo 2003).

been trapped as high as 2,575 meters (8,700 feet). Harley Shaw (The Juniper Institute, personal communication) stated that bobcats are common at 7,000 to 9,000 feet in the mountains of Arizona. Young (1978) reported no records of bobcats above 12,000 feet and speculated that the boreal conditions that exist at such altitudes are unsuitable.

Information on the presence of bobcats in Mexico is increasing. The Mexican bobcat is known to wander throughout the Sierra Madre Occidental on the west coast and Sierra Madre Oriental on the east coast, as well as the desert mountains of Sonora and Baja California (Delibes et al. 1997). During the 1950s, bobcats were reported to be uncommon in central Mexico (Leopold 1959), but some have been killed as far south as Zacatecas and Oaxaca (Goodwin 1963). Rolley (1987) reported that there was little published information on the status of the bobcat south of the border before 1987, but in 1996 biologists using a camera trap (a remote camera activated by an infrared motion sensor) recorded the presence of a male bobcat in the Chamela-Cuixmala Biosphere Reserve on the western coast of Mexico, near Jalisco (Lopez-Gonzalez et al. 1998). Other researchers have now examined bobcat food habits in southern Baja California (Delibes et al. 1997) and ranging behavior on Colima Volcano, also near Jalisco (Burton et al. 2003). The IUCN Cat Specialist Group has called for more research on the distribution and status of bobcats in the western Mexican Sierra, in light of deforestation and degradation of the dry scrub, oak, and pine habitats (IUCN 1996).

The Eurasian lynx and Spanish lynx have had their historical ranges substantially reduced due to conflict with humans. The Canada lynx currently ranges across almost all of Canada and Alaska and may have roamed parts of the northern continental United States in the past, retreating in the 1800s in the face of settlement of the midwestern United States and southern Canada (Quinn and Parker 1987). Only the bobcat retains most of its original range. However, although adaptable, the bobcat can be displaced. It has been largely eliminated from the densely populated states along the mid-Atlantic coast and from the intensely cultivated midwestern states, most notably Iowa, Illinois, and large portions of Indiana, Ohio, Michigan, and Wisconsin. Woolf and Hubert (1998) explained that the decline of the feline in the midwest was primarily due to habitat changes resulting from intensive agriculture and secondarily due to hunting and trapping by humans because of real or perceived attacks on livestock. More recent evidence indicates that the resilient bobcat is rebounding throughout the Midwest. State wildlife officials report that sightings are increasing, but the population status is unknown (see Figure 1.3). Illinois delisted bobcats as threatened in the state in 1999 (Bluett et al. 2001), and in 2000 the Pennsylvania Game Commission approved their first legal harvest in more than 30 years (Lovallo 2001).

It is the bobcat's ability to live in close proximity to humans that prevented its extirpation from even larger regions of North America. The cougar and Canada lynx have not been so fortunate. The key to the bobcat's existence in an area seems to be the presence of prey and cover. Cover refers to vegetation and topography that allow the bobcat to remain hidden while stalking prey (stalking cover) and to escape detection. The felines avoid areas of intense agricultural development, such as the Corn Belt of the midwestern United States, where habitat has been destroyed and prey eliminated. Certain types of logging and fire management techniques followed in second-growth forests, as well as agricultural practices that leave adequate cover and prey, can actually benefit bobcats. Some researchers speculate that during the early 1900s the bobcat's range expanded into northern Minnesota, southern Ontario, and Manitoba as timber harvest, fire, and farming opened the dense, unbroken coniferous forests of these areas. This northward expansion occurred at the same time the Canada lynx's distribution was retreating northward (Rollings 1945; Quinn and Parker 1987; Rolley 1987). Bobcat researcher Gary Koehler of the Washington Department of Fish and Wildlife (personal communication) believes there is insufficient evidence of a northward retreat of Canada lynx range. As he pointed out, lynx are still present in Maine and Minnesota, and records further south may represent transient or migrating individuals. Susan Morse (personal communication) believes that bobcats have always been present in these northern areas, although not in the higher mountains and boreal forest zones.

Koehler (personal communication) agreed: "I think snow conditions, especially deep and dry powdery snow present at high elevation and northern latitudes, may inhibit bobcats and prevent them from encroaching on lynx habitat."

Subspecies and Status

When a species is as broadly distributed as the bobcat, regional variations in physical appearance occur. For instance, bobcats from British Columbia look somewhat different from bobcats from Florida, a fact that relates to the different habitats in which the bobcat lives. Wildlife taxonomists recognize these regional variations by dividing *L. rufus* into geographic races or subspecies, scattered across North America. This is similar to the different races or breeds of the domestic cat. In scientific nomenclature, the subspecies name follows the genus and species. For example, the Montana bobcat is *Lynx rufus pallescens,* or *L. r. pallescens* (Hall 1981).

Disagreement arises again among taxonomists and other biologists regarding the legitimacy of some subspecies of bobcats. Criteria used to define these groups usually consist of subtle differences in pelage and skull. Hall (1981) listed 12 subspecies (see Figure 1.4), whereas Young (1978) recognized only 9. Samson completed a statistical analysis of the skull characteristics among bobcats that generally supported the 12 recognized subspecies, except that he divided *L. r. rufus* into an eastern and a western subspecies (Samson 1979; Anderson 1987; Anderson and Lovallo 2003). During his study of the geographic variations among bobcats in the south-central United States, Read (1981) came to a much different conclusion, suggesting that there were far fewer valid subspecies than those posited by Hall or Samson. Biologists Chet M. McCord and James E. Cardoza pointed out that the designation of subspecies has little meaning in contiguous bobcat populations that lack geographic barriers. Possible exceptions are *L. r. fasciatus,* which is separated from *L .r. pallescens* by the Cascade Mountains, and the endangered *L. r. escuinapae* of central Mexico (McCord and Cardoza 1982). Rolley agreed that recognition of subspecies helps to acknowledge morphological differences across the geographic range of a species, but he concluded that "the inability to accurately classify individuals to subspecies by either pelage or skeletal characteristics severely limits the usefulness of this taxonomic rank in the management of bobcats" (Rolley 1987:671).

The lack of agreement on the number of valid subspecies and the inability to assign individual bobcat pelages to subspecies has ramifications beyond mere taxonomy. With passage of the federal Endangered Species Act (ESA) in 1973, the terms *species* and *subspecies* have taken on legal definitions. The U.S. Fish and Wildlife Service (USFWS) recognized only one subspecies, the Mexican bobcat (*L. r. escuinapae*), as endangered in 1976 under the ESA. However, the ESA includes a "look-alike" clause that allows an entire species to be fully protected throughout its range if one or more subspecies within its range is considered endangered.

1. *L.r. baileyi*
2. *L.r. californicus*
3. *L.r. escuinapae* (endangered)
4. *L.r. fasciatus*
5. *L.r. floridanus*
6. *L.r. gigas*
7. *L.r. oaxacensis*
8. *L.r. pallesceus*
9. *L.r. peninsularis*
10. *L.r. rufus*
11. *L.r. superiorensis*
12. *L.r. texensis*

Figure 1.4
Subspecies of bobcat in North America (Hall 1981; Anderson 1987).

Similar protection is provided by CITES, which regulates the international trade in wildlife, such as bobcat pelts. CITES originally listed the Mexican bobcat in Appendix I, which recognized the feline's endangered status and restricted its commercial trade. All other bobcat subspecies were listed in Appendix II for reasons of similarity of appearance to the Mexican bobcat. Appendix II allows for international trade, but only under close monitoring and with required permits. The dilemma here was that, if no reliable method existed to distinguish bobcat subspecies on the basis of pelage or other physical characteristics, there was no way to be certain Mexican bobcats were not entering international trade. The subspecies was originally described from only two immature male specimens on the basis of color and cranial differences (Allen 1903). Sansom's analysis of a variety of bobcat skull measurements indicated that *L. r. escuinapae* is similar to *L. r. californicus* and *L. r. texensis* (Samson 1979). In addition, the range of *L. r. escuinapae* overlaps with that of *L. r. baileyi* and *L. r. texensis* (see Figure 1.4). Because of the uncertainty of its validity as a subspecies, the United States successfully proposed downlisting the Mexican bobcat to Appendix II in 1992. Currently, the entire species is listed in Appendix II, indicating that international trade in Mexican bobcats has been reopened, but without threatening the species with extinction (CITES 2004) (see Table 1.1).

On July 8, 1996, the USFWS received a petition from the National Trappers Association, Inc., of Bloomington, Indiana, requesting that the Mexican bobcat be delisted (removed from the list of endangered species) under the ESA. The petition contained information on bobcat taxonomy, present population status and trends, and threats. It also took the position that downlisting the Mexican bobcat to threatened status would not be an appropriate alternative. Due to staffing and budget constraints, the USFWS was unable to respond to the petition until June 2003. At that time, they found that the petition presented substantial information indicating that the requested action may be warranted and solicited public comments. Two comments were received from the Mexican government, and they did not object to the delisting. A third comment in favor of delisting was received from Mr. Lawrence G. Kline, who submitted the original petition on behalf of the National Trappers Association. Mr. Kline pointed out that there is no evidence of taxonomic differences between bobcat populations in the United States and Mexico, and that the bobcat population in Mexico does not constitute a discrete population separate from the U.S. bobcat population. The only dissenting comment came from the Center for Biological Diversity, a nongovernmental conservation organization, who opposed the delisting because of a lack of population data. They further argued that continued listing was necessary to help prioritize research and that development along the U.S.-Mexico border was likely to increase, thereby reducing genetic flow between bobcat populations in Mexico and the United States. In the May 19, 2005, issue of the *Federal Register*, the USFWS announced in its 12-month finding that the petition to delist the Mexican bobcat (*L. r. escuinapae*) was warranted. The finding stated, "The best available information indicates that the Mexican bobcat may not constitute a separate subspecies and does not constitute a distinct population segment (DPS). Despite habitat modification by humans, the bobcat remains abundant throughout Mexico. Accordingly, we herein propose to delist the Mexican bobcat under the Act." At the time this book went to press, USFWS was seeking data and comments from the public on this proposed rule (USFWS 2005).

On March 24, 2000, the USFWS designated the Canada lynx as threatened in the contiguous states where the species is known to occur. This includes Colorado, Idaho, Maine, Michigan, Minnesota, Montana, New Hampshire, New York, Oregon, Utah, Vermont, Washington, Wisconsin, and Wyoming. The USFWS stated, "Because a substantial amount of lynx habitat in the contiguous United States occurs on federally managed lands, particularly in the West, we conclude that the factor threatening lynx in the contiguous United States is the lack of guidance in existing Federal land management plans for conservation of lynx and lynx habitat." The designation included a special regulation that allows for take and

Table 1.1
Status and Legal Protection of the Lynxes

Common and scientific name	U.S. Fish and Wildlife Service Threatened and Endangered Species System (year listed)	IUCN[a] Red List of Threatened Species (year assessed)	CITES[b] listed species database (Appendix no. and year listed)
Bobcat (*Lynx rufus*)	Not listed	Not rated	Appendix II (1977)
Mexican bobcat (*Lynx rufus escuinapae*)	Endangered (1976)	Not rated	Appendix II (1992) [formerly listed as *Felis* (*Lynx*) *rufus escuinapae* on Appendix I, now included with *Felis* spp.]
Canada lynx (*Lynx canadensis*)	Threatened (2000)	Not rated	Appendix II (1977)
Spanish lynx (*Lynx pardinus*)	Endangered (1970)	Critically Endangered as *Lynx pardinus* (2002)	Appendix I as *Lynx pardinus* (1990)
Eurasian lynx (*Lynx lynx*)	Not listed	Near Threatened (2002)	Appendix II (1995)

[a]IUCN is the World Conservation Union, an international organization that promotes the protection and sustainable use of living resources.
[b]CITES is the Convention on International Trade in Endangered Species of Wild Fauna and Flora. Parties to this agreement, signed in 1975, agreed to restrict their commercial trade of endangered plant and animal species. Appendix I lists species that are the most endangered among CITES-listed animals and plants; Appendix II lists species that are not necessarily now threatened with extinction but that may become so unless trade is closely controlled.

export of lawfully obtained captive-bred lynx (USFWS 2000). A species is listed as threatened when it is likely to become endangered throughout all or a significant portion of its range in the foreseeable future.

The Spanish lynx has been designated as an endangered species throughout its range (Spain and Portugal) since June 2, 1970. With fewer than 300 animals remaining in the wild, the Spanish lynx may be the rarest felid species (Gaona et al. 1998). Additionally, CITES has listed the Canada lynx on Appendix II since 1977, and the Spanish lynx was added to Appendix I in 1990.

In 2002, the IUCN placed both the Spanish lynx and the Eurasian lynx on its Red List of Threatened Species. The IUCN 's mission is to influence, encourage, and assist societies throughout the world to conserve the integrity and diversity of nature and to ensure that any use of natural resources is equitable and ecologically sustainable. It considers the Spanish lynx to be "Critically Endangered" throughout its range in Spain and Portugal, and IUCN biologists estimate its population to number less than 250 mature animals. Major threats include habitat loss, prey loss, human-caused mortality (trapping, snaring, netting, shooting, and vehicle collisions), and no subpopulation containing more than 50 mature breeding individuals. The Eurasian lynx is "Near Threatened" throughout much of its range in Europe, Central Asia, Siberia, and East Asia due to ongoing habitat loss and degradation, hunting, and changes in the cat's prey base (IUCN 2004). CITES listed the Eurasian lynx on Appendix II in 1995. The USFWS does not list the Eurasian lynx, nor any of its subspecies, as threatened or endangered, and IUCN does not rate either the Canada lynx or the bobcat (see Table 1.1).

Appearance and Size

> As I worked my fingers into Billy the bobcat's fur, I was struck by how soft, short, and dense it was.

Their species name, *rufus,* is Latin for red, but the actual color of their fur varies with their geographic location. In the Pacific Northwest and western Canada, where little sun penetrates the dense forest canopy, bobcats are a dark reddish-brown. In the more arid regions of the southwestern United States, a light gray-brown pelage predominates (Koehler 1987). Their pelage has also been described as light gray, buff, brown, and yellowish brown. Arizona wildlife ecologist Christine Hass (personal communication) reported that bobcats around Tucson can be quite red. The coat along the middle of the back is usually darker, giving the subtle appearance of a sporty racing stripe. They molt twice a year, with some populations exhibiting a reddish coat during the summer and a grayer coat in winter (McCord and Cardoza 1982). There are distinct dark brown or black spots covering the back and legs. The white belly fur has distinct black spots, whereas the back of the ears is black with a large white spot in the center. Koehler (1987:399) explained, "The spotted pelage is very effective camouflage in places [where] the sun casts dappled shadows among the undergrowth allowing this elusive predator to meld into its environment."

With such variety in bobcat pelage coloration, it is not surprising that both black (melanistic) and white (albinistic) color phases have been documented. Florida seems to be the hotbed of black bobcats. Biologists Tim Regan and Dave Maehr (1990) documented ten occurrences between 1939 and 1990, all of them in southern Florida. Stanley Young (1978) described an albino bobcat that survived four years in the wild before being captured and placed in a Texas zoo.

Although its color can vary, the most distinguishing features of the bobcat are the tufted ears, the facial ruff, and the short tail. Although not as pronounced as in the Canada lynx, the bobcat's ears are tipped with a short tuft of black hairs, and there are distinctive white splotches on the back of each ear. A ruff or collar of fur, frequently streaked with black, extends along the side of the face, giving the appearance of enormous sideburns. The distinctive short tail averages 14.8 cm (6 inches) in adult males and 13.7 cm (5 inches) in adult females and is white underneath with dark bands on top (McCord and Cardoza 1982; Rolley 1987; Lariviere and Walton 1997; Sunquist and Sunquist 2002; Anderson and Lovallo 2003).

Canada lynx can be distinguished from bobcats by their larger feet, slightly shorter tail, longer black ear tufts (<2.5 cm [1 inch]), and less well defined spots on the coat. The fur of the Canada lynx is grayer than the reddish-brown of the bobcat. The bobcat's tail is banded only on the upper surface, whereas the tail of the lynx is brownish or pale buff white and ends in a black tip that entirely encircles the tip (Lariviere and Walton 1997; Anderson and Lovallo 2003). However, visually distinguishing these characteristics in the outdoors can be a challenge, even for those with a practiced eye. Wildlife biologist Kerry Murphy has had ample opportunity to learn to recognize the two species while working in and around Yellowstone and Grand Teton national parks, where both cats are present, and reported that "[t]he feet or tracks are the best diagnostic, when they are visible." Canada lynx have large furry foot pads that can spread up to almost 12.7 cm (5 inches) when measured along the outline of the hair impression. Bobcat feet and tracks are half as large (Rezendes 1999). Murphy continued, "The tail is the next best diagnostic. The lynx tail tip is black all around, as if dipped in chocolate. The bobcat tail is only black on the dorsal side with partial rings. Color (pelage) is not diagnostic unless you are close to the animal because the mottled light of northern latitudes makes it hard to distinguish a plain from a spotted coat. Ear tufts on the Canada lynx are longer, but hard to see from a distance" (Kerry Murphy, National Park Service, personal communication).

Like the proverbial fish story, predators seen in the wild, even small ones, take on enormous proportions during the retelling at the local barber shop. The reality is that the bobcat is not a very large feline. They are medium-size wild cats, twice the size of the domestic cat, but slightly smaller than the Canada lynx (McCord and Cardoza 1982; Sunquist 1991; Lariviere and Walton 1997) and much smaller than the mountain lion. Canada lynx frequently appear larger than bobcats because the long legs and dense fur of the more northern feline exaggerate its body size. Only on Cape Breton Island in New Brunswick, Canada, do bobcats outweigh Canada lynx; there, adult male bobcats are 40% heavier than adult male lynxes (Parker et al. 1983).

Bobcats also have shorter legs and smaller feet than the Canada lynx. Weight and physical dimensions vary with age, season, nutritional condition, and geographic location (Rolley 1987; Sunquist and Sunquist 2002). Male bobcats average 10 kg (22 pounds) and may stand 46 cm (18 inches) at the shoulder. The head and body length is about 77 cm (30 inches), with a 14.8-cm (6-inch) tail. Females average 7.3 kg (16 pounds), with a head and body length of 70 cm (27 inches) and a 13.7-cm (5- inch) tail (McCord and Cardoza 1982; Sunquist 1991; Sunquist and Sunquist 2002). Bobcats in northern latitudes are larger than those in more southern regions (Rolley 1987; Sunquist and Sunquist 2002). During his work on bobcats in Minnesota, Berg (1979) found that adult male bobcats averaged 13 kg (28.6 pounds) in the winter, and adult females averaged 9.2 kg (20.2 pounds). The largest bobcat on record came from this same study, tipping the scales at 17.6 kg (38.7

pounds). Rolley (1983) found Oklahoma bobcats to be much smaller. Adult males averaged 8.9 kg (19.6 pounds), and females averaged 5.8 kg (12.7 pounds). In biology, Bergman's Rule asserts that the body size of a species increases with latitude and elevation. The classic explanation is that a lower surface-to-volume ratio has thermal advantages (Boyce 1979). Animals tend to have smaller body size in warmer climates, where they must radiate heat, and larger body size in cooler climates, where they must retain body heat. Bobcats certainly seem to follow this pattern. However, Wigginton and Dobson (1999) examined 950 bobcat skulls and concluded that bobcat body size is probably more closely related to seasonal food abundance and the energy demands of cold weather, rather than Bergman's Rule. There is also a pronounced difference in skull structure between the sexes. Male skulls are much larger, longer, and more sharply ridged than those of females of the same age (Read 1981; McCord and Cardoza 1982; Sikes and Kennedy 1992).

Male bobcats are up to 10% longer and can weigh from 25% to 80% more than females (McCord and Cardoza 1982; Anderson 1987; Lariviere and Walton 1997; Sunquist and Sunquist 2002; Anderson and Lovallo 2003). Researchers Sikes and Kennedy (1993) analyzed 1,056 adult bobcat skulls from the eastern United States to identify geographic variation in sexual dimorphism. It was most pronounced in mountainous regions and occurred less frequently in areas of little topographic relief. Bobcat authority Eric Anderson (1987) suggested that there may be a number of advantages to sexual dimorphism. Female bobcats may mate with several males during the breeding season. Under such a polygynous mating system, larger males have the advantage in competing for breeding opportunities, so natural selection favors the larger males. Another suggestion is that, because predators of different sizes hunt prey of different sizes, sexual dimorphism reduces competition between males and females for food (Fritts and Sealander 1978b). Finally, with the constraints on their mobility and the energy demands of rearing kittens, female bobcats have evolved physically and behaviorally to more efficiently and intensively hunt close to home. Anderson (1987) emphasized that all of these factors probably work in combination to select for size difference.

Determining the sex of a bobcat can be a challenge for amateur and professional alike. The male genitalia of felids are much less prominent than those of most other mammals. Untrained biologists, as well as trappers and hunters, have often misidentified the sex of a bobcat (Rolley 1987). The most frequent error is identifying males as females. Although adults are sometimes misidentified, juveniles are more frequently a source of error. Pelt examination alone is unreliable for identifying sex, because the male genitalia usually are not attached (Henderson 1979). The most reliable method to accurately determine sex is an internal examination of the carcass by trained personnel. This is also important in quantifying sex ratios (the ratio of males to females) in harvested populations. P. D. Friedrich and his colleagues at the Michigan Department of Natural Resources developed a technique for determining sex based on measurements of the maximum cross-sectional area of the lower canine teeth (fangs). This was obtained by multiplying the maximum canine root width by the maximum root thickness for each bobcat. In their two-year sample, 88.7% of the juveniles and 96.9% of the adults were correctly classified as to sex by this method (Friedrich et al. 1984). When handling live-trapped bobcats, sex is determined by carefully palpating the genitals (Rolley 1987).

2 The Petite Predator

We keep the big carnivores in here," announces Karen Cebra, pulling open the doors of a large wooden cabinet. From the shelves within, rows of enormous skulls stare down at us with large, empty eye sockets. The bone has a yellow cast under the fluorescent light. There are bear, jaguar, and African lion.

"The lynxes and bobcats are over here," she says turning to face a row of five metal specimen cabinets. "Skulls and postcranial skeletons here," she says pointing to one of the end cabinets. "And study skins over here." She steps forward and removes each containers' front panel. Both are filled with stacked wooden drawers.

We are in the main collection room of the California Academy of Sciences in San Francisco. As Collections Manager in the Department of Ornithology and Mammalogy, Karen oversees one of the largest bird and mammal collections in North America. She also assists the hundreds of academics, scholars, students, writers, and artists who use the collection each year. "The mammal collection has 23,931 specimens," she explains. "We're in the process of inventorying and updating the scientific names of all specimens, as well as putting the names on a computerized database. Come get me if you have any questions," she smiles, then disappears around a corner.

Pulling a chair up to the first cabinet, I carefully pull out the top drawer. It is filled with assorted small cardboard boxes. Opening one of the containers I find the skull and jaw of a Eurasian lynx. The identification tag tells me that cat was collected in December 1939 by A. S. Loukashkin in the Great Kingdom Mountains of Northern Manchuria. Another box reveals another Chinese lynx donated by Loukashkin, and there are others. Mr. Loukashkin was a busy man.

The next drawer brings me to the bobcats. I examine the skull and jaw of a California bobcat collected on December 10, 1909, in Santa Barbara. The skull fits comfortably in my palm. The bone appears polished, and the empty orbits stare blankly from the skull. The teeth are worn but intact, indicating it was probably an adult. The second upper premolar is missing, reflecting the bobcat's unique 28 teeth instead of the usual 30 found in most cats. I am struck by how delicate this most deadly part of the bobcat's anatomy appears.

Next I open a cardboard box measuring only 5 × 7 × 4 inches. Inside is the complete postcranial skeleton of a bobcat (everything but the skull and jaw). It is a male and dates from 1913. Again the bones are surprisingly light and delicate. Even the large leg bones seem small. A few caudal vertebrae, once supporting the distinctive short tail, roll around in the bottom of the box. I carefully lay out the bones and am amazed that the box does indeed contain a complete skeleton. My respect for the efficiency of the design deepens.

I examine several other boxes before moving to the cabinet at the other end of the row to examine the study skins. A study skin is the preserved hide of a collected animal. The organs, muscles, and skeleton have been removed and replaced with cotton stuffing and wire to help keep its shape. Seven bobcat skins lie nestled in the wooden drawer like furry loaves of bread. Most are gray and brown, but the color has faded. Six of them date from the late 1800s, and one was collected in 1945. Cotton stuffing is visible where the eyes once were. I pick one up to examine it. The pelt is stiff and brittle with age. As I turned it in my hands, a familiar discomfort returns.

Like many college biology students, I spent countless hours studying preserved specimens in similar collection rooms. Such exposure is basic training for any biologist. At the time, I found the skulls and skins fascinating but preferred observing live animals in the field. Today, I am more ambivalent about the value of collecting. The millions of preserved specimens that are stored in collections today are the foundation of much of our knowledge of the living world. They also represent enormous carnage. In the Academy's collection room, my youthful fascination is tempered by a profound sense of the macabre.

I ask Karen about the age of the specimens and about the Academy's collection policy. She explains that the Academy's collection is always being added to, but most specimens now come from salvage, such as beached marine mammals. The most recent specimens died in zoos. The most recent bobcat added to the collection was a 1990 roadkill. The Academy does no active collecting. In a world where wild animals face so many obstacles to survival, there is no need to add to the carnage simply to add to the collection.

■

Anatomy of a Hunter

Felines are the pinnacle of carnivore evolution. Their anatomy, behavior, and cosmopolitan distribution are testimony to their success. Among the carnivores, cats also show the greatest relative variation in body size, ranging from the tiny rusty-spotted cat (*Prionailurus rubiginosus*) at 1 kg (2.2 pounds) (Sunquist and Sunquist 2002) to the majestic Bengal tiger (*Panthera tigris*) at 258 kg (568 pounds). The Siberian tiger, a subspecies found in eastern Asia, may be even larger, but documenting accurate weights is difficult (Sunquist and Sunquist 2002). Because they are the most exclusive of meat-eaters, almost every feature of a cat's body is related to the way it detects, catches, and kills its prey. The bobcat's spotted coat, keen senses, muscular body, claws, paws, teeth, jaws, gut, and remarkable adaptability make it ideally suited for a predatory existence.

Hiding and Detecting Prey

Like most wild felines, bobcats are not capable of extended chases, so they must get close to their prey, without being seen, before launching their attack. Their spotted coats provide excellent camouflage against vegetation or the ground. Such camouflage is especially effective in the dappled light of the forest. For small cats such as the bobcat, and for the young of all species, camouflage also protects against larger predators. Variations in the bobcat's pelage occur throughout its range. Northwestern populations seem to have more colorful coats and more distinctive spots than eastern or southern bobcats. Wildcats inhabiting the desert southwest are paler in color (Koehler 1987).

Cats have extraordinary vision. The eyeball, pupil, and lens are proportionately larger than in other carnivores. The eyes of a domestic cat are only slightly smaller than those of humans, but the cat's pupil can open to a maximum area three times larger than that of a human. This increases light-gathering ability and enhances night vision (Kiltie 1991). The amount of light entering the eyeball is controlled by the pupil, and the pupil in smaller felines of the domestic cat lineage is elliptical. This allows it to open as wide as possible at night but close almost completely in bright light, protecting light-sensitive cells. Bobcat eyes are prominent, and the pupils are elliptical, reflecting a somewhat lesser dependency on nocturnal hunting. They may hunt at any time during the day or night but are primarily active during the twilight hours of dawn and dusk. As a result, their eyes are proportionately smaller than those of more nocturnal cats, making bobcats suited to hunting both in daylight and at night (Buie et al. 1979; McCord and Cardoza 1982; Kitchener 1991).

After passing through the pupil and lens, light strikes a layer of light-sensitive cells at the back of the eye called the retina. There are two kinds of light receptor cells in the retinas of mammals: rods and cones. Rods function in low light levels and are sensitive to shades of black and white, whereas cones operate in high light levels and are sensitive to color. Not surprisingly, the eyes of cats consist primarily of rods, although there is a concentration of cones near the center of the retina, as in our own eyes. Therefore, felines may be able to see some color, at least during daylight. There is evidence that cats can see green, blue, and possibly red, but these colors are probably much less saturated than what humans see (Kiltie 1991; Kitchener 1991; Sunquist and Sunquist 2002).

Behind the retina is a thin layer of reflective cells called a *tapetum lucidum*, meaning "bright carpet." The tapetum reflects light back through the rods and enhances low-light images, giving the bobcat a second chance to discern what it is looking at. The tapetum is responsible for the characteristic eyeshine of reflected light that is frequently seen in mammals at night (Sunquist 1987; Kiltie 1991; Kitchener 1991; Sunquist and Sunquist 2002). Another characteristic of feline vision is that the eyes are close together and facing forward. This allows the field of vision of the two eyes to overlap, giving them enhanced binocular vision. Binocular vision provides excellent depth perception and the ability to precisely judge distance; cats have the most highly developed binocular vision among carnivores (Sunquist and Sunquist 2002). The domestic cat's total visual field spans 186 degrees, with a binocular overlap of 98 degrees (Hughes 1976; Kitchener 1991). Larger felids, such as the puma, with their larger and more protruding eyeballs, can have a total visual field that covers 287 degrees, with a binocular overlap of 130 degrees (Tansley 1965). The bobcat's visual field probably lies somewhere between those of the domestic cat and the puma. Enhanced depth perception is a valuable adaptation for a predator that stalks its prey and attacks from a short distance.

Having such a wide visual Weld also gives cats highly developed peripheral vision, which may contribute to their reputation of being aloof and mysterious. "Because its peripheral vision is so good, a resting cat focuses its eyes infrequently," explained Mel and Fiona Sunquist. "The result is the cat's typical wide-eyed staring-into-space look that some people Wnd so unsettling (Sunquist and Sunquist 2002:10)." A cat that appears to be gazing blankly into space may in reality be carefully watching everything.

Although a bobcat's extraordinary vision seems to give it a distinct advantage over its prey, nature has a way of compensating for advantages. The concentration of rods and the presence of a tapetum have increased the cat's sensitivity to low light, but at the sacrifice of visual acuity, the ability to discern detail in bright light. Rods do not allow for much discrimination between light wavelengths, and the reflection from the tapetum further blurs the image the cat sees. As a result, cats' vision at night is six times better than that of humans, but humans have better visual acuity in daylight (Ewer 1973; Sunquist 1987; Kiltie 1991; Kitchener 1991).

In prey species such as the cottontail rabbit, the eyes are on the side of the head. This arrangement does not allow good depth perception but increases the total field of view and, hence, the ability to detect predators. Cats have a heightened sensitivity to movement, and biologists believe that it is the movement of prey that triggers the bobcat to attack (Hubel 1959). This may explain why prey animals typically freeze after detecting a predator (Dixon 1982). In the world of predator and prey, there seems to be a defense for every offense.

Although little research has been done on hearing in bobcats, it is known that most felines can hear in the 65- to 70-kHz range, well beyond the human range of 15 to 20 kHz. Rodents, the primary prey of many small cats, communicate in the ultrasound range of 20 to 50 kHz, giving felines a decided advantage in detecting and catching dinner (Sunquist and Sunquist 2002). However, ultrasound does not carry very far, and it is most useful for short-range communication in dense vegetation. To enhance their ability to detect sounds, cats have developed large external ear flaps or pinnae, which can be moved together or independently to isolate those sounds (Kitchener 1991). The serval (*Leptailurus serval*) uses its enormous ears to pinpoint prey in the grasslands of Africa (Sunquist and Sunquist 2002). Bobcats have large ears, and one of their most unique features is their ear tufts. The purpose of these small spears of hair remains a mystery. Stanley Young believed that the hairs aid the cat's hearing by acting as antennae in collecting sound impulses. He has further stated, "Experiments made with a number of animals held in captivity certainly showed that those having the spears clipped at the tip of the ears did not respond to sound effects as did those with hair spears intact" (Young 1978:21).

Cats have another feature that may enhance their hearing. On the underside of the skull are two bulbous projections called auditory bullae. They form a chamber that surrounds the three ear bones or auditory ossicles. Their specific function is poorly understood, but the bullae appear to vary in size in relation to the feline's lifestyle, particularly the detection of low-frequency sounds. Desert animals, such as the sand cat and the kangaroo rat, have enlarged bullae compared with animals of similar size that dwell in forest habitats. The hot dry air of the desert absorbs sound, so if enlarged auditory bullae increase sensitivity to sound, especially to the movement of prey, it would be a helpful predatory adaptation indeed (Kitchener 1991; Sunquist and Sunquist 2002).

Bobcats, like all species of the Felidae, have a surprising repertoire of vocalizations. "Meow" types of calls are common to all cat species, although the meow of an African lion sounds noticeably different from the meow of a domestic cat. Calls can vary considerably in intensity, duration, pitch, and tonality, depending on the species, function, and motivation of the vocalizing individual. Low-intensity meows usually occur between mothers and kittens at close range; high-intensity meows are used by adult males and females for territorial advertisement and mate attraction. A caterwauling female bobcat in heat is an example of a high-intensity meow. In agonistic situations, such as being held in a trap or snare, vocalizations are also fairly uniform, and they generally occur in association with specific body postures and facial expressions. Under such circumstances, all species spit, hiss, and growl. In friendly, close-contact situations, felids frequently purr. This rhythmic pulsing can vary from the sound of cooing pigeons to the sound of bubbling water. Purring is most common between mother cats and their kittens in the den and in other situations of undisturbed close contact (Young 1978; Peters 1991; Sunquist and Sunquist 2002).

Experts speculate that, in most cats, vision and hearing are most important for hunting, whereas smell plays a more active role in social behavior. Felids produce and deposit odors from their anal sacs, as well as from glands on their cheeks and paws. I do not know what Billy the bobcat was trying to communicate while he was cheek-marking my neck and face, but he was certainly enthusiastic. Cats also deposit urine and feces at strategic locations throughout their home ranges. All are thought to be a means of communication. Although there are accounts of cats tracking prey by scent, the canid sense of smell is much more highly developed than that of felids (Sunquist and Sunquist 2002). The longer muzzle of a dog boasts almost 50 square inches of olfactory cells, compared with the cat's 6 square inches, and 5% of canine brain volume is committed to the sense of smell, compared with 3% for cats (Kitchener 1991). How much a bobcat uses its sense of smell in hunting remains an area of speculation.

Both bobcats and cougars seem to share their domestic cousin's attraction to catnip or catmint. The catnip plant (*Nepeta cataria*) seems to have a soothing effect on feline nervous systems, similar to that of mild opiates in humans (Kitchener 1991). The active ingredient in catnip is *cis-*, *trans*-nepetalactone, which is active in small concentrations (Albone and Shirley 1984). Responses to catnip vary dramatically among species and age of felids (Hill et al. 1976; Cherfas 1987). However, experiments in captivity showed that bobcats, tigers, and pumas did not respond, even though hunters insist all three species are very attracted to catnip. The oil of the catnip plant has been used as an effective lure by both bobcat trappers and wildlife photographers. Young discussed attempts by the U.S. Department of Agriculture to synthesize catnip oil for use as a lure for predator control. He also related his own efforts to use catnip as a lure when photographing bobcats and pumas in northern Coahuila, Mexico (Young 1978).

Cats have an acute sense of touch, particularly with the tip of their nose, paws, and toes. A cat's whiskers or vibrissae are specially adapted as tactile sensors on the muzzle, above the eyes, and on the cheeks and wrists. Thicker than body hairs and embedded more deeply in the skin, vibrissae are highly sensitive to movement. Each sits in a tiny fluid sac, pivoting like a straw in a soda bottle. Any object brushing against a hair sends a signal down the hair shaft to the fluid sac, which is lined with a dense supply of nerve endings. This detection system is delicate enough to sense minor changes in air currents, enabling even blindfolded cats to navigate obstacles without touching them (Sunquist and Sunquist 2002). When hunting, the bobcat spreads its whiskers out on either side of the face like a fan. During prey capture, the muzzle whiskers are extended like a net in front of the mouth, allowing the cat to detect the direction of any evasive movements. Even while carrying its prey, the bobcat wraps its whiskers around the mouse or rabbit to detect any sudden movement that might allow escape. In domestic cats, the areas of the brain that control vision and touch lie adjacent to each other, perhaps indicating that the animals use the two senses together to interpret their world (Kitchener 1991; Sunquist and Sunquist 2002).

Capturing and Consuming Prey

The familiar adage, "Form follows function," is superbly demonstrated in the anatomy of cats. As stealthy, solitary hunters who stalk and ambush their prey, cats must be both fast on approach and strong during capture and killing. The compromise between speed and strength is exemplified in their skeleton and muscles. Cats have a heavy musculature attached to a light but strong skeleton. The majority of a feline's body weight is muscle and sinew, with only a relatively small portion made up of bone and viscera. Long, muscular legs and a flexible backbone allow strong extended strides. Leg movement is further accentuated by a reduced collarbone and by the positioning of the shoulder blade on the side of the body rather than on the back, which allows it to swing along with the leg. A larger pelvis and longer rear leg bones enhances their springing ability, making the bobcat's rear legs longer than its front legs. This adaptation for jumping is valuable both for catching prey and for moving through rugged terrain. One of the most distinguishing anatomical features of the bobcat, and all other lynxes, is the absence of a long tail. Biologists have long speculated as to the purpose of tails, but the bobcats' short tails do not appear to hinder their success as hunters (Kelson 1946; Kiltie 1991; Kitchener 1991).

Cats and many other carnivores walk upright on their toes, a stance known as digitigrade, as opposed to the plantigrade stance found in humans and bears (Kiltie 1991). Webbed skin and fur between the toes muffle sound as the cat walks. Bobcat tracks are generally round and reveal four toe pads in front of a smooth, calloused, three-lobed plantar pad. Because bobcats are digitigrade, they do not have a heel as plantigrade animals do. There is a fifth toe located higher up on the front foot, but it never shows in the track. Adult tracks average 5.1 cm (2 inches) in width and 6 cm (2¼ inches) in length, with a plantar pad about 3.9 cm (1½ inches) wide (see Figure 2.1.) During normal walking, the claws are retracted, but

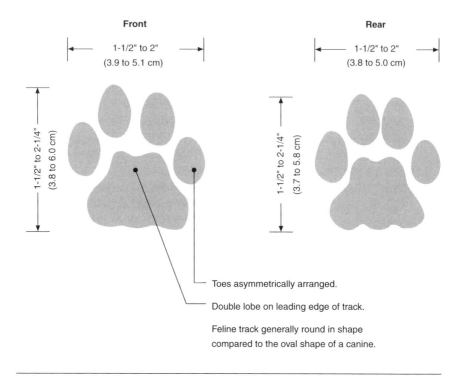

Front

1-1/2" to 2"
(3.9 to 5.1 cm)

1-1/2" to 2-1/4"
(3.8 to 6.0 cm)

Rear

1-1/2" to 2"
(3.8 to 5.0 cm)

1-1/2" to 2-1/4"
(3.7 to 5.8 cm)

Toes asymmetrically arranged.

Double lobe on leading edge of track.

Feline track generally round in shape
compared to the oval shape of a canine.

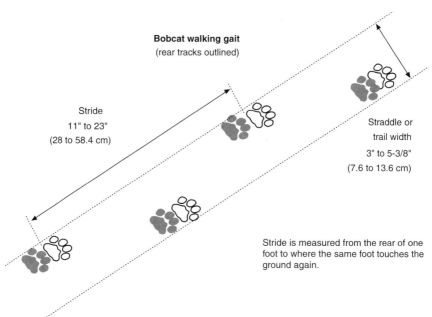

Bobcat walking gait
(rear tracks outlined)

Stride
11" to 23"
(28 to 58.4 cm)

Straddle or
trail width
3" to 5-3/8"
(7.6 to 13.6 cm)

Stride is measured from the rear of one
foot to where the same foot touches the
ground again.

Figure 2.1
Bobcat tracks and walking gait (Rezendes 1999; Hass 2001).

during quick acceleration they are extended and used for traction (Rezendes 1999; Hass 2001).

If a bobcat is stalking or walking on snow or on a muddy surface, its track sequences shows a direct register of tracks. This means that the rear feet are placed almost directly in the corresponding impression of the front feet. If it is walking normally, an overstepped register or slightly oVset direct register occurs. The rear feet are placed on top of or forward of the front feet impressions. The normal walking gait has a stride length ranging from 28 to 58.4 cm (11 to 23 inches) and a trail width from 7.6 to 13.6 cm (3 to 5³/₈ inches) (Rezendes 1999; Hass 2001) (see Figure 2.1.)

Sharp claws are important for seizing and controlling prey so that the killing bite can be delivered. To keep their claws sharp, bobcats have spring-like ligaments that keep the claws retracted inside fleshy sheaths and elevated above the ground most of the time. Retraction of the claws is passive, requiring no conscious effort on the part of the cat. In use, the muscles in the forelegs contract, which in turn protracts the claws, and the bobcat is ready for action (Kiltie 1991).

The skull is short and round and displays a dentition unique to cats. The teeth are few and highly specialized in function. Incisors are chisel-like teeth in the front of the jaws, which are used in plucking the fur or feathers of prey before feeding. The large canines or fangs are the primary killing weapons, and they tend to be longer, stronger, and more rounded than those of dogs. The premolars and molars are specially adapted for feeding on meat. In most felids, there are 15 teeth on each side of the adult skull: 3 upper and 3 lower incisors, 1 upper and 1 lower canine, 3 upper and 2 lower premolars, and 1 upper and 1 lower molar. This dental formula is expressed as I 3/3, C 1/1, P 3/2, M 1/1 = 30. Bobcats and lynxes differ from other cats in that they lack an upper premolar, which gives them 14 teeth in the upper jaw and 14 in the lower jaw, with a dental formula of I 3/3, C 1/1, P 2/2, M 1/1 = 28 (McCord and Cardoza 1982; Jackson et al. 1988; Kitchener 1991).

Dental features are used to classify bobcats as kittens, juveniles, or adults. Experience with hand-raised bobcat kittens has shown that milk (baby) teeth begin to erupt at 11 to 14 days after birth and are complete by nine weeks of age. During this time the molars are missing, giving kittens a dentition of I 3/3, C 1/1, P 2/2, M 0/0 = 24 (Jackson et al. 1988). Permanent teeth begin to erupt at 16 to 19 weeks of age and are complete by 34 weeks. This schedule of tooth replacement is used to age kittens younger than 240 days (34 weeks). It also indicates that there is a period of several weeks when kittens possess an impressive collection of both milk teeth and permanent teeth. The root canals of permanent canines (fangs) remain open until 13 to 18 months of age, allowing researchers to distinguish between juveniles and adult bobcats (Crowe 1975a; Tumlison and McDaniel 1984a; Jackson et al. 1988).

Counting the layers of cementum annuli in cross-sections of canine teeth provides the most reliable estimate of adult age (Crowe 1975a; Anderson 1987). Cementum is the bonelike tissue that forms the outer surface of the root of a tooth.

Annuli are the circular layers of the cementum that are deposited each year. The first layer (annulus) is not deposited until late in the bobcat's second winter, so the animal is one year older than the total number of annuli (Rolley 1987). Other methods have been evaluated that allow classification of bobcats into general age groups, including skull measurements, epiphyseal and cranial suture closings, and eye lens weight. Pelt quality and body measurements are too variable and lack precision for age determination (Conley and Jenkins 1969; Mahan 1979; Anderson 1987).

Bobcats have a powerful bite because of the reduced length of their jaws and their large jaw-closing muscles, the temporalis and masseter. Atop its skull, the cat has a bony ridge called the sagittal crest, which provides a large surface for the attachment of the temporalis, the larger and stronger of the two muscles, and the one that lifts the jaw up and back. The other end of the temporalis attaches to the lower jaw. At a wide gape, such an arrangement gives the temporalis a greater mechanical advantage in driving the large canine teeth through the prey's muscle and bone. The masseter originates on the zygomatic arch, a bony arch on the side of the skull, attaches to the outside of the mandible, and pulls the jaws together. The masseter is more important as the jaws close at the end of the bite and when the cat uses its carnassials during feeding (Ewer 1973; Kiltie 1991; Kitchener 1991). Even the bobcat's tongue is specially adapted, with sharp, horny protuberances that help remove meat from bone and also aid in grooming (Kiltie 1991).

Cats have a relatively short digestive tract, compared with those of other carnivores. This is because the meat that makes up the majority of the feline diet is easier to digest than the vegetable matter that augments the diets of other predators such as canines. Compared with dogs, cats have a smaller cecum (a blind pouch at the beginning of the large intestine that helps in digesting vegetation) and a shorter large intestine. Cats also seem unable to tolerate low levels of nitrogen (protein) in their diets (Kiltie 1991; Kitchener 1991). David Houston of Glasgow University suggested that the shorter and lighter gut of cats benefits their ambush hunting method. Cats depend on quick acceleration to capture prey, and a short intestine reduces body weight and inertia (Houston 1988).

What's on the Menu?

Size is of critical importance in the world of predator and prey. The bigger the cat, the bigger the prey it can catch and kill. Kitchener (1991:107) pointed out, "It is advantageous for cats to prey on the largest possible prey, in order to get the maximum energetic return, but the potential costs of tackling large prey are possible failure, wastage if too much food is caught and injuries caused in any struggle." In the case of the diminutive bobcat, it is best suited for killing prey weighing from 700 g to 5.5 kg (1.5 to 12 pounds) (Rosenzweig 1966; Anderson and Lovallo 2003), which generally means rabbits, hares, and large rodents. Cottontail rabbits, snowshoe hares, and jackrabbits are the most frequently documented items (Bailey 1974; Berg 1979; Dibello et al. 1990; Knick 1990), sometimes making up more than 90% of the bobcat's diet (Bailey 1979; Parker and Smith 1983). Rodents on the menu include the cotton rat in the south and east and wood rats in the west (McCord and Cardoza 1982). Being more of a generalist predator than either the cougar or the Canada lynx, the bobcat will also kill and eat several species of mice, squirrels, birds, and reptiles, as well as beaver, baby coatis, opossums, bird eggs, domestic fowl, sheep, goats, and other bobcats (Beasom and Moore 1977; Fritts and Sealander 1978b; Jones and Smith 1979; Knick et al. 1984; Rolley 1985; Delibes 1997). Ambitious male bobcats sometimes take white-tailed deer (*Odocoileus virginianus*; Marston 1942; McCord 1974a; Petraborg and Gunvalson 1962), mule deer (*Odocoileus heminonus*; Bailey 1979; Koehler and Hornocker 1989), pronghorn *(Antilocapra americana*; Beale and Smith 1973), and bighorn sheep *(Ovis canadensis*; Koehler and Hornocker 1989). Large prey may also be consumed as carrion, roadkill, or animals crippled by sport hunting (Fritts and Sealander 1978b).

Before 1970, studies of bobcat diet made up the majority of research. This is because it is relatively easy to collect and analyze stomachs from harvested animals or to collect scats (feces) in the wild (Anderson 1987). Scat analysis tends to reveal only those food items that are not digested, such as bone, so it underestimates the occurrence of prey that is highly digestible. The advantage is that it causes no harm to the animal. Stomach content analysis, on the other hand, requires killing of the animal and may provide no information if the stomach is empty. However, bobcats usually are not killed simply to analyze their food habits.

Once diet information is collected and analyzed, it is usually expressed either as the frequency of occurrence of a prey species in the scats or stomach contents or as the percentage by volume or weight of the total amount of food in the stomach. The primary limitation of these two approaches is that neither reflects the actual weight or biomass of the animal consumed (Kitchener 1991). During her study of bobcat food habits in northern California, researcher Jennifer Neale used a computer program to more accurately estimate the amount of fresh prey consumed. The program used correction factors based on feeding trials to infer the amount of prey consumed from food remains in scat samples. For example, from a certain amount of deer hair present in a scat, it was possible to estimate the amount of deer consumed. This was expressed as a percentage of the estimated total fresh weight of prey (%FWP). Neale was able to estimate her bobcats' biomass consumption of deer, sheep, lagomorph, squirrel, woodrat, pocket gopher, kangaroo rat, chipmunk, vole, mouse, mole, bird, insect, unknown rat, and unknown mouse (Neale 1996).

From 1980 to 1982, Canadian biologists Christopher Matlack and Alison Evans conducted one of the largest bobcat diet examinations ever attempted. They analyzed stomach contents of some 1,099 bobcat carcasses, obtained from trappers, hunters, fur buyers, and taxidermists from across Nova Scotia. Snowshoe hares were the most frequent prey item found, followed by white-tailed deer and small rodents (Matlack and Evans 1992). In the warmer climate of Florida, researchers David Maehr and James Brady (1986) picked through the remains of 413 bobcat stomachs collected from 1977 to 1983 and discovered that the hispid cotton rat was at the top of the feline's menu, followed by rabbits, gray squirrels, and white-tailed deer. Steven Knick and his colleagues in Washington found that bobcats in the western portion of the state preferred mountain beaver (*Aplodontia rufa*) and snowshoe hares, whereas bobcats in the eastern portion had a more diverse menu, including rabbits, hares, red squirrels, deer, and voles (Knick et al. 1984). Northern California bobcats divide their take between wood rats, lagomorphs, voles, and reptiles (lizards and snakes), according to Jennifer Neale's analysis of 242 scats (Neale 1996). In the middle of their North American range, Arkansas bobcats follow a similar pattern and dine most frequently on cottontail rabbits, squirrels, rats, and mice, based on the examination of 150 stomachs collected between 1970 and 1972 by Fritts and Sealander (1978b). Illinois bobcats prefer to dine on small rodents (32.8%), rabbits (22.7%), squirrels (19.3%), and birds (10.1%) (Woolf and Nielsen 2002).

Table 2.1
Bobcat Diet by Geography

Location	Sample size	Common prey	Author
Arizona	176 scats	Lagomorphs, woodrats	Jones and Smith 1979
Arkansas	150 stomachs	Cottontails, squirrels	Fritts and Sealander 1978a
British Columbia	70 stomachs	Red squirrels, deer	Apps 1995b
California	242 scats	Woodrats, lagomorphs	Neale 1996
Florida	413 stomachs	Cotton rats, lagomorphs	Maehr and Brady 1986
Idaho	233 stomachs	Lagomorphs, rodents	Bailey 1979
Illinois	91 stomachs	Small rodents (32.8%), rabbits (22.7%), squirrels (19.3%), birds (10.1%)	Woolf and Nielsen 2002
Maine	170 stomachs	Snowshoe hares, white-tailed deer	Litvaitis et al. 1986a
Minnesota	215 stomachs	snowshoe hares, white-tailed deer	Berg 1979
New Hampshire	388 stomachs	Cottontails, white-tailed deer	Litvaitis et al. 1984
Nova Scotia	1,099 stomachs	Snowshoe hares, white-tailed deer	Matlack and Evans 1992
Texas	125 stomachs	Cotton rats, cottontails	Beasom and Moore 1977
Utah-Nevada	53 stomachs, 81 intestinal tracts	Lagomorphs, mule deer	Gashwiler et al. 1960

Surprisingly, deer is an important food for bobcats. Early researchers believed that most of the deer eaten was carrion obtained as a result of sport hunting or winter starvation (Rollings 1945; Pollack 1951a). It is now known that bobcats regularly kill deer, usually fawns or does in poor physical condition, although healthy adult bucks have been taken as well. Predation on deer is most prevalent in the winter, usually in the Northeast and Northwest, where deep snow makes them more vulnerable to attack (Marston 1942; Young 1978:68,73; Beale and Smith 1973; McCord 1974a). John Litvaitis and his fellow researchers (1986a) examined winter diets of bobcats in Maine and found that the white-tailed deer was the most important prey of both adult and yearling males but was insignificant in the rodent-dominated diets of females and juveniles. Apps (1995b) found a similar pattern among the bobcats of southeastern British Columbia. Adult males consumed ungulates more often than did adult females or kittens/juveniles. With female bobcats specializing in lagomorphs and rodents and males killing deer, competition between the sexes is reduced. The key to this partitioning of food resources appears to be body size.

"It's almost as if male bobcats are a different species than females," said Seth Riley during his study of bobcats north of San Francisco. "Their weights and foraging habits are so different. Males are more muscular and their heads are larger. In my study area males weigh 20 to 22 pounds, while females weigh 11 to 13 pounds" (Seth Riley, National Park Service, personal communication). The male bobcats' larger and more muscular body gives them an obvious advantage in attacking and killing bigger prey, such as deer. Their larger size also allows them to defend carcasses from competing bobcats and other predators. In addition, because of their ability to kill deer, male bobcats can survive the severe conditions of winter better than females can. Litvaitis and his fellow investigators in Maine (1986a) and Apps in British Columbia (1995b) found that male bobcats in both regions carried more body fat. Conversely, female bobcats face the dual handicap of being too small to kill deer and entering winter with smaller fat deposits due to the cost of lactation earlier in the year. During his inventory of bobcat diets in western Washington, S. J. Sweeney (1978) observed that male stomachs contained almost twice the weight of prey as female stomachs, suggesting that females not only feed on different prey but also need to feed more frequently. Additionally, studies in Oklahoma (Whittle 1979) and Oregon (Toweill 1980) found that juvenile bobcats (younger than one year) ate more rodents and fewer rabbits and hares than did yearling and adult bobcats.

When the abundance of their primary prey declines, bobcats have even been known to change their diet. This occurred in Big Bend National Park in western Texas, where cougars and male bobcats usually feed on deer. When the mule deer population crashed in 1980–1981, both cat species were forced to switch to peccaries and lagomorphs, the next largest prey (Leopold and Krausman 1986). During a major decline in rabbit and hare populations in eastern Idaho, Ted Bailey (1974) noted a reduced occurrence of lagomorphs in bobcat scats and an increased occurrence of rodents and birds. Conversely, an increase in prey availability can also greatly influence feeding preferences. Researchers Samuel Beasom and Rebecca Moore examined 125 bobcat stomachs from south Texas in 1971 and 1972. Bobcats consumed 21 different species, with 80% being cotton rat, white-tailed deer, or cottontail rabbit. A dramatic population increase in cotton rats and cottontail rabbits in the second year led to a decline in the variety of prey eaten, from 21 species to 6 species. Of the six species taken the second year, 96% were cotton rats and cottontails (Beasom and Moore 1977). Further complicating the predator/prey picture for bobcats, James Jones and Norman Smith looked at 176 bobcat scats in central Arizona and found that the frequency of occurrence of rodents and lago-morphs did not vary significantly, even though the populations of both prey groups varied considerably over the year of the study (Jones and Smith 1979).

Although much is known about what bobcats eat, their energy and nutritional needs are poorly understood. In 1965, Frank Golley and his colleagues at the University of Georgia monitored eight captive bobcats trapped in the field and fed a diet of chicken, rabbit, or deer for up to 100 days. They found that the caged felines ate about 138 kcal/kg/day but could maintain their physical condition on half that amount. The cats also digested 91% of the food they ate. It appears that bobcats can survive for extended periods with little food; then, when prey is caught, they can efficiently metabolize large amounts of food (Golley et al. 1965). Later research at the University of New Hampshire revealed that different prey yielded different amounts of energy. Four adult bobcats were fed diets of snowshoe hare, white-tailed deer, gray squirrel, and small mammals. The bobcats digested 77% of the gross energy of the snowshoe hares, 95% of the white-tailed deer, 87% of the gray squirrels, and 83% of the small mammals (Powers et al. 1989).

It is known that domestic cats require almost five times more protein than dogs or humans (adjusted for body weight) (Anderson 1987:9). Domestic cats also have a mean digestive efficiency for total energy of 79%, as opposed to 89% for the domestic dog (Kitchener 1991). Obviously, the digestive tracts of felines must be adapted to efficiently metabolize such high levels of protein. Biologists Mark Johnson and Don Allred compared prey digestibility in bobcats and coyotes. Bobcats were able to digest 99% of the bones of both gray squirrels and eastern cottontails, whereas coyotes dissolved 91% and 93%, respectively. When it came to hair, bobcats processed 93% of the gray squirrel hair and 88% of the cottontail hair, compared with 80% and 43%, respectively, for the coyotes (Johnson and Allred 1982). Feline digestive enzymes seem to handle a high-protein diet, but their livers are unable to alter the levels of these enzymes to allow the cats to process vegetable protein. In addition, cats are unable to convert beta-carotene into vitamin A, so they must obtain it from the liver, lungs, adrenals, or kidneys of their prey (Scott 1968).

Many studies have shown that grass is incidentally ingested by bobcats from the digestive tracts of their prey. Miller and Speake (1979) found grass in 66% of the scats they examined in south Alabama. But the large boluses of grass frequently found indicate that grass may be eaten intentionally to assist digestion or as a purgative for accumulations of tapeworms in the intestine (Rollings 1945; Toweill and Anthony 1984; Neale 1996; Anderson and Lovallo 2003).

Little is known about bobcats' water requirements. They have been observed drinking from streams and springs, but when water is scarce they apparently can exist for long periods without it. This seems particularly evident in some of the desert areas of the Southwest. Kitchener (1991) believed that, even when wild felids have access to free water, part of their liquid requirement probably comes from their prey.

Killing for a Living

Bobcats are stalking and ambush predators. Like most cats, with the notable exception of cheetahs, they attempt to catch their prey unaware rather than chase it down. They are master hunters that employ patience, speed, and precision rather than brute force. The cat is silent on approach, quick on the attack, and efficient in making the kill (Sunquist and Sunquist 2002; Anderson and Lovallo 2003).

Bobcats are not strictly nocturnal, as many once thought. Rather, they are active when their prey are active, and rabbits, hares, and rodents tend to be active at dawn and dusk. Animals that are active during the twilight of dawn and dusk are said to be crepuscular. Bobcats are on the move most frequently during early morning and late afternoon or early evening. Little activity has been observed at midday or midnight (Hall and Newsom 1978; Buie et al. 1979). Not surprisingly, eastern cottontails and hispid cotton rats, two of the bobcat's favorite prey, are also most active around sunrise and sunset (Anderson 1987). The bobcat's excellent night vision makes it well suited for stalking during these low-light periods. Bobcats in South Carolina seem to be more active during daylight hours in the winter (Buie et al. 1979).

The bobcat actually employs two hunting strategies: the first involves searching the home range until prey is encountered, and the second involves waiting in ambush until prey comes within range of attack. The two techniques are also used in combination (Anderson and Lovallo 2003). The mobile strategy is most likely used when prey is scarce, forcing the bobcat to cover more ground while hunting. The bobcat is a relentless hunter. The search for prey is driven by the cat's hunger and, in the case of a female, the need to feed growing kittens. The hungrier the cat, the greater the tendency to roam, with effort focused on areas where prey was previously found. The bobcat navigates its home range in a zigzag course, repeatedly searching thick vegetation along streams, brushy areas in old agricultural fields, or timber regeneration sites, while skirting open areas and taking advantage of available cover. Keen senses are focused to pick up the slightest movement, sound, or odor. How frequently the cat encounters prey depends on the number of prey in its home range, the density of cover, and the bobcat's searching behavior. The hunter frequently stops, sits, crouches, waits and watches from lookouts near well-worn game trails (Rollings 1945; McCord 1974a; Hamilton 1982; McCord and Cardoza 1982; Sunquist and Sunquist 2002).

Because of the bobcat's skill as a stealthy hunter, few people have actually witnessed a bobcat make a kill in the wild. Most accounts have been inferred from radiotelemetry studies, snow tracking, or observations of captive animals (Rolley 1987). Paul Leyhausen (1979) has performed extensive research on predatory behavior in domestic and wild cats. It is now believed that prey-capture behavior is very similar in all species of wild cats. After locating a rabbit or rodent, the bobcat fixes its gaze on the animal, lowers itself to the ground in a crouch, and begins to maneuver closer, taking care to remain hidden. It assumes an alert watching posture: head stretched forward, whiskers spread wide, and ears erect and turned toward the front. The cat will hold this position for more than ten minutes if necessary, following the prey's slightest movement with its head. Cats are notoriously patient, and bobcats are no different. Marshall and Jenkins (1966) told of one Louisiana bobcat that took 13 minutes to move one meter before pouncing on and trapping a hispid cotton rat with its forefeet. When the prey draws within 10 m (33 feet) or less, *Lynx rufus* gives chase (McCord and Cardoza 1982; Sunquist and Sunquist 2002). But the bobcat is built for speed, not endurance, and if the prey is not caught within 3 to 18 m (10 to 60 feet), the pursuit is abandoned (Rollings 1945; Pollack 1951a).

When bobcats are foraging for mice or voles in long grass, an extended stalking approach is not possible. Here the wildcat employs a brief stalk followed by a high, curved jump, similar to what a fox uses to catch a mouse. Such an approach allows the bobcat to pounce directly on its prey, trapping the animal against the ground with its forepaws. This behavior was observed many times by Seth Riley and Pamela Donegan during their study of bobcats and foxes in the Marin Headlands area of Golden Gate National Recreation Area north of San Francisco. The study area's rolling, grassy hillsides were home to an abundant population of California voles. Donegan explained in her thesis that the bobcats she observed were primarily "sit-and-wait" predators. After the cat located a vole, there was a period of stalking, followed by a crouch and pounce. Two other sequences involved a sit-crouch-pounce and a stand-crouch-pounce technique. Another sequence was described as walk-pounce. This occurred when a bobcat happened upon prey, and the subsequent pounce was more reflexive than premeditated (Donegan 1994; Seth Riley, National Park Service, personal communication).

When hunting rabbits or hares, bobcats employ a more passive hunting strategy, making use of hunting beds or "lookouts." In such cases, the bobcat selects a spot where game is plentiful, crouches, and waits (Rollings 1945; Marshall and Jenkins 1966; McCord 1974a). Occasionally, the cat rotates its position to change its angle of view. The resulting circular bed of packed snow shows front paw prints along its edge. Susan Morse pointed out that lookouts are often strategically positioned near a swamp or thicket, or on a ledge or outcrop. Bobcats spend considerable time in these beds, dozing, napping, and watching for a possible meal. It is not unusual to find hair imbedded into the packed snow. Attacks on prey are sometimes launched directly from the bed, or stalking may be necessary, depending on prey location and movements (Susan Morse, Keeping Track, Inc., personal communication).

Once the rodent, hare, or rabbit is seized and pinned with the bobcat's forepaws and claws, it is usually killed with a bite to the nape of the neck or head (Sunquist and Sunquist 2002). The nape bite is faster if the feline's teeth can penetrate the prey's skull or sever the spinal cord. Leyhausen identified the nape bite as the most common killing technique among felines (Leyhausen 1979).

When hunting deer, the bobcat actively stalks and attacks this formidable quarry while it is resting on the ground. Leaping on the bedded deer, the bobcat either attempts to deliver a killing bite to the base of the skull or, more frequently, directs its attack at the throat. The diminutive predator's ability to bite quickly allows it to puncture the major blood vessels and crush the trachea, resulting in strangulation. A throat bite requires death by strangulation and takes longer than a bite to the nape of the neck (Marston 1942; Matson 1948; McCord and Cardoza 1982). Stories of bobcats attempting to take such large prey initially produced skepticism among wildlife officials, but numerous accounts have been documented. Young (1978:78) told of an incident in which a deer hunter and guide heard a loud noise alongside an old logging road in New Brunswick in 1949:

> While the men waited, the brush parted about thirty feet ahead and a deer bounded into the open. On its back was a bobcat, hunched low over the deer's shoulder and struggling to bring its quarry to the ground. This gruesome and one-sided contest had apparently been going on for some time, for the deer was badly winded and lurched unsteadily on its feet. Still trying to 'shake' the ferocious cat, the deer ran twenty-five yards farther along the road. Then collapsed in a heap. [The guide] fired at the bobcat but raised only a bit of fur, and it disappeared into the bush. The deer was stone dead when the men reached it. A jagged hole about three inches deep had been chewed through the hide near the shoulders and there were no other marks on it.

During his study of bobcats in the Salmon River Mountains of central Idaho, Koehler also observed evidence of the violence of bobcat attacks on mule deer. "These attacks are likely real rodeos for the bobcat. I have seen where the hair of both the deer and the bobcat are impaled on rocks and shrubs. But the bobcat's tenacity often wins in the long run" (Gary Koehler, Washington Department of Fish and Wildlife, personal communication).

The speed of the bobcat's bite is impressive, a fact to which biologist Chet McCord can painfully attest. While he was attempting to feed a five-month-old captive kitten, it suddenly attacked his exposed hand. Despite a quick, reflexive withdrawal of his hand, the feline bit to the bone four times (McCord and Cardoza

1982). Such biting speed has obvious advantages when trying to bring down large prey such as deer.

After a successful kill, cats rarely feed immediately. They typically leave the captured prey where it was killed, get up, and explore their immediate surroundings, sniffing the ground and occasionally making short grooming movements, then pick up the prey again. This process may be repeated several times and may serve to work off any excitement not expended during the capture and kill. At some point, however, the bobcat carries or drags the carcass to a protected spot, such as under a tree, and begins to feed (Leyhausen 1979).

Small prey are usually eaten whole on the spot or carried to a secluded location and eaten later. Females with small kittens sometimes return to the den with food (Sunquist and Sunquist 2002). Larger carcasses are fed on, cached, and then revisited for later dining. The bobcat, like other small cats, crouches and eats its prey without using its paws (Gary Koehler, personal communication). The big cats, such as the tiger and the African lion, crouch or lie down and hold their prey with their forepaws while they feed. Small cats usually begin to eat their prey by the head, ignoring the viscera, larger bones, and skin. Big cats start at the abdomen or between the hind legs and either eat the viscera or bury it. Because of the articulation of their jaws, felines can use only one side at a time. This is why cats turn their heads to the side when they are biting through tissue while feeding. Cats do not chew their food; rather, they use their carnassials to cut their prey up into small pieces or strips, which are swallowed whole (Leyhausen 1981; Kitchener 1991).

After feeding on a large kill, the bobcat attempts to hide what remains of the carcass for later feeding. Using its forefeet, it scrapes leaves, pine needles, twigs, dirt, or snow over the carcass (Sunquist and Sunquist 2002). This is usually accompanied by a lot of sniffing of the site. Deer cached in this manner frequently have large amounts of their hair removed and mixed with the covering material (McCord and Cardoza 1982). Hiding the carcass protects it from scavengers, such as coyotes and ravens, and keeps the meat fresher. The bobcat remains in the vicinity of its kill, making frequent trips back to feed and to protect the carcass from other bobcats, carnivores, or scavengers. Sometimes a bobcat buries the uneaten portions of its prey. Young (1978:106) stated, "Instances have been found where a pile of the intestines of a squirrel were covered with a mound of dust and pine needles scraped from a trail. Nearby were observed spots of blood showing where the animal had eaten its meal and in the dust along the used trail were plain cat tracks leading to the scratched-up mound of dust and pine needles."

Determining the hunting success of bobcats is difficult, again due to their stealthy lifestyle. Investigators in South Carolina watched a bobcat make eight attempts to catch prey, succeeding three times (37.5%), resulting in capture of two cotton rats and a cottontail rabbit (Marshall and Jenkins 1966). One Louisiana bobcat was reported to be successful in only one of six attempts (17%) to catch rabbits and rodents (Hall and Newsom 1978). Pamela Donegan observed hunting success during her study of bobcat foraging behavior in northern California. She found that 45% of all capture attempts were successful. Not surprisingly, she found that adults were more successful (54%) than subadults (25%) (Donegan 1994).

Bobcats are primarily solitary hunters, but females and their kittens sometimes forage together in late winter. McCord observed courting pairs of bobcats cooperatively hunting in a spruce plantation on the Quabbin Reservation in Massachusetts: "[T]he cats moved through the plantation about 10 to 15 meters apart and appeared to alternate stopping as the other moved forward 10 to 20 meters" (McCord 1974b). Cooperative hunting has been more commonly observed in the Eurasian lynx and the Canada lynx. Kitchener (1991) suggested that this sort of hunting may be an important part of lynx education. However, Koehler (personal communication) countered that this idea is very speculative: "It is questionable how much learning or 'education' is involved in gaining skill to hunt effectively. Trial and error may be more important than 'watching' and being educated."

The specific impact predators have on prey populations is one of the least understood and most controversial areas of study in wildlife science. In nature, predation is the rule, not the exception. All animals compete for the resources their environment provides, and there are few animals that are not subject to some kind of predation. Prey populations are influenced by many factors, some of the more important being availability of food, denning sites, disease, migration, emigration, and predators.

Traditional thinking was that predators slaughtered everything in sight and were capable of decimating entire prey populations. It was believed that eradication of predators would cause the prey populations to increase, resulting in more game for human hunters. As a result, the Scottish wildcat was almost eradicated by the early 20th century; lions and leopards in African game parks were "controlled" until recently (Kitchener 1991); and the cougar was exterminated in the eastern two-thirds of North America (Hansen 1992). The bobcat's occasional taste for mutton and chicken did not help the situation.

The next evolution in predator/prey theory suggested that predators weed out old or sick individuals, thereby improving the overall health of the prey population. This is sometimes referred to as "sanitation." Although the sanitation hypothesis has elements of truth, it is more frequently a distorted and oversimplified interpretation of Darwin's theory of natural selection (Shaw 1989). Bobcats prey on both healthy and sick animals, and whether the cat selects for unhealthy prey is unsubstantiated. Both healthy and weak are vulnerable because of the bobcat's ambush-hunting method.

Without predators or disease, a prey population could increase until it runs out of space or food. At this point, the population could stabilize if reproduction rates match the rates of death and emigration. More likely, the prey population will enter a cycle of increase and decrease as it responds to the fluctuating levels of food availability and predation. The best historical example of this cyclic pattern is the Canada lynx and its primary prey, the snowshoe hare. Fur trapping records collected over 200 years show a constant 10-year population cycle, with Canada lynx lagging just behind snowshoe hare. Because the Canada lynx is a specialist predator that depends almost exclusively on a snowshoe hare diet, its fate is closely tied to that of its prey (Elton and Nicholson 1942). However, more recent work by Koehler and Aubry (1994) showed the cycle in hare and lynx populations to be absent from populations in the southern parts of their ranges. These southern populations exhibited the same feeding habits, home range sizes, densities, and reproductive characteristics of northern Canada lynx populations during low hare numbers. The difference may be due to the noncycling pattern of snowshoe hare populations and their chronic low numbers in the southern range, as well as a wider variety of alternative prey, habitat patchiness, and a wide array of predators and competitors (Aubry et al. 2000).

Clair Rollings studied bobcats in Minnesota in 1938–1939 and believed that their populations exhibited similar cyclic fluctuations based on cyclic variations in snowshoe hare numbers (Rollings 1945). However, McCord and Cardoza (1982) stated that this cyclic phenomenon has not been demonstrated in bobcats. The fact that the bobcat is a more generalist predator than the Canada lynx and therefore is better able to switch prey probably reduces the its vulnerability to decreases in prey numbers. If snowshoe hares become unavailable, bobcats can switch to other species of rabbits, rodents, or even deer. However, more recent evidence indicates that, if bobcats are present in areas where hare populations vary widely, the felids may show some of the characteristics of a cycling Canada lynx population. During their work in southeastern Idaho, Bailey (1974) and Knick (1990) examined the impact of two periods of cyclic decline in jackrabbits on the local bobcat population. There was a ninefold decrease in bobcat numbers over three years. Home ranges increased in size, forays outside home ranges increased, adult mortality increased, and recruitment of young bobcats into the population dropped to zero.

There is no question that bobcats respond to changes in prey availability. What role, if any, bobcats play in suppressing prey numbers is harder to determine. Anderson (1987:7) emphasized that "the suppressing effect of bobcat predation on prey populations is difficult to separate from the combined effect of all predators, but may be significant at times and in certain areas." In his study of cotton rat populations in South Carolina, Schnell (1968) felt that hawks, foxes, and bobcats were holding the rodent population at a "predator-limited carrying capacity." Beale and Smith (1973) documented high bobcat predation on pronghorn fawns in western Utah and believed it was limiting the population. According to Disney and Spiegel (1992), bobcat predation was a major cause of death of the endangered San Joaquin kit fox (*Vulpes macrotis mutica*) in California.

Kitchener (1991:93) pointed out that predators can have a wide range of impacts on prey populations: feral cats introduced to islands have caused the extinction of resident bird species; mountain lions are thought to reduce wide fluctuations in deer populations; and African lions in the Serengeti have little impact on the migrating ungulate herds. He added, "In other cases, the predator populations seem to be controlled by the prey populations, apparently reducing the predator's role to that of a macroparasite." Whether bobcats limit prey numbers or prey numbers limit bobcat populations remains largely a biological chicken-and-egg question with no simple answer. Where bobcats fall on the continuum, from agent of extinction to macroparasite, depends on the circumstances—and the circumstances are complex indeed.

3 From Den to Death

Harley, I think I found one."

Harley Shaw walks over and follows my gaze to the ground at my feet. Slipping off his pack, he squats for a closer examination. Nestled in the loose dirt is the outline of a mountain lion track—a big one.

"Good eyes," he says, smiling. "Looks like you're getting the hang of it. It's a big tom—the first male we've seen this year."

As I try to burn the image of the track into my mind, Harley glances around. "Here's some more," he says, pointing at the ground farther up the road. He squats to examine the others, then glances up the canyon with a puzzled look.

"What is it?" I ask.

"I think he has a kill cached up this canyon somewhere. These tracks are going up the canyon," he says pointing at the ones near his feet, then gestures to the ones near my feet, "those are coming back down."

While I doubted his interpretation of the sign, I knew it was based on equal parts experience and instinct. After 26 years as a research biologist with the Arizona Game and Fish Department, much of it spent studying mountain lions, and after writing two books on the big cats, Harley Shaw knows a thing or two about cougars (as the cats are also known). That is why I quickly accepted the offer to join him for a week of tracking in the Huachuca Mountains of southern Arizona. Due to their stealthy nature, *counting lions in the wild is practically impossible with current research technology. Harley is trying to develop a tracking technique that will allow him to determine the relative presence of cougars in an area using minimum tracking effort.*

Farther up the road, Harley drops off the side and makes his way down to the dry streambed near a culvert running under the road. His dog, Shy, ambles through the nearby brush, her nose hard at work. Shy is a redbone lion hound, specially bred to track mountain lions. I'm fascinated how Harley uses the dog as a sixth sense in the woods.

"Come look at this," he calls to me.

Climbing down the embankment, I find Harley examining another track. This time it's not a mountain lion.

"Bobcat," he says pointing at the much smaller imprint. "I don't see these very often around here."

Just then Shy lets out with her distinctive howl from farther up the canyon. Harley and I quickly abandon the bobcat track and make our way up the road. It takes a while to locate Shy's howl, but soon we are pushing through thick brush up the south side of the canyon. Harley leads the way, and we find Shy milling around an oak tree. The dog is pawing at a pile of leaves near the base of the tree.

Harley kneels and brushes away the leaves. Just then the odor hits me.

"Well look at that," announces Harley. Buried among the leaves are the decaying remains of a bobcat. The skull is crushed and much of the abdomen is missing, but the remaining fur and the size of the carcass tells the story.

"I guess your hunch was right," I say, covering my nose to reduce the stench. "Do you think it met up with that lion?"

"Yeah, and the predator became the prey."

■

Birth

From birth to death, bobcats face endless obstacles to their survival. Staying alive is a full-time job. But although they may leave this world in a variety of ways—such as meeting up with a mountain lion—all bobcats enter the world the same way.

When a pregnant female bobcat senses the imminent arrival of her kittens, she seeks refuge in a cave, under a rock ledge or rock pile, in a hollow log, under a brush pile or the upturned roots of a fallen tree, or even in an abandoned beaver lodge. She does not prepare an elaborate den but selects the location for privacy and protection from predators (foxes, owls, adult male bobcats) and to shield the litter from heavy rain and hot sun (Gashwiler et al. 1961; Zezulak and Schwab 1979; Miller 1991; Lovallo et al. 1993). She sometimes brings moss and dry leaves into the shelter to enhance its comfort. In isolated areas, the expectant mother may even choose a den under or in ranch buildings (Young 1978). In eastern Idaho, bobcat researcher Ted Bailey (1979) observed a litter in an abandoned nuclear reactor cooling tower and another inside an abandoned storage shed. The female is probably familiar with the location of potential den sites throughout her home range before she selects a natal den. Outside the entrance to her selected natal den, she frequently deposits scat (fecal) mounds—possibly as biological warnings to other bobcats that the site is occupied (Bailey 1974, 1979, 1984b).

Before her first contractions occur, the female licks her nipples and genitalia clean. After her water breaks, she continues to vigorously lick her vaginal region as the first kitten is born. Newborn bobcat kittens enter the world as balls of blind and helpless fur weighing 150 to 340 g (5.2–12 ounces) and open their eyes in 9 to 18 days (Pollack 1950; Young 1978; Stys and Leopold 1993). They have distinctive facial markings, and their fur is covered with dark spots (Sunquist and Sunquist 2002). The female separates the newborn from the placental membrane and severs the umbilical cord, and the kitten immediately begins to nurse while being licked by the mother. This process is repeated as each kitten is delivered. Litter sizes range from one to six, but two to four is most common (Guggisberg 1975; Anderson 1987; Miller 1991). After giving birth, the mother lies with her kittens to keep them warm. As they suckle, she comforts and reassures them with soft calls, licks, and nuzzles. The mother stays with her kittens for the first two days, eating the iron-rich placenta, feces, and any stillborn young (Sunquist and Sunquist 2002). This keeps the den clean and provides her with highly nutritious food. It allows her to remain with her kittens longer and delays the need for her to leave the den to hunt. Throughout the birth, the warm air outside the den indicates that it is spring—the season when most bobcats are born (Bailey 1979; Crowe 1975a, 1975b).

Measuring reproduction is fundamental to understanding changes in bobcat populations. Observing litters directly is the most accurate method (Gashwiler et al. 1961), but it is such a rare event in studies that it is of little value. Wildlife biologists more frequently rely on techniques that require the dissection of bobcat carcasses obtained from hunters and trappers. The size of litters is estimated by counting the number of corpora lutea (Gashwiler et al. 1961), embryos (Fritts and Sealander 1978a), or placental scars (Parker and Smith 1983; Johnson and Halloran 1985; Rolley 1987). Corpora lutea are yellowish scars that develop in the ovaries on the sites where an egg is released. Corpora lutea counts are the least accurate estimate of bobcat fertility, because corpora lutea may form even if a shed egg is not fertilized, and because multiple ovulations during the same season may lead to inflated estimates of litter size. Embryo counts are of little value, because most bobcats are harvested (killed by trappers or hunters) before the breeding season. Placental scars are probably the most accurate index of bobcat reproduction, even though they reflect the number of eggs implanted and not the number of kittens produced (Beeler 1985; Knick 1990).

Kittens are helpless at birth. Their eyes are closed, they have poor coordination, and they cannot regulate their body temperature. As a result, they depend on their mother for both food and warmth. She rarely leaves them during the first two days, nursing almost constantly. As in all mammals, the first milk the bobcat kittens receive is colostrum, which contains critical antibodies for defense against disease. Kittens also develop an affinity for a certain nipple and use it exclusively (Kitchener 1991). This nipple ownership is thought to reduce conflict among littermates (Mellen 1991). Suckling kittens purr and perform a treading motion against their mother's belly to enhance milk flow (Ewer 1973).

Lactation is metabolically expensive for the female bobcat. Her energy requirements might increase two to three times during pregnancy (Kitchener 1991) and probably reach a peak during the second month of nursing a large litter. This is the period of greatest lactation, when the kittens are not yet eating meat. The mother may lose weight as body fat is converted to milk for the voracious young. Another effect of increased lactation is that the mother hunts more intensely within her home range. Her movements are most concentrated after the birth, then expand as the kittens are able to accompany her on hunts (Sunquist and Sunquist 2002). However, one study conducted in North Carolina found that female bobcats with kittens maintained home ranges of the same size and traveled the same distances each day but moved faster when they were active, indicating a more intensive hunting effort (Lancia et al. 1986). The mother expends an enormous amount of energy feeding her growing litter. As a result, the density of prey in the home range affects how well she can provide for her young, which in turn influences their likelihood of survival (Bailey 1974; Knick 1990).

Yearling females generally produce smaller litters than older females do (Knick et al. 1985; Anderson 1987). There is speculation that this may reduce the stress on first-time mothers, allowing them to develop their skills in rearing young. The percentage of females that actually conceive increases with age and levels off after about three years. The pregnancy rates of yearling females in Oklahoma ranged from 26% to 46%, whereas those in Nova Scotia for females three years and older averaged 73% to 90% (Rolley 1983; Parker and Smith 1983). The availability of prey and the density of the bobcat population may influence pregnancy rate and litter size. During his bobcat research in Idaho, Knick (1990) observed a crash in the jackrabbit population and a subsequent decrease in the pregnancy rate of adult bobcats, from 100% to 12.5%. In Lembeck and Gould's (1979) California study area, only half of the females became pregnant when population density was high, compared with 100% when density was low. Although bobcats usually produce one litter each year, if the litter is lost shortly after birth the female may cycle into heat again and produce a second litter that same year (Winegarner and Winegarner 1982; Beeler 1985; Stys and Leopold 1993).

While nursing her kittens, the mother must eventually leave the den to hunt. She must hunt to sustain herself and replenish her milk. While hunting, searching for a mate, or raising young, the female bobcat remains within a territory called a home range. Varying in size from 1 to 38 km^2 (0.4 to 15 square miles) for females, home ranges are specific areas that bobcats use for hunting, resting, and rearing young (see Table 4.1 in Chapter 4). Biologists refer to the bobcats that occupy home ranges as residents (Anderson 1987; Anderson and Lovallo 2003; Sunquist and Sunquist 2002). Possession of a home range is critically important to a female bobcat, because it increases the chances for survival of her litter by guaranteeing an established hunting area for the mother.

The reproductive potential of bobcats is high. Females reach sexual maturity during their second year (18 to 24 months of age), and they can reproduce annually for six to eight years or longer. With an average litter size of three, a potential lifetime output of 18 to 24 kittens is possible for females in unharvested populations (McCord and Cardoza 1982; Sunquist and Sunquist 2002).

Growing Up and Leaving Home

Bobcat kittens grow quickly. Once their eyes are open, they begin to explore their den. Weighing 150 to 340 g (5.2–12 ounces) at birth, a well-fed kitten gains 10 g (0.35 ounces) or more each day (Scott 1976; Hemmer 1979). However, growth rates vary depending on prey availability and the hunting skill of the mother. Guggisberg (1975:62) described this stage of growth:

> The kittens, delightful bundles of short, but nevertheless thick and soft fur, express their well-being by purring and utter little plaintive mews when in distress. When five weeks old, they come out of the den, especially between dusk and nightfall, and romp about with considerable zest. At first they quickly tire and may fall asleep in the middle of the game, but they rapidly gain in strength and vigor. They are nursed for about two months, and while they are still small, the mother may restrict her hunting to an area of approximately one-mile radius around the den. When three to five months old, the kittens are led from the den and begin to accompany their mother on her forays. On these outings, the female's upturned tail and conspicuous ear patches probably help them to keep her in sight as they trail behind through dense vegetation at night.

Female bobcats with kittens may change their den site if it becomes fouled with food or feces or if it is disturbed. Female bobcats with new litters in south-central Florida moved their kittens to new dens every one to six days during the first two months after the birth (Wassmer et al. 1988). Researchers in southern California observed a female bobcat move her kittens to a new den two to three weeks after giving birth, but the cause of the move was a mystery (Lembeck 1986). When transporting particularly young kittens, the mother picks the youngster up by the scruff of the neck, to which it responds by remaining limp and passive until it is set down again. This behavior is common in all cats and appears again in a variation later in the bobcat's life, when it reaches adulthood and engages in mating (Kitchener 1991).

Once they begin to venture from the den, kittens are vulnerable to wandering off and getting lost, as well as falling victim to predators. The danger of straying is reduced by the kittens' strong tendency to stay together, especially when they move any distance from the den. It also makes it easier for the mother to locate them on her return. Bobcat kittens also have a pronounced reaction to a parental alarm call. Biologists have witnessed such behavior in bobcat kittens in Utah (Gashwiler et al. 1961). One minute the youngsters may be playing together, oblivious to any danger; then there is a sudden growl from their mother. The kittens instantly vanish, scattering in all directions, taking advantage of any available cover and remaining absolutely still until the danger has passed and the mother gives the all-clear signal.

Like most female cats, the female bobcat is the consummate single parent. The male plays no part in rearing of the young (Bailey 1974; Sunquist 1987; Miller 1991). In fact, the only time the female is tolerant of the male's presence is during breeding. Although some differences in this behavior have been observed in captive bobcats, in the wild, the female is on her own in raising and protecting the young. However, it is possible that the paternal male plays a role in providing an umbrella of spatial protection for the female without having much contact with her. Male home ranges typically overlap multiple female home ranges (Sunquist and Sunquist 2002), so the paternal male may keep out other roaming males. Observations in south-central Florida suggest that the male of a pair may keep other males from a female with kittens (Wassmer et al. 1988).

Purring is a common behavior in cats, although its purpose is not well understood. R.F. Ewer, in her classic book, *The Carnivores*, stated that purring is probably an "all's well" signal between the nursing mother and her young and may assist in forming the original bond. Purring also occurs between siblings in a litter and between males and females during mating (Ewer 1973; Peters 1991). Anyone who has experienced the pleasure of holding a purring cat on his or her lap can vouch for its hypnotic and contentment-inducing effect.

Weaning is a gradual process. A female bobcat begins to bring prey to the den before the kittens are capable of digesting meat. They sniff at it and play with it. At this stage, the mother eventually eats it. Such behavior allows the young to learn what prey looks like and what is locally available. As the kittens mature and begin to augment their diets with flesh, the mother begins to bring back wounded or live prey for the young to play with. This allows them to practice stalking, handling, and killing prey (Mellen 1991).

Play is a much-discussed topic among animal behaviorists. As with purring, its function is poorly understood. Play certainly is fundamental to the development of strength, endurance, general motor control, and prey capture skills. It may also have social benefits among siblings in a litter, allowing young kittens to stay together and entertain themselves while their mother is away hunting. Kittens play-fight, wrestle, and chase each other. This allows them to practice social skills in the safety of their den, before their teeth and claws can cause damage. As their agility and coordination develop, they begin practicing the stalking, rushing, and pouncing skills they will use in hunting (Mellen 1991). In more social carnivores, such as canids, play may allow the establishment of a dominance hierarchy within the litter and reduce the need for serious conflicts over rank later on. Although play diminishes as kittens mature, it never completely disappears. However, biologist Andrew Kitchener pointed out that play is not the only way kittens learn to be successful predators. Other methods include watching mother or siblings hunt, hunger, sibling motivation, and a kitten's own experience (Ewer 1973; Leyhausen 1979; Kitchener 1991).

However skills are acquired, a hunter cannot hunt without a weapon, and a bobcat has two: claws and teeth. Both develop quickly in kittens. Young (1978) related the story of a physician from Palm Springs, California, who fed and housed what he thought were three stray domestic cats. Not long after their arrival, the doctor attempted to pet one of the animals and was severely clawed. While having his wounds treated, he was informed that his feline guests were bobcat kittens. A study of tooth development in captive bobcats at Mississippi State University indicated that deciduous (baby) teeth began to appear 11 to 14 days after birth, and were all present by nine weeks of age. Permanent teeth began to erupt at 16 to 19 weeks and were all present by 34 weeks of age. Permanent canines (fangs) erupted to the inside of the deciduous canines and became functional before the deciduous teeth were lost. This resulted in the bobcats' having two sets of canines for up to two weeks. Despite this apparently awkward mouthful of teeth, the kittens were able to eat without difficulty (Jackson et al. 1988). Because bobcats depend on their canines to kill prey, they cannot become independent until their permanent canines have appeared.

Weaning is complete by seven or eight weeks of age, as the kittens slowly convert to a diet of meat (Young 1978). Growth continues at a rapid pace, and juvenile males appear to grow more quickly than females. At six months, a male kitten can be 20% heavier than his sister (Crowe 1975a). By autumn, kittens weigh 3.6 to 4.5 kg (8–10 pounds), an almost tenfold increase since birth. Young (1978) told of one captive bobcat that gained 3.1 kg (7 pounds) in four months and another that gained 8.1 kg (18 pounds) in eight months. Male bobcats continue to increase in weight until at least 3.5 years of age, whereas the weight of females levels off at 2.5 years (Rolley 1987).

At three months, bobcat kittens regularly follow their mother on daily training hunts, watching and learning (Bailey 1979). Bobcats, like many species of cats, possess white patches of fur on the back of their ears. These spots may serve as a signal to the kittens, making it easier for them to follow their mother in heavy vegetation. They may also serve to enhance threat postures (Mellen 1991). Kittens remain with their mothers into winter and even begin to make their own kills. As they grow stronger and more skilled at stalking, they may separate from their mother for days at a time and hunt on their own. They will remain alone within their mother's home range, occasionally making short explorations outside, before rejoining her, perhaps after several days of unsuccessful hunting. This growing independence is a precursor to young bobcats' leaving their mother and seeking their own home range (Sunquist and Sunquist 2002).

The departure of young bobcats from their mother's home range is called dispersal, and it is a time when the young bobcats are especially vulnerable; they must now kill enough prey to feed themselves, without the alternative of food provided by their mother. These young bobcats, now called transients, disperse from their mother's home range before the next year's litter is born (usually between six and ten months of age) (Crowe 1975a; Kitchings and Story 1984). Dispersal can occur as early as nine months of age or as late as almost two years, depending on how quickly the juvenile bobcat masters its hunting skills. The pattern of dispersal varies as well. Some juveniles abruptly leave their mother's home range and rapidly travel several kilometers; others are more reticent to leave, and the process may take months. Sometimes an immature bobcat takes up residence within or adjacent to its natal range, but this is usually due to the death or departure of its mother or father. It is important for all transients to find a suitable home range as soon as possible, because residence is a prerequisite for successful mating (Knick 1990; Sunquist and Sunquist 2002).

It is unknown whether a mother and her young grow apart, with the young leaving of their own accord, or whether she abandons them or becomes aggressive toward them, as do female black bears with their young. It is most likely a combination of the two. Bobcat expert Ted Bailey (1974:435) related an incident that occurred in the Snake River Plains of southeastern Idaho: "One mother led one of her kittens, a nine-month-old male, out of his familiar range and returned several days later alone. He did not return. No kittens were captured within their mother's home range after she had her next litter." In south-central Florida, two 10-month-old bobcats confined their wanderings to the edge of their mother's home range before dispersing three to four months later. Aggressive encounters between the juveniles and their mother during the breeding season and pregnancy may have discouraged the young from staying (Wassmer et al. 1988). Once juvenile bobcats are finally on their own, their mother will come into heat again and breed. Although maternal intolerance, aggressive breeding males, and competition for prey are all important factors, the timing of dispersal depends on the complex interplay of a variety of social and environmental circumstances (Sunquist and Sunquist 2002). Crowe (1975b) speculated that widespread dispersal of juveniles is unnecessary in populations that are heavily harvested, because vacant home ranges are readily available.

Transients often wander far from the familiar home range of their mother, and their hunting skills are not as efficient as those of older resident cats. This nomadic existence is characterized by the bobcat's lingering in potential home ranges for a few days to several months before moving on (Griffith et al. 1981;

Kitchings and Story 1984; Knick 1990). In one area, bobcats quickly located new home ranges in two to six days, but elsewhere the search lasted five to ten months. The time it takes a transient to locate a suitable home range varies depending on the density, home range size, and disappearance rate of residents in the area (Sunquist and Sunquist 2002). The longest recorded distance traveled by a dispersing transient bobcat is 182 km (113 miles) (Knick and Bailey 1986). There are other records of dispersing bobcats traveling more than 100 km (62 miles), but these long treks are usually made by subadult males abandoning an area of severe lagomorph decline (Bailey 1974; Knick and Bailey 1986). Dispersal distances of 20 to 40 km (12 to 25 miles) are more common (Griffith et al. 1981; Hamilton 1982; Knick 1990), and some youngsters travel as few as 10 km (6.2 miles) (Kitchings and Story 1984). Young males typically disperse and travel longer distances in search of suitable unoccupied territory, whereas young females often settle near, or partially within, the range of their mother. Transients can also be older bobcats that have been displaced or are shifting home range (Sunquist and Sunquist 2002; Anderson and Lovallo 2003).

The advent of radiotelemetry in the 1960s made it possible for wildlife biologists to understand how bobcats move through a landscape (Anderson 1987). Radiotelemetry involves capturing a wild bobcat and fitting it with a collar containing a small battery-powered transmitter that sends out a radio signal at a specific frequency. By using a special antenna and receiver, the field biologist takes bearings from two or three locations, and the animal is assumed to be near the point where the bearings cross (the location or "fix"). Triangulation of bearings is the basic approach in most radio tracking. Ideally, bearings should cross at a 90-degree angle and should be taken as close to the animal as possible. By following the radio signals in the field and plotting the bobcat's locations on a topographic map, biologists can learn the size of its home range, when it is active, the travel routes it uses, which habitat it prefers, the density of bobcats in the area, and the social structure of the population. Radiotelemetry can also reveal how far and in what direction transient bobcats disperse from their mother's home range.

In southern British Columbia, wildlife ecologist Clayton Apps (personal communication) found that male bobcats in his study area appeared to be on the move or generally transient over their entire second year (about 9–21 months of age). In the one case that he was able to document, home range establishment coincided with the breeding season of that year (at about 22 months). He speculated that the onset of sexual maturity is probably the driving force for home range establishment. Although they may be sexually mature, there is tremendous variation as to when bobcats become reproductively active (or productive). Apps found one three-year-old female that had not produced kittens. Productivity is related to many factors, such as environmental conditions, prey availability, and experience.

The dispersal of subadult bobcats out of their birth areas is important, because it prevents overcrowding, prevents overexploitation of prey, ensures that new areas will be occupied, and reduces inbreeding. Once a transient bobcat settles into a home range, it familiarizes itself with the best hunting areas and adjacent neighbors and becomes a resident. Secure in its new surroundings, the resident bobcat can turn its attention to mating.

Mating

Female bobcats can breed during their first year (9–12 months of age), but they rarely do. Males are not sexually mature until their second year. The onset of sexual maturity may depend on prey availability and may be delayed in high-density bobcat populations (Crowe 1975a; Rolley 1985; Knick et al. 1985). Females are seasonally polyestrous (having more than one period of estrus or heat in a breeding season), and males appear to be fertile all year. However, evidence from Wyoming suggests that sperm production in bobcats may be reduced or arrested in July and August, resuming in September or October (Crowe 1975a). The estrous cycle normally lasts 44 to 46 days, with females in heat for 5 to 10 days. The female bobcat may cycle through up to three estrous periods during a single season if she does not become pregnant (Crowe 1975a; Mehrer 1975; Fritts and Sealander 1978a; Anderson 1987a; Stys and Leopold 1993).

The period during which a juvenile bobcat is dependent on its mother can have a profound influence on her estrous cycle. As discussed earlier, there is a significant time interval between weaning and independence of the bobcat young, during which the mother must kill for the young until they are strong enough and experienced enough to survive on their own. During this period, the mother's estrous cycle is suppressed. The physiological causes of this inhibition are not understood, nor is it clear what stimuli the kittens provide.

Breeding has been documented as early as November and December and as late as August and September, but the peak breeding season appears to be from February to April (Duke 1954; Gashwiler et al. 1961; Rolley 1987; Lariviere and Walton 1997; Sunquist and Sunquist 2002) (see Table 3.1). In the southern region of the bobcat's range, breeding appears to occur earlier and may take place any time of the year (Fritts and Sealander 1978a; Blankenship and Swank 1979; Wassmer et al. 1988). The timing of breeding can be influenced by latitude, longitude, altitude, climate, photoperiod, nutritional condition, prey availability, and age composition of the population (McCord and Cardoza 1982).

When it comes time to mate, the first challenge facing male and female bobcats is finding one another. Solitary and territorial by nature, bobcats are frequently scattered over miles of rugged terrain. Further, females are receptive to males for only a few days of each estrous cycle (Crowe 1975a; Mehrer 1975). However, it appears that an intriguing combination of evolved behavior and keen senses allows them to surmount these obstacles and come together.

Polygyny seems to be the rule for bobcats (Provost et al. 1973). Males mate with as many females as possible. Males occupy home ranges that are two to three

Table 3.1
Bobcat Breeding Season

Location	Sample size	Method	Breeding season	Author
11 western states	365	Plotted the frequency of embryonic litters by month	February–April	Duke 1954
Arkansas	74 males, 64 female	Examined reproductive tract	December–April	Fritts and Sealander 1978a
Florida	13	Backdated litters	February–March (range, August–March)	Wassmer et al. 1988
Illinois	4 females	Examined fetuses	November–March	Woolf and Nielsen 2002
Michigan	15 males, 35 females	Examined uteri, ovaries, and blood clots in urine	January–March	Erickson 1955
South Carolina	N/A	N/A	February–March	Griffith and Fendley 1986b
Texas	97	Examined reproductive tracts	November–July	Blankenship and Swank 1979
Utah	356	Backdated embryonic litters (47)	January–July	Gashwiler et al. 1961
Wyoming	161	Used follicles, corpora lutea, and embryos to backdate to ovulation dates	January–July	Crowe 1975a

times larger than those of females, and a resident male with a large home range typically overlaps or encompasses the home ranges of several resident females (Anderson 1987; Sunquist and Sunquist 2002). In stable bobcat populations with established home ranges, females probably mate most frequently with the resident male.

Bobcats communicate using visual and olfactory signals. The most common of these is scent marking. Adult bobcats use feces, urine, and anal glands to delineate home ranges, dens, and travel routes and to advertise sexual availability or facilitate mutual avoidance (Bailey 1974, 1979, 1984a). Territoriality and scent marking are discussed in depth in the next chapter, but here it is important to understand the role that scent marking appears to play in attracting a mate.

Adult male bobcats probably spend most of their time sleeping, hunting, and searching for receptive females. Males also urinate more frequently when females are in heat, and they increase their home ranges to maximize contact with estrous females. On encountering a site where a female has urinated, a male bobcat sniffs the location, drawing the fragrance over a special organ in the roof of his mouth. This organ allows the male to detect the presence of sex hormones in the urine (Estes 1972). While doing this, the male exhibits a lip-curling grimace on his face known as a flehmen. The flehmen response is common in all cats. It is often interpreted as a sign of displeasure, when just the opposite is the case (McCord and Cardoza 1982; Kiltie 1991; Kitchener 1991).

If scent marking is effective and the male and female bobcat find each other, then courtship can begin. Female bobcats are also known to vocalize frequently when in heat, similar to the familiar caterwauling of domestic cats. This may also aid in attracting mates. In the wild, caterwauling can be heard from a mile away (Young 1978; Sunquist and Sunquist 2002).

Courtship is a delicate phase in bobcat relations in which two solitary and well-armed predators must come together in intimate contact without hurting each other. Initial contact between the male and female usually involves some form of playful fighting. Ewer (1973:315) explained how two factors prevent the play from becoming lethal in courting carnivores:

> The first is the existence of highly ritualized forms of fighting in which attacks are specifically directed to particular parts of the body, where even a bite that is too hard will not have serious consequences; the second is an inhibition which operates in the male against biting a female. The inhibition is not reciprocal and a smaller and weaker female may bite quite viciously to defend herself against the importunities of a male whom she is not yet prepared to accept, while the rules that govern his behavior prevent him from retaliating.

Although few bobcat courtships have actually been witnessed by researchers, those that have seem to follow Ewer's "rules of engagement." Biologist Chet McCord indirectly observed courting bobcats on three occasions in Massachusetts by following and interpreting the signs they left in the snow. What transpired was an exuberant choreography of running parallel to each other, bumping, chasing, ambushing, cooperative hunting, and, finally, copulation (McCord 1974b).

Mating also involves considerable visual and vocal communication, usually in the form of physical posturing and the caterwauling that is characteristic of domestic cats. Both may reassure the male and female that their intentions are mutual. In *Wild Cats of the World*, Edmund C. Jaeger (quoted in Guggisberg 1975:62) related a fascinating account of mating bobcats in the desert southwest:

> I was awakened near midnight by an interrupted series of ferocious hisses, shrill screams, harsh squalls, and deep-toned yowls. No alley strays could ever have half-equaled this cat concert of the desert wilds. Luckily, it was moonlight, and I was able to see the animals almost perfectly. The female most of the time lay crouched upon the ground, while the big male, which

must have weighed twenty pounds, walked menacingly about her. Sometimes they both sat upright, facing each other. The loud and ludicrous serenade was kept up for almost half an hour, and it ended with a dual climax of discordant, frightening squalls as mating took place.

Most of what is known about bobcat mating behavior comes from observations of captive animals. Before the onset of estrus, the female bobcat increases the rate at which she rubs against objects with her head and neck, increases scent marking, and makes loud and frequent vocalizations. There is also more tail flicking, holding the tail erect to indicate receptiveness, and an increased interest in males (Jackson et al. 1988). There may be sex hormones present in the female's feces, urine, and body secretions that advertise her reproductive status during this period. Rubbing against objects in her home range and frequent urination advertise her presence to the male and signal that she is ready to mate (Kitchener 1991; Sunquist and Sunquist 2002). The female resists the male's initial advances, often by biting or clawing. Eaton (1976) and Kitchener (1991) speculated that the female tests the male's persistence to ensure that he is in fact the dominant male in the area. However, Koehler (personal communication) emphasized that this interpretation is speculative and believed that scent marking is more important than testing persistence in the female's identification of the dominant male. Eventually, the female becomes more provocative, presenting her rump to the male and possibly rubbing against him. Now it is the male who resists the female's advances. When she is ready to copulate, the female bobcat crouches on the ground with her rump slightly raised (lordosis) and her tail turned aside. The male then straddles the female and grips the back of her neck in his teeth. This has a calming effect on the female—similar to the carrying reflex in kittens (Kitchener 1991; Mellen 1991). Swaying continuously on his hind legs, the male uses a series of thrusts to insert his penis into the female bobcat's vagina (intromission) (Anderson and Lovallo 2003). During copulation, the female remains silent or emits a low, barely audible growl—what Sunquist and Sunquist (2002) called the copulatory cry. After copulation, she rises and dislodges the male, then engages in more urinating, rolling, and rubbing on objects (Anderson and Lovallo 2003). As estrus passes, the female may allow the male to mount her, but she refuses intromission. She frees herself from his grasp with a violent jerk, snarl, and swipe of her paw (Mehrer 1975).

Actual copulation can last up to five minutes and is repeated up to 16 times a day (Mehrer 1975). Such frequent copulation is also thought to induce ovulation, the release of the eggs from the ovaries to make them available for fertilization. Further support for the induced ovulation argument can be found in the structure of the bobcat's penis. Bobcats have a baculum, a small bone in the head of the penis, and keratinous spines on the shaft of the penis (Maser and Toweill 1984; Tumlison and McDaniel 1984b). Both are thought to help facilitate penetration and stimulation of the female's vagina. However, more recent evidence indicates that domestic cats, Canada lynx, and bobcats ovulate spontaneously. Spontaneous ovulation is involuntary, possibly triggered by hormones, as opposed to induced ovulation. As mentioned earlier, studies show that female bobcats may cycle through as many as three estrous periods in a single season if they do not breed (Crowe 1975a; Fritts and Sealander 1978b; Stys and Leopold 1993). Obviously, females can ovulate without the help of a male, but copulation may induce or hasten ovulation (Anderson and Lovallo 2003). In the cold climate of the northern latitudes, the breeding season is so restricted that induced ovulation may be more efficient. It is also possible that bobcats may be induced ovulators in years of low prey density, when there is less chance of finding a mate, and spontaneous ovulators in years of high prey density, when the chances of meeting a mate and producing a surviving litter are high. Age may also affect the type of ovulation, with younger cats more likely to be induced ovulators (Kitchener 1991). Ewer (1973:328) pointed out, "The difference between spontaneous and induced ovulation may therefore be one of degree rather than of kind and the fact that some carnivores do ultimately ovulate without copulation does not preclude the existence of some normal triggering effect of the stimuli resulting from mating."

After ovulation, the egg and sperm eventually come together and gestation begins. Gestation can range from 50 to 70 days, with 63 days being the average (Mehrer 1975; Young 1978; Miller 1991; Lariviere and Walton 1997; Sunquist and Sunquist 2002). Birth may occur in any month of the year (Berg 1979; Fritts and Sealander 1978a; Gashwiler et al. 1961; Young 1978), with most occurring from late April through June (Bailey 1979; Crowe 1975a, 1975b). Research by Steven H. Fritts and John A. Selander (1978a) indicated that bobcats in Arkansas that produce litters as late as September may be first-time breeders. Bobcats usually raise one litter per year.

Death

All bobcats die, but how they die varies. A bobcat can meet its demise through starvation, disease, parasites, injury during prey capture, predation by other animals, cannibalism, or old age. Survival became even more problematic with the arrival of Europeans in North America. The list subsequently expanded to include death by poison, snare, trap, collisions with cars, electrocution, getting shot, or loss of habitat. More bobcats die at the hands of humans than from any other cause (Anderson 1987; Anderson and Lovallo 2003).

Rates and causes of death in bobcats vary with age. To better understand mortality, researchers divide bobcats into three age periods: kitten (<1 year old), yearling (1–2 years old), and adult (>2 years old). Measuring mortality presents different challenges in each age group. Kittens are difficult to radio collar or monitor without influencing their survival, so kitten survival is poorly understood. Yearlings are usually transients. They have left maternal care and protection behind and are now in search of their own home range, which exposes them to a wide variety of risks. Adults are usually residents in their own home ranges and generally experience lower mortality. However, even though adult and yearling mortality rates may differ considerably, they are often combined and reported as an adult survival rate (Anderson and Lovallo 2003).

As with measuring reproduction, measuring bobcat survival is fundamental to understanding changes in bobcat populations. One technique long used to estimate bobcat survival rates analyzes the age structure of harvested animals using a life table. A life table is a mathematical model that allows biologists to project a schedule of survivors over time. Scientists use a combination of collected data (e.g., age structure of harvested bobcats) and assumptions about the living population to construct the life table. Does the harvested sample represent a sample of the living population or a sample of the dying? Is the age structure of the population stable? Is the population increasing or decreasing? Life tables were used to estimate annual kitten survival rates of 26% in Wyoming (Crowe 1975b), 29% in Texas (Blankenship and Swank 1979), and 33% in Michigan (Hoppe 1979). Assumptions made while developing the model can obviously bias the subsequent analysis and must be given careful consideration (Bolen and Robinson 1999). Anderson and Lovallo (2003) believed that, because bobcat kittens are generally underrepresented in annual harvests, survival rates calculated from life tables are unreliable.

Kitten survival depends primarily on prey availability and on how well the mother is able to protect the young from hunters, trappers, adult bobcats, and other predators. After crashes in the rabbit population in Idaho, Bailey (1974) and Knick (1990) found no bobcat kittens alive by the following autumn, despite high survival during previous years of greater prey abundance. During such times of food scarcity, the mother most likely feeds herself first and leaves the kittens to starve. In northeastern California, Zezulak (1981) observed two of three radio-collared juveniles succumb to malnutrition and parasitism. Kitten survival is generally lower than that of adults but can greatly vary. Crowe's estimate of annual kitten survival in Wyoming fluctuated between 18% and 71% (Crowe 1975b). Despite occasional failures, the female bobcat's primary job is to keep her kittens alive long enough for them to disperse.

After dispersal, survival of juvenile bobcats still depends largely on food supply, but now they can no longer rely on their mother for food and must hone their own hunting skills as quickly as possible (Bailey 1974). How quickly a bobcat attains hunting proficiency is probably a function of natural ability and practice. If prey is scarce and the juvenile is successful in only 10% of its attempts to capture dinner, it will frequently go hungry and may starve The more prey that is available, the more practice the bobcat gets, and the better it eats (Crowe 1975b). The situation is further complicated by the onset of winter, a time when hunting and trapping seasons are typically open and there is a decline in food supply (Anderson and Lovallo 2003). In addition, the transient juvenile must also locate and settle into a permanent home range. Eastern Idaho bobcats are usually eight to ten months old during their first autumn and winter, so they still frequently remain behind in the den while the mother hunts alone. They therefore encounter fewer sets left by trappers than do older, more mobile adults. When they reach one to three years of age, their vulnerability to trapping increases as they disperse and become highly mobile, searching for places to live, and they are not yet as efficient hunters as older adults (Bailey 1979). Harvest records in Texas (Blankenship and Swank 1979) and in Nova Scotia (Parker and Smith 1983) show an increase in the proportion of kittens taken as the trapping season progresses, reflecting increased mobility and independence from maternal care.

Adult and yearling annual survival rates have been measured using life tables and radiotelemetry (Anderson 1987; Anderson and Lovallo 2003). Most experts believe that radiotelemetry provides the best estimates (Heisey and Fuller 1985; Anderson and Lovallo 2003). The transmitter worn by the bobcat usually contains a mortality sensor that activates if the transmitter is motionless for an extended period, such as eight hours. This is detected by the receiver as a change in signal rate. After a mortality signal is detected, the researcher can search for the carcass to confirm and determine the cause of death. Adult annual bobcat survival rates range from 56% to 67% when heavily exploited populations and periods of dramatic prey decline are excluded (Anderson and Lovallo 2003). During his bobcat study in Oklahoma, Rolley (1985) estimated an annual adult survival rate of 56% using life tables and 53% using radiotelemetry. Although radiotelemetry has been a powerful tool in expanding knowledge of bobcats, Rolley (1987) cautioned that it has limitations. If the radio signal is lost due to a dead battery or a slipped collar, is the animal assumed to be alive or dead? If such animals are assumed to be alive, then survival may be overestimated. If they are assumed to be dead, then survival could be underestimated. Another limitation of this technique is that it is costly to obtain samples large enough for precise estimates of survival.

Measuring bobcat mortality in protected populations is difficult because, even in areas that are closed to trapping and hunting, bobcat numbers are affected by both illegal and legal harvest in adjacent areas. Even so, adult survival rates in unexploited populations appear to be much higher than in exploited populations. During his three-year study on the closed Idaho National Engineering Laboratory (INEL), Ted Bailey (1974) observed death by natural causes in only 3 of the 35 resident adults, for an apparent annual adult survival rate of 97% (Crowe 1975b). While studying bobcats in the same area in 1982–1983, Knick (1990) concluded that the annual survival rate for INEL bobcats was 78%, due to high prey densities (rabbits and hares), low disturbance, and high security restrictions on the INEL. Adult bobcats in an unharvested population in Mississippi demonstrated an even higher annual survival rate of 80% (Chamberlain et al. 1999). Clayton Nielson and the late Alan Woolf performed a survival analysis on 75 bobcats (39 females, 36 males) in southern Illinois from 1995 to 2000. Their combined estimates of annual and seasonal survival ranged from 84% to 94% and were among the highest reported for an unexploited population of bobcats (Nielsen and Woolf 2002a). Unfortunately, even in supposedly unexploited populations, human-caused mortality is common. Of the 20 bobcat deaths reported during Bailey's (1974) three-year study of an unharvested population in Idaho, 16 were caused by humans. Fur trappers killed seven of the radio-collared bobcats, three deaths were study related, and six kittens were electrocuted while climbing powerline poles.

Today, hunting and trapping are the most prevalent known causes of death in bobcats. While studying the ecology of Missouri bobcats, Dave Hamilton (1982) found that 50% of juvenile and 80% of adult annual mortality was caused by humans. In Oklahoma, Robert Rolley (1985:283) observed that exploitation was the sole source of non–study-related death in his radio-collared bobcats. He went on to state, "Continued harvest of already low density bobcat populations may further depress the populations and result in local extirpations. Reduction of harvest during periods of negative rates of increase is recommended." Todd Fuller and his colleagues (1995) analyzed eight radiotelemetry bobcat survival studies: two each in Maine, Minnesota, and Idaho, and one each in Massachusetts, Missouri, and Oklahoma. They discovered that 47% of all deaths were attributable to legal harvest. In Minnesota, Berg (1979) and Fuller et al. (1985a) found that 82% of mortalities were caused by harvest. In Fuller's study area, 100% of mortality was due to legal or illegal harvest, and adult male annual survival was only 8%. Knick (1990) used a computer simulation model of the female bobcat population in his Idaho study area to determine that the bobcat population could not sustain itself if annual adult female survival was less than 52%.

Nine states and one Canadian province give the bobcat complete protection, while most of the remaining states and provinces classify the bobcat as a game species that may be killed under the restrictions of a specified season and method of capture (usually tracking and treeing with dogs, or trapping). Some tribal nations also allow hunting and trapping of bobcats (Woolf and Hubert 1998). According to the International Association of Fish and Wildlife Agencies (IAFWA), 36,674 bobcats were killed and tagged in the United States during the 1997–1998 season. This is a substantial drop from the 1987–1988 season, when 85,879 bobcats were killed, but a substantial increase over the 13,854 taken during the 1990–1991 season (see Figure 5.3 in Chapter 5).

Legal harvest can have an indirect impact on kittens. Because they depend on their mothers until they are eight to ten months old, premature removal of the mother by a hunter or trapper orphans the kitten and leads to high kitten mortality (Anderson and Lovallo 2003). Knick (1990) noted that kittens orphaned before independence in Idaho did not survive.

The annual rate at which adult bobcats die is not constant for all age groups. Mortality rates in exploited populations decrease after the first year of life or remain constant until age four or five years, then increase again (Fritts and Sealander 1978b; Blankenship and Swank 1979; Litvaitis et al. 1987). The decrease in mortality is probably due to improved hunting proficiency and the establishment of home ranges (Bailey 1974).

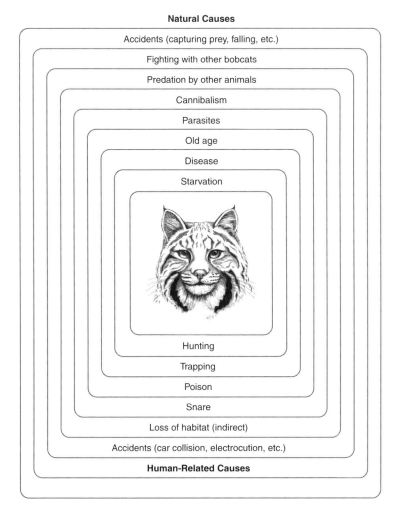

Natural Causes
Accidents (capturing prey, falling, etc.)
Fighting with other bobcats
Predation by other animals
Cannibalism
Parasites
Old age
Disease
Starvation
Hunting
Trapping
Poison
Snare
Loss of habitat (indirect)
Accidents (car collision, electrocution, etc.)
Human-Related Causes

Figure 3.1
The bobcat's obstacles to survival.

Male and female bobcats are also killed at different rates during harvest. Male mortality is higher, especially during the first few years as adults. Males may be more susceptible to trapping because of their larger home ranges and their tendency to wander greater distances, which is thought to increase their chance of encountering traps or a hunter (Anderson and Lovallo 2003). However, Chet McCord and John Cardoza questioned this assumption. They suggested that females use their smaller home ranges more intensively, so, although the probability of a trapper's setting traps in a male bobcat's larger home range may be greater, the chance of a female's encountering a trap once set would be greater (McCord and Cardoza 1982). Under such circumstances, the overall density of males is lower than that of females. As Koehler (personal communication) pointed out, "That males are more vulnerable to harvest and study capture efforts holds true for a variety of species, from bears to deer mice, and is likely the result of greater vulnerability due to behavioral differences, including larger home ranges, perhaps greater inquisitiveness, boldness, etc."

Bobcat mortality also fluctuates with the season. Survival rates are lowest during the winter months, when hunting and trapping seasons are generally open. Additionally, weather can increase the vulnerability of bobcats to trapping. In Minnesota (Petraborg and Gunvalson 1962) and in Idaho (Koehler and Hornocker 1989), bobcats were more vulnerable to trapping during severe winters. Winter and early spring are the times of greatest starvation, because lagomorph and rodent populations are lowest and environmental stresses are greatest (Petraborg and Gunvalson 1962). In the midst of the cold winter months in north-central Minnesota, Fuller and his colleagues (1985a) observed 14 bobcat deaths during the December-January bobcat trapping and hunting season and no deaths during July-September. Harvest during the furbearer season in Oklahoma was the cause of all non–study-related deaths reported by Rolley (1985) on his study area. This is a crucial period for bobcat kittens and yearlings due to the absence of maternal care and still-developing hunting skills (Bailey 1974).

Predator control programs present yet another obstacle to the bobcat's survival. The U.S. Department of Agriculture's Wildlife Services program killed 2,503 bobcats during fiscal year 2003 because of attacks on domestic livestock, such as lambs, ewes, and chickens. Most of these (2,454) were target (intended) animals, but 49 were nontarget (unintended) animals. Texas was responsible for 83% of all bobcats killed (2,070). The Lone Star state allocates more money, $13,330,425 in fiscal year 2003, and takes a more aggressive approach to predator control than any other (Wildlife Services 2005).

Bobcats also fall victim to other carnivores. Kittens are vulnerable to foxes, owls, and adult male bobcats (Crowe 1975b; Young 1978). Mountain lions and coyotes are known to kill adult bobcats (Lembeck 1978; Young 1978; Knick 1990; Fedriani et al. 2000). Stanley Young probably had his tongue firmly planted in his cheek when he described a bobcat's falling victim to a mountain lion as "a case of cat eat cat" (Young 1978:38). Studying bobcats near San Diego, Lembeck (1986) observed domestic dogs kill six of the wild felines, 20% of his recorded mortality. Koehler (personal communication) found depredation by cougars to be a significant cause of bobcat mortality in central Idaho, particularly during winter, when bobcats, coyotes, and cougars are confined to smaller winter ranges and encounter each other at ungulate carcasses.

As with most wild mammals, bobcats are subject to a variety of diseases and parasites. No large-scale die-offs have been documented in bobcat populations due to infestations or infections. The feline's solitary lifestyle and penchant for frequently changing its dens and resting areas may reduce its vulnerability to parasites and disease (McCord and Cardoza 1982). However, in some populations they are a major cause of direct mortality. At the Archbold Biological Station in south-central Florida, Douglas Wassmer and his colleagues found that 73% of the bobcat deaths studied were caused by feline distemper or Notoedric mange (Wassmer et al. 1988). Up north in Massachusetts, researchers attributed 37% of bobcat mortalities to gastric enteritis (Fuller et al. 1995).

Viral diseases found in bobcats include rabies, panleucopenia (also known as feline distemper and feline infectious enteritis), rhinotracheitis, feline leukemia, feline calicivirus, and feline infectious peritonitis (McCord and Cardoza 1982; Anderson and Lovallo 2003). Rabies has been more frequently documented in bobcats than in Canada lynx (Quinn and Parker 1987). In a survey of carnivores infected with rabies in the United States from 1960 to 1997, bobcats accounted for 402 cases, making it seventh on the list of species reported with the disease (Krebs et al. 1999). Feline distemper is known to be highly infectious and frequently fatal (Povey and Davis 1977). Bacterial diseases include tularemia (Bell and Reilly 1981), sylvatic plague (Poland et al. 1973), salmonellosis, leptospirosis (Labelle et al. 2000), and brucellosis (Witter 1981). Bobcats are also susceptible to the protozoan parasites toxoplasma (Riemann et al. 1975) and feline infectious anemia (Glenn et al. 1982).

An extensive list of internal and external parasites has been documented. Eric Anderson provided a comprehensive table of endoparasites in bobcats arranged by geographic regions in his review of bobcat literature (Anderson 1987). The bobcat's gut is home to an assortment of tapeworms, flukes, roundworms, and spiny-headed worms, while its fur is host to both fleas and mange mites (Anderson and Lovallo 2003). Bobcats and coyotes in south Texas were found to have severe infestations of hookworms, which were suspected to account for some mortality in wild populations (Mitchell and Beasom 1974). Although it is known that some diseases and parasites are fatal to bobcats, they may play a greater role, one that is not fully understood, in predisposing the felines to other forms of mortality, such as starvation, predation, or accidents. Additionally, because bobcats are both harvested and live in ever-increasing proximity to humans, they can be a route for infection of humans. Rabies, sylvatic plague, and toxoplasmosis are diseases that have been transmitted to humans from wild bobcats and Canada lynx (Anderson and Lovallo 2003).

When not avoiding or fighting other predators to stay alive, bobcats sometimes kill and eat each other. Bobcat flesh and fur were found in several stomachs examined in Utah and eastern Nevada (Gashwiler et al.1960). Researcher David Zezulak (1981) reported that an adult male bobcat ate another bobcat it had killed in northeastern California. In eastern Maine, biologist John Litvaitis and his colleagues observed an adult female bobcat that killed and ate a kitten. They suggested that this instance of cannibalism may have been partly due to territorial behavior, because it took place on the edge of the adult's home range. However, the female was also underweight and may have eaten the kitten due to hunger (Litvaitis et al. 1982). With such scant evidence, it appears that cannibalism is not a major source of bobcat mortality and therefore has little effect on its population dynamics (Anderson and Lovallo 2003).

Finally, accidents happen, even to a wild animal as alert and agile as a bobcat. As predators, bobcats practice a high-risk lifestyle. Chasing, catching, and killing prey at high speed in rugged terrain continually exposes the cat to injury or death from collisions with rocks and trees, falls from ledges, or combat with prey. The latter is especially true in the case of male and female bobcats that attack prey larger than themselves, such as deer and bighorn sheep. Stanley Young described a bobcat that was injured when attacked and struck by the forefeet of a doe in British Columbia (Young 1978). Apps (1995a) documented a large (35 pounds), healthy male bobcat that died from a punctured abdomen, apparently sustained while attempting to kill a deer. A debilitating injury such as a broken bone can lead to starvation for the bobcat. In Minnesota, several bobcats died excruciating deaths from porcupine quills after tangling with the prickly rodent (Berg 1979, Fuller et al. 1985a). Human-related accidents further complicate survival. No cumulative statistics exist on how many bobcats are killed each year on roads and highways by collisions with motor vehicles, but Illinois researchers Alan Woolf and Clayton Nielsen documented the highest reported rates of vehicle-caused mortality for bobcats. Of the 19 bobcats that died during their study, 10 (52%) were struck by automobiles and 2 (11%) were hit by trains. They suspected that the deaths could be attributed to the relatively high road density in southern Illinois (Nielsen and Woolf 2002a). Over a two-year study in southern Texas, a team of biologists found 25 dead bobcats along a 32-km (20-mile) section of highway (Cain et al. 2003). Bobcats in California (Williams 1990) and in Idaho (Bailey 1974) were electrocuted after climbing poles supporting high-voltage transmission lines.

Removed from the gauntlet of survival they must navigate in the wild, captive bobcats have lived to be 32.2 years of age (Jones 1982; Anderson and Lovallo 2003). In the wild, life spans exceeding 16 years are rare (Knick et al. 1985, Anderson and Lovallo 2003). Reproductive capabilities are retained until death (Crowe 1975a; Miller 1991). The oldest bobcat found during Woolf and Nielsen's study of a protected population in Illinois was a radio-collared female aged 13 years (Woolf and Neilsen 2002). Maximum life spans of harvested bobcats have been estimated at 12 years in Wyoming (Crowe 1975a) and 12 to 13 years in Texas (Blankenship and Swank 1979). Tooth analysis of a bobcat harvested in New Mexico in 1986 showed it to be an impressive 23 years old (Matson and Matson 1993; Sunquist and Sunquist 2002). A more common scenario is that old bobcats experience extreme tooth wear and loss of weight, making them less efficient hunters, resulting in starvation.

4 Bobcats at Home

Welcome to bobcat heaven-on-earth," announces Susan Morse, gesturing around us.

We are standing in a lush, mixed conifer and hardwood forest in northern Vermont, just a few miles outside the small town of Jericho. Above us stretch the branches of beech, birch, maple, hemlock, and red spruce. Springing from the rich, black soil beneath our feet is a mixed understory foliage of witchhobble, as well as saplings of yellow birch, sugar maple, striped maple, and American ash. Dappled sunlight falls all around. As I gaze up into the canopy, Susan motions to a cliff face a few yards away. This vertical slab of gray, metamorphic schist is broken by fissures and ledges and is covered with patches of green moss and lichen. These rocky outcrops occur frequently in this part of what is called the Northern Forest.

"Those ledges are critical to good bobcat habitat," she explains. "The cats use them for daytime resting sites, natal denning areas, and to escape predators such as coyotes and possibly fishers. When I'm tracking bobcats in the winter, these cliff faces show a lot of activity, in the way of tracks and scent-marking sign."

Wildlife habitat specialist, forester, and expert tracker, Susan Morse is more at home in the outdoors than anyone I know. Because she is an authority on forest carnivores, especially the bobcat, I paid her a visit.

During our time together in the woods, I was awed by her encyclopedic knowledge and boundless affection for the Northern Forest and its wild residents. She constantly preached the gospel of wildlife habitat protection. She spoke of how the bobcat, lynx, cougar, and bear need refugia that will be protected in perpetuity. Back in her restored cabin, I spent hours perusing the floor-to-ceiling bookshelves that covered every wall. In addition to an impressive collection of natural history books and technical papers, I found the complete works of Shakespeare (Susan's major in college), Robert Frost's poetry, D.H. Lawrence, Henry David Thoreau, and other classical literature. Her library is so well known that the local folks refer to her home as the town library.

Leaving the cliff face, Susan leads me down the remnants of a logging road toward a marshy wetland. Her eyes miss nothing. Along the way she points out where a deer has rubbed its antlers against a bush and where a black bear has left claw marks on a beech tree. The ground grows progressively soggy.

"Good bobcat habitat contains rocky, steep terrain with wetlands. It must have trees of different age classes, a variety of cover types, and different vegetation structures, and a corresponding smorgasbord of prey species."

Suddenly we hear splashing from below. Susan signals silence and then grins. "That's either a moose or a bear. Follow me." She quickly moves out through the dense vegetation with the stealth of, well, a bobcat. A short while later we are sitting on a hillside watching through the foliage as a moose cow and her two calves feed in the pond below. They are the first moose I have ever seen.

"Beaver populations are increasing in Vermont," Susan whispers as we watch. "Their dams are causing an expansion of these wetlands, which in turn produces good habitat for wildlife like moose and bobcat. The moose feed on the aquatic vegetation and the bobcats hunt in the thick, riparian vegetation that grows along the edges of the ponds and streams."

Later, while slogging through a small meadow downstream, Susan motions for me to stop and crouches to point out a bobcat track in the middle of the muddy trail. I am pleased with the find but admit to mild disappointment. While in bobcat heaven-on-earth, I had expected to catch a glimpse of at least one bobcat. Susan smiles and explains how rare it is to actually see the stealthy feline. She also reminds me not to be misled by the lush August landscape and talk of plentiful prey. The Northern Forest can be very unforgiving, especially in the winter.

Earlier that day, from atop a rocky promontory she called Cougar Knob, Susan had pointed to another ridge about two miles distant. "One day last winter I tracked a bobcat all the way from here to that ridge and back. He was hunting, so he didn't travel in a straight line and covered a lot of additional ground in between. He probably traveled more than five miles that day, through the snow and cold, and never did catch anything to eat."

■

Where Bobcats Live

In the bobcat's world, success is determined by how long the feline stays alive and produces offspring. Under such circumstances it is not the strong that survive, but the most adaptable. The ability to use and live in a variety of landscapes is a big advantage, and few predators can do this as well as the bobcat.

The bobcat inhabits more of North America than any other native wild feline (Anderson and Lovallo 2003)—from southern Canada to central Mexico and from the Atlantic to the Pacific coast. The bobcat thrives in the thick chaparral of southern California (Lembeck and Gould 1979), the coniferous-hardwood forests of northern Wisconsin (Lovallo and Anderson 1996a), and the abandoned pasture and cropland of South Carolina (Kight 1962). They hunt prey in the sagebrush plains of southeastern Idaho (Bailey 1974; Knick 1990), the ponderosa pine and aspen of British Columbia (Clayton Apps, wildlife ecologist, personal communication), and the oak-pine forests of the Ozark Mountains (Hamilton 1982). Bobcats wander the mixed stands of eastern hemlock and hardwoods in Massachusetts (McCord 1974a), citrus groves and tree plantations in south-central Florida (Wassmer et al. 1988), and the bottomland hardwood forests of Louisiana and Alabama (Hall and Newsom 1978; Miller 1980). The key characteristics these varied habitats share are sufficient prey, dense cover, protection from severe weather, availability of rest areas, availability of den sites, and freedom from disturbance (Rollings 1945; Pollack 1951b; Erickson 1955; Bailey 1974).

Bobcats still seem to be rare in the dense urban populations along the mid-Atlantic coast and in large portions of the midwestern states (see Figure 1.3 in Chapter 1), including eastern South Dakota, southern Minnesota, Wisconsin, and Michigan, as well as northern Iowa, Illinois, Indiana, and Ohio, and portions of western Pennsylvania and New York. In the midwest, the bobcat was displaced during the 20th century, probably due to removal of cover and the subsequent extirpation of prey as a result of intensive agricultural development, as well as persecution by humans (Erickson 1981). However, recent work by Woolf and Nielsen (2002) showed that the bobcat is doing well in southern Illinois. Sightings and roadkills of the felid are increasing across southern Iowa (Iowa Department of Natural Resources [DNR] Wildlife 2003). Reports of bobcats are on the rise as well in eastern South Dakota (Huxoll 2002), southern Indiana (S. Johnson, Indiana DNR, personal communication), and eastern Ohio (Ohio DNR 2005). Regrowth of cover, increased prey numbers, restricted harvest, and improved management are all factors that may be contributing to the recovery.

Even abundant prey is of no value to a bobcat if it cannot be caught. This is why the presence of cover is so important. Bobcats either crouch and wait for prey to approach close enough to ambush or they actively stalk, then ambush. Both hunting techniques require the bobcat to get close to the prey before pouncing from a short distance (Sunquist and Sunquist 2002; Anderson and Lovallo 2003). Cover refers to the terrain and vegetation that allows the cat to stay out of sight while lying in wait or stalking. Habitats that have good stalking cover attract bobcats. Cover also helps protect the female bobcat's vulnerable kittens. For example, a dense brush thicket or pile of boulders that is used as a den also serves as concealment (Bolen and Robinson 1999).

Habitat is equally important to prey, and it must contain the appropriate combination of food and cover. Because most bobcat prey species are herbivores (plant-eating rodents, rabbits, and deer), they use both resources differently. Prey animals are attracted to vegetation that is both edible and dense enough to allow them to remain hidden while eating or resting (protective cover). Where the bobcat requires stalking cover, prey animals need a dense tangle of vegetation in which they can escape a pursuing bobcat. Any researcher who chooses to study bobcats on their home ground develops an intimate appreciation of why it chooses such dense vegetation. Apps (personal communication) fondly referred to the dense cover favored by the bobcats in his study area in southeastern British Columbia as "shit tangle."

Habitat characteristics dictate the diversity, abundance, and stability of prey populations, which in turn influence bobcat density and home range size (Anderson and Lovallo 2003). Some of the highest bobcat densities and smallest home ranges have been documented in openings in the bottomland hardwood forests of southern Alabama (Miller and Speake 1979), the broken desert scrub/desert grassland of Arizona (Jones and Smith 1979), and the thick chaparral vegetation of southern California (Lembeck 1986; Riley et al. 2003). Conversely, some of the lowest bobcat densities occur in areas with low prey productivity, such as the oak-pine forests of the Ozark Mountains (Hamilton 1982), the sagebrush-grasslands of southeastern Idaho (Bailey 1974), and the coniferous forests of Minnesota (Berg 1979; Fuller et al. 1985b) (see Table 4.1).

Different prey choose and use habitat in different ways. For example, Shaw (personal communication) pointed out that wild turkeys tend to avoid extremely dense shrubby habitat, because they are physically adapted to see and flee (fly). They have a fairly long periscope of a neck, with sharp eyes at the top. This is attached to a body designed for quiet escape on foot, or rapid, violent, and confusing escape in the air in an emergency. They need space to see and to get their wings unfolded. Similarly, pronghorn are see-and-flee creatures, and they go virtually unmolested by stalking predators such as mountain lions, unless circumstances force them to use brushy or broken country (Beale and Smith 1973). An examination of the spatial relations among bobcat, Florida panther, and white-tailed deer in south Florida revealed a degree of habitat separation among all three species.

The deer experienced some level of constant predatory tension from both cat species. It appeared that at least a segment of the deer herd used open marsh habitats to avoid Florida panther predation in forest cover, but this behavior made them vulnerable to bobcat predation in the marsh. Thus, the avoidance of one may increase susceptibility to the other (Maehr et al. 2002). Perhaps no prey species will live in a habitat ideally suited for its predators. For this reason, predators live under a "habitat stress," possibly full time. They must satisfy their own comfort and survival needs yet exploit prey on its home ground, which is selected via evolution to give the prey survival advantage. This give-and-take phenomenon in predator/prey habitat has not been well studied.

The cover most used by bobcats and their prey grows near the ground in what is referred to as understory vegetation. The density of vegetative cover is measured in both the horizontal and the vertical plane. The density of horizontal cover is measured using a cover board—a board that is divided into designated sections and held vertically at a sample point. An observer stands at a specified distance from the board and records the proportion of the board obscured by vegetation (Bolen and Robinson 1999). To a bobcat, the best horizontal cover is transparent enough to allow the feline to see its prey but dense enough for it to remain undetected while stalking and launching its final attack.

The density of the vegetation above the ground, in the higher branches and canopy of the forest, is also important to bobcats. The layers of vegetation from ground to canopy are called vertical cover or crown closure. This is measured as the percentage of ground surface covered by vegetation if one could look straight down on a landscape. It can be divided into ground layer cover, shrub layer cover, tree cover, and so on. Knowles (1985) found that bobcats in north-central Montana selected habitats with more than 52% vertical cover (crown closure). Although these habitats supported the highest prey densities, she thought that cover was also important to the bobcat's stalking and ambush hunting style. In southern Illinois, bobcats tend to use locations with dense understory vegetation during summer and winter, and more than 50% vertical vegetative cover during summer (Kolowski and Woolf 2002). This is probably the result of the bobcats' selecting for daylight resting locations with adequate cover. Anderson (1990) observed that bobcats in southeastern Colorado chose resting sites in steep-sloped, rocky areas with dense vertical cover. Juveniles were observed climbing trees to escape approaching biologists and once to avoid a coyote. He speculated that, in addition to providing concealment and escape cover, dense vertical cover provides protection from extreme temperatures and wind.

Bobcats do indeed appear to select habitat that protects them from severe weather. Thermal cover is especially important in the northern part of their range. The lowland conifer stands and swamps frequented by Minnesota bobcats (Fuller et al. 1985a) and the mixed stands of hemlocks and hardwoods frequented by Massachusetts bobcats (McCord 1974a) shelter the felines from the deep snow, high wind, and low temperatures common to upland deciduous sites. During the harsh

Canadian winters common to British Columbia, Apps (personal communication) found that bobcats move down to lower elevations, make use of south- and west-facing slopes, and seek out mature stands of trees that minimize snow depth and provide thickets of understory vegetation. Zezulak and Schwab (1979) found that bobcats in the Mojave Desert of southern California made use of boulder piles to avoid high temperatures and heavy rain. While hunting in nearby desert plains during the winter months, the cats rested under bushes or next to fallen Joshua trees (*Yucca brevifolia*).

Vegetation is not the only type of cover a bobcat needs. Numerous studies have documented the importance of cliff and ledge habitat for bobcats. In northern Vermont, Morse (personal communication) is convinced that cliff and ledge habitat is highly significant for bobcats and serves a variety of needs. This is particularly true if cliff refugia are found within valley and foothill habitats, which offer an abundance and diversity of prey and milder climates. During winter and spring, bobcats need to manage their energy budget. They need to rest and sun themselves in a safe place. South- and west-facing cliffs are best for thermoregulation in winter. Cliffs also provide natal denning habitat and a refuge from predators such as dogs, coyotes, and possibly fishers. Morse (personal communication) has observed bobcat fidelity to cliff refugia during three distinct times of year. The first period is deep winter, when they are used for safety, thermoregulation, and resting habitat. The second period is late February and March, when they serve as rendezvous sites, especially within the cliff refugia used by females. Males converge at or near these refugia, where scent-marking dramatically increases. The third period is late April to mid-June, when they are used for natal and rearing dens.

Just to the south of Morse's Vermont study area, in Massachusetts, McCord also showed that bobcat courtship activities seem to center on ledges, and that such areas seem to be gathering places for the otherwise solitary felines. He further pointed out that bobcats are primarily found in the western two-thirds of the state, where ledges are common. In the east, where there are no ledges, bobcats are scarce or absent (McCord 1974a). Missouri bobcats favor bluffs, brushy fields, and logged oak habitats. The bluffs are used for cover and social interaction, and the brushy fields and oak regeneration offer plentiful prey (Hamilton 1982). In Idaho (Bailey 1974) and in California (Zezulak and Schwab 1979), rocky terrain and boulder piles may serve the same function as ledges and bluffs in eastern habitats, however, during his study in northern California, Riley (personal communication) did not observe bobcats using rock outcrops as often as reported by others. Bobcats frequented such sites because of abundant prey and because of the shelter they afforded. During their study of bobcat habitat use in southern Illinois, Kolowski and Woolf (2002) found that rock outcroppings were not often used in summer but were more likely to be used in winter. In the southern part of their range, where ledges and rocky formations are rare, bobcats made use of dense vegetation for resting sites and natal dens, as well as hunting. While studying bobcats in the Salmon River Mountains in central Idaho, Koehler (personal communication) concluded that they used cliffs and bluffs as a refuge from coyotes and cougars. Shaw (personal communication) observed bobcat tracks associated with limestone ledges on Mingus Mountain in central Arizona. In midwinter, with a snow cover of 8 to 10 inches, he found signs of bobcats hunting cottontails, which in turn were on the ledges eating the leaves of cliffrose, a plant that stays green and produces leaves all along its stems right to their base at snow level. In this case, the bobcats' ledge selection was related to the feeding behavior of rabbits, which in turn was a result of the ancient presence of a sea in what is now Arizona, plus subsequent patterns of uplift and tilt.

Bobcats appear to shift their use of habitat with the seasons. In summer, they prefer higher elevations and are less selective in the habitats they frequent (Koehler and Hornocker 1989). In winter, habitat selection is most inXuenced by snow conditions, with bobcats preferring low elevations, south- or southwest-facing slopes, rocky terrain, and open areas (Koehler and Hornocker 1989; McCord 1974a). Wisconsin bobcats used lowland conifer stands more often, and unforested areas and upland deciduous forests less often, in winter (Lovallo and Anderson 1996a). Seasonal shifts in habitat use have also been observed in Minnesota (Fuller et al. 1985b) and in Oklahoma (Rolley and Warde 1985). Both shifts probably occurred in response to seasonal changes in energy demands due to reproduction, weather, and availability of prey. In southern Illinois, Kolowski and Woolf (2002) examined bobcat habitat use during summer and winter. During the warmer summer months, bobcats were most frequently found in areas with thick cover, close to distinct edge (change in cover type), and close to permanent streams and water sources. With the arrival of winter, bobcats still frequented areas of thick cover, but rock ground cover and log-wood ground cover as well. They were found even closer to water sources than during summer. During both seasons, bobcats were likely to be resting in tall, dense grass or brush.

There is evidence that male and female bobcats use habitat differently. Females appear to use better-quality habitat than males do, probably because they must capture more prey from a smaller area, especially when providing for dependent kittens (Bailey 1981; Anderson and Lovallo 2003). While analyzing bobcat habitat selection in Pennsylvania, Lovallo (1999) found that males used a broader range of habitats than females, resulting in twice the amount of suitable habitat being available in the state for males than for females. In the Ozark Mountains of Missouri, Hamilton (1982) also most frequently located breeding females in areas where large amounts of preferred habitats were nearby. They preferred bluffs, brushy fields, and oak regeneration areas more than other types. During their work in Oklahoma, Rolley and Warde (1985) found that females preferred deciduous or mixed pine-deciduous forests, and males preferred grass fields and brush. In Wisconsin, male bobcats frequented lowland conifer forests and avoided upland conifer stands, upland deciduous forest, and mixed savanna cover types. Females showed similar preferences but also selected for lowland deciduous forests and avoided unforested areas. Males and females differed in diet, activity periods, and seasonal habitat preferences, suggesting partial niche partitioning (Lovallo and Anderson 1996a). An examination of bobcat habitat selection in central Mississippi showed that females preferred pine (*Pinus* spp.) stands that were less than 8 years old, whereas males selected pine stands 9 to 15 years old and mature pine habitats (Chamberlain et al. 2003).

If there is one characteristic that contributes most to the survival of the bobcat, it is the feline's ability to live in close proximity to humans. Harrison's (1998) survey of 2,600 households in central New Mexico revealed that bobcats used residential areas and were active in the vicinity of houses, including areas with high densities of homes. Almost 30% of the respondents reported having seen bobcats less than 25 m (27 yards) from houses. In southern Illinois, Nielsen and Woolf (2001a) found that bobcats generally avoided areas around human dwellings. They concluded that, although some individual bobcats tolerate human presence and influences, they appear to select cores areas that offer a retreat from human activity. A study of 35 bobcats and 40 coyotes (*Canis latrans*) in the Santa Monica Mountains National Recreation Area of Los Angeles demonstrated the remarkable adaptability of both animals. Both species occupied mostly natural home ranges. Although the bobcats had lower levels of "urban associations" than the coyotes, both species managed to move through the fragmented landscape with relative ease, and survival rates were relatively high (Riley et al. 2003).

Roads and trails can affect bobcats in a variety of ways. They can be a source of direct mortality from collisions with vehicles (see Chapter 3), and they can influence spatial use, fragment habitat, increase access for hunters and trappers, or provide access during winter for competing carnivores (Anderson and Lovallo 2003). Wisconsin bobcats chose home ranges with higher trail densities and lower densities of secondary highways. They also crossed paved roads less frequently than expected (Lovallo and Anderson 1996b).

Some human land-use practices can actually enhance bobcat habitat. In Louisiana and Alabama, bobcats favor open areas in bottomland hardwood forests, which are created by farms, timber cuts, roads, pipelines, and prescribed burning. Such activity maintains areas in early successional stages, resulting in dense growths of briars, vines, and grasses—good habitat for prey species as well as ideal hunting and daytime resting sites for bobcats (Hall and Newsom 1978; Miller and Speake 1979). In eastern Oklahoma, bobcats most frequently used clearcut areas less than 10 years old, because such habitat supported larger populations of eastern cottontail rabbits (*Sylvilagus floridanus*) and hispid cotton rats (*Sigmodon hispidus*) (Rolley and Warde 1985). During our walk in the forest near her cabin in Vermont, Susan Morse showed me where she had made two small, irregularly-shaped patch cuts of about one-half acre each. She explained that, if done properly, such forestry practices enhance the habitat for snowshoe hare, grouse, rodents, and white-tailed deer. It has been suggested that the clearing of dense, unbroken coniferous forests for agriculture displaced the Canada lynx from the southern portion of its range, allowing the bobcat to expand its range into northern New England, northern Minnesota, southern Ontario, Manitoba, and Cape Breton Island (Rollings, 1945; Rolley 1987; Quinn and Parker 1987). Again, Koehler (personal communication) questioned this assertion: "I suspect the southern ranges were occupied by lynx during cyclic highs in the North resulting from lynx dispersal and these occurrences were documented and became viewed as 'lynx range.' As agriculture expanded and lynx became more 'rare' in these areas this 'lack of presence' was attributed to habitat loss."

Even the best habitat with abundant prey cannot support an unlimited number of bobcats. Any given area of land can support only a certain number of animals. Ecologists refer to this limiting concept as carrying capacity. Dasmann (1981) listed three important ways in which carrying capacity has been defined: (1) the number of animals of a given species that are actually supported by a habitat, measured over a period of years; (2) the upper limit of population growth in a habitat, above which no further increase can be sustained; and (3) the number of animals that a habitat can maintain in a healthy, vigorous condition. Caughley and Sinclair (1994:117) proposed a more comprehensive definition of carrying capacity that includes animals and vegetation. They use the term "ecological carrying capacity" and defined it as "the natural limit of a population set by resources in a particular environment. It is one of the equilibrium points that a population tends toward through density-dependent effects from lack of food, space (e.g., territoriality), cover, or other resources." They also differentiated ecological carrying capacity from economic carrying capacity. Economic carrying capacity is "the population level that produces the maximum offtake (or maximum sustained yield) for culling or cropping purposes."

It is important to understand that carrying capacity is not a static but a dynamic condition. The availability of resources within a given habitat and the animals' needs for those resources fluctuate over time in response to changes in environmental conditions such as weather. Fire, flood, drought, disease, predation, logging, and other forms of human development can have dramatic effects on carrying capacity. A habitat's carrying capacity can also vary seasonally, with regular bottleneck periods, such as winter or the dry season, when the number of animals the habitat can support is less than during the rest of the year. Bobcat survival rates are lowest during the winter months, an already stressful time when hunting and trapping seasons are open as well (Anderson and Lovallo 2003). Additionally, winter and early spring are the most likely periods of starvation, because rabbit, hare, and rodent populations are lowest at that time (Petraborg and Gunvalson 1962). However, this may be true only in colder climates. Shaw pointed out that winter in the desert Southwest can be a period of high survival. During his study of the social organization of bobcats in Idaho, Bailey (1974) discovered that winter and early spring are critical times for juveniles, because maternal support is being withdrawn and the hunting skills of the young are still developing. Brand and Keith (1979) studied Canada lynx in Alberta and found decreased amounts of fat in the individuals they examined in late winter during a snowshoe hare decline. They suggested that lynx experienced a negative energy balance during hare scarcity. Lynx pregnancy rates and litter sizes also decreased during the population decline. The complex and dynamic nature of carrying capacity underscores the difficulties in attempting to quantify the precise carrying capacity of a given habitat for a particular species at a specific point in time.

So, although the bobcat occupies an enormous range, encompassing a variety of habitats, it does not use all areas equally. In the northern part of its range, the feline prefers rough, rocky country interspersed with dense cover. This includes conifer stands, cliffs, riparian areas, and swamps. In the south, the wildcat favors mixed forest and agricultural areas with a mosaic of vegetation. Bobcats seem to select cover and terrain that provides a diversity of plentiful food, good resting and denning sites, protection from bad weather, and refuge from predators.

Home Range

Within bobcat habitat, adults space themselves out and confine their movements to individual territorial areas known as home ranges. Home range should not be confused with geographic range, which is a broader term indicating the entire geographic area in which the bobcat occurs (Dasmann 1981). Bobcat home ranges include hunting areas, travel routes, water sources, resting areas, lookout positions, and denning sites where kittens are reared. Adult bobcats that occupy a home range are called residents, and possession of a home range enhances a bobcat's chances of more consistently finding prey, locating mates, and successfully producing young (Kitchener 1991).

Possession of a home range enhances the bobcat's survival as a solitary predator. By having a fixed area of land to hunt in, the bobcat is better able to consistently locate prey. It roams its home range, learning the terrain, where the best cover is, and where prey most likely can be found. This is why survival for a transient bobcat is more precarious than for a resident bobcat. Transients move through unfamiliar terrain as young animals that have not yet perfected their hunting skills or as animals too old to defend prime habitat.

Radiotelemetry has allowed wildlife biologists to identify and map the movements and home ranges of a variety of species, including bobcats. One technique used to delineate and estimate home ranges is the minimum convex polygon. After compiling a number of radio locations and marking them on a topographic map, researchers connect the outermost locations or fixes to create a polygon that represents the bobcat's home range. This minimum convex polygon is the smallest (convex) polygon that contains all locations the animal has visited (see Figure 4.1). But although a resident animal generally confines its movements within the boundary of the minimum convex polygon, it does not use all of its home range equally, and there are areas the animal never visits (Kenward 1987). The felid focuses its activity where it can most easily find prey, escape and resting cover, and, in the case of females, natal dens. These selected areas of concentrated use within home ranges are called core areas (Kaufman 1962; Chamberlain et al. 2003). Core areas

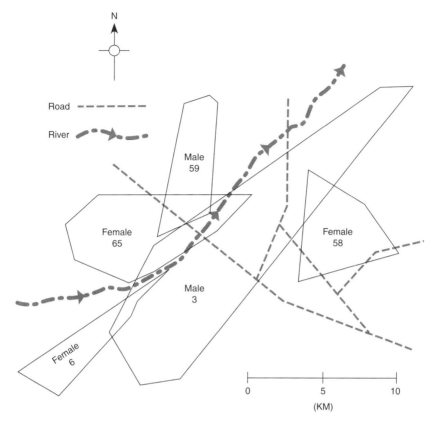

Figure 4.1
Home ranges of resident male and female bobcats in Ted Bailey's study area in
southeastern Idaho. (Bailey 1974.)

are defined mathematically as a percentage of the home range, usually the inner-
most 50% of radiotelemetry locations. These are bounded areas within the larger
home range that represent where animal spends the most time.

The size of bobcat home ranges, the degree of overlap between sexes, and the
extent of overlap between cats of the same gender vary widely across the cat's geo-
graphical range. Anderson and Lovallo (2003) urged caution when comparing
home range characteristics among studies. Variations in the number of bobcats
tracked, their social status, the number of radiotelemetry locations used, the season of sampling, and the technique employed to estimate home range size can
confound and confuse comparisons. However, there are some consistent generalizations that can be made about bobcat home ranges.

Home ranges tend to be larger in the northern latitudes of the bobcat's range
than those in the south, probably due to lower prey density, colder temperatures,
and larger body size (Anderson and Lovallo 2003). Maine bobcat males wander

home ranges that average 112 km² (43 square miles) (Litvaitis et al. 1987), whereas Alabama bobcat males need only 2.63 km² (1 square mile) (Miller and Speake 1979). In New York's Adirondack Mountains, male home ranges average an impressive 325 km² (127 square miles), whereas those of females average 86 km² (34 square miles) (Fox 1990). These are some of the largest home ranges recorded, but the cats in this region prey primarily on white-tailed deer, which requires constant travel. To the south, in the Catskill Mountains, deer and rabbits are more abundant, and male and female bobcat home ranges are 36 km² (14 square miles) and 31 km² (12 square miles), respectively (Fox 1990; Sunquist and Sunquist 2002). The bottomland hardwood forests of southern Louisiana offer the bobcat abundant prey and no hunting pressure, resulting in adult male home ranges of only 4.9 km² (2 square miles) and adult female home ranges of 0.9 km² (0.35 square miles) (Hall and Newsom 1978; Sunquist and Sunquist 2002) (see Table 4.1).

Table 4.1
Estimated Bobcat Home Range Size

| State | n | Home Range in square kilometers (square miles) | | | Author |
		Male	n	*Female*	
Alabama	6	2.63 (1.03)	6	1.12 (0.44)	Miller and Speake 1979
California		1.55 (0.60)		0.84 (0.33)	Lembeck 1986
California	16	3.21 (1.25)	19	1.55 (0.60)	Riley et al. 2003
Idaho	4	42.1 (16.4)	8	19.3 (7.5)	Bailey 1974
Idaho	7	53.0 (20.7)	13	28.5 (11.1)	Knick 1990
Illinois	22	52.4 (20.4)	30	16 (6.2)	Nielsen and Woolf 2001b
Maine	10	95.7 (37.3)	8	31.2 (12.1)	Litvaitis et al. 1986b
Minnesota	22	58.3 (22.7)	11	36.6 (14.3)	Fuller et al. 1985a
Minnesota	16	62 (24.2)	6	38 (14.8)	Berg 1979
Mississippi	35	Breeding 17.69 (6.8)	68	Breeding 8.63 (3.36)	Chamberlain et al. 2003
	28	Kitten-rearing 15.28	62	Kitten-rearing 8.70	
	23	(5.96)	42	(3.39)	
		Winter 18.77 (7.32)		Winter 8.55 (3.33)	
Missouri	9	60.4	8	16.1	Hamilton 1982
Oklahoma		43.4 (16.7)		14.8 (5.7)	Rolley 1983
South Carolina	3	20.8 (8.1)	3	10.35 (4.0)	Buie et al. 1979
South Carolina	4	2.56 (0.99)	3	1.14 (0.44)	Fendley and Buie 1986
Tennessee	2	76.8 (29.9)	3	25.9 (10.1)	Kitchings and Story 1984
Wisconsin	6	60.4 (23.5)	6	28.5 (11.1)	Lovallo and Anderson 1996b

n = number of animals.

Male home ranges are typically two to three times larger (sometimes four to five times larger) than those of females (Hall and Newsom 1978; Kitchings and Story 1979; Witmer and DeCalesta 1986). They usually overlap or encompass several female home ranges, and occasionally they overlap those of other resident males (Bailey 1974; Berg 1979; Lovallo and Anderson 1996b). Female home ranges tend to be more exclusive and rarely overlap (Bailey 1974; Berg 1979; Lembeck and Gould 1979; Hamilton 1982; Lawhead 1984) (see Figure 4.1). Exceptions to this pattern do exist. Studies in Alabama (Miller and Speake 1979) and in Oklahoma (Rolley 1983) showed no overlap between male home ranges, and researchers in northern California (Zezulak and Schwab 1979) observed a bobcat population with 36% overlap of female home ranges. Nielsen and Woolf (2001b) found substantial home range overlap among bobcats in southern Illinois. Annual overlap was 36% between female home ranges, 47% between male home ranges, and 54% between male and female home ranges. They stated, "Although intrasexual home range overlap was extensive, core areas were nearly exclusive, implying that core areas confer benefits to bobcats by reducing competition for resources and may represent areas of more aggressive territoriality within the home range." They also suggested that this pattern of spatial organization may result from several factors, including higher bobcat densities in southern Illinois. However, Plowman (1997) found that male bobcats in central Mississippi established core areas that overlapped female core areas, apparently to maximize breeding opportunities.

Bobcats are not territorial in the sense of defending their home ranges to exclude all other bobcats. Rather, the cats have evolved a land tenure system, in which home ranges are maintained by resident bobcats but not transient bobcats. Adjacent resident bobcats and transient bobcats will not permanently settle in an area already occupied by a resident. Transients simply pass through areas occupied by adults and seem to be tolerated, regardless of how exclusive the home ranges are to the resident adults (Provost et al. 1973; McCord 1974a; Miller and Speake 1979). Bobcats also show strong fidelity to their home ranges over time (Bailey 1974; Litvaitis et al. 1987). Residents usually move their home range only if an adjacent occupant dies (Lovallo and Anderson 1995) or lack of prey causes the social organization to collapse (Bailey 1974; Knick 1990). When a resident is killed, either by harvest or natural mortality, the vacant home range is filled by a transient or by an adjacent resident. This happens most frequently with males (Bailey 1974; Miller and Speake 1979; Anderson 1988) and less so with females (Bailey 1974; Lovallo and Anderson 1995). The shift in the home range matrix when a vacancy occurs indicates that bobcats are aware of the varying quality of home ranges and that bobcat habitat use is influenced by the location of adjacent residents (Anderson and Lovallo 2003). On the Tallahalla Wildlife Management Area (TWMA) in Mississippi, Benson and colleagues (2004) documented 10 cases in which the home ranges of deceased male and female resident bobcats were filled by transient or neighboring bobcats. For males (n = 5) and females (n = 5), respectively, an average of 85% and 79% of each replacement cat's home range overlapped with the former resident's home range. This extensive overlap supports the land tenure system for bobcats and the filling of home range vacancies by transients or neighboring residents of the same sex. However, as discussed later, bobcat social organization may be more complex than previously reported.

In areas where home ranges overlap, bobcats seem to avoid each other. This mutual avoidance is thought to be accomplished primarily through sight and smell. Visual markers include scat (feces) piles and scrapes. A scrape is a small mound of soil, leaves, twigs, or duff that the bobcat scrapes together with its hind feet and on which he will urinate and sometimes defecate. Scent marking facilitates olfactory communication (Hornocker and Bailey 1986; Kitchener 1991; Mellen 1991). Adult bobcats scent mark using mouth glands, feces, urine, scrapes, and anal glands (Bailey 1974). This form of communication is far more sophisticated than it appears. Kitchener (1991:153) explained, "Urine and feces are the common language in the felid world, which they use to maintain a stable living space where they survive and breed."

Bailey (1974) examined the use of marking by bobcats during his research in Idaho. He noticed that young bobcats did not scent mark, and that near natal dens the kittens always attempted to cover their feces. Later in the autumn, when the kittens were older, they abandoned this habit. Adults deposited their feces in what he called fecal marking locations. These were frequently in the same location, usually in conspicuous areas along travel routes such as rocky ridges and rims of volcanic craters. Another frequent location was near natal or temporary dens of females with kittens. Kight (1962) found similar fecal mounds in South Carolina, with one single marking site containing 254 scats. Provost and colleagues (1973) believed that female bobcats used their feces to mark the boundaries of home ranges, but Bailey (1974) concluded that they were used primarily to mark special places within their home ranges. He found that resident bobcats also scent-marked with urine, squirting small amounts on rocks, bushes, and snow banks as they traveled. They sprayed urine one to five times per mile. Scrapes were usually made with their hind feet after scent marking with urine or feces. Scrapes consisted of two parallel grooves, 25 to 30 cm (10–12 inches) long and 10 to 15 cm (4–6 inches) wide. Bailey noticed that the odor of urine was present in all fresh scrapes he examined.

How bobcats use their anal glands in scent marking is not well understood. Bailey (1974) found that the anal glands of adult males contained a dark brown, paste-like secretion; in females, this was light yellow, and in juveniles it was white to slightly yellow. He detected anal scent on fresh feces in fecal marking locations and in sprung traps. In south-central Florida, Guenther (1980) observed a seasonal change in marking behavior, with many more scats deposited in scrapes at marking sites in February than in July and August.

Experts speculate that scent markings function as biological bulletin boards within and between home ranges. By either depositing feces or urine or sniffing the feces or scrape of other individuals, bobcats may send and receive a variety of messages. Male residents can announce their presence, female residents can stake claim to a natal den, transient bobcats or females with dependent kittens can avoid male residents, and females can find males when they are ready to mate. Two bobcats with overlapping home ranges can both use a common area because scrapes allow them to use the area at different times. Biologists refer to this as temporal spacing (Kitchener 1991; Mellen 1991).

As might be expected, male and female bobcats use their home ranges differently. It is thought that female bobcats select home ranges to secure the necessary resources for survival and the survival of their kittens, whereas males establish home ranges to maximize breeding opportunities (i.e., female home ranges) within the area (Bailey 1979; Anderson 1987; Sandell 1989; Anderson and Lovallo 2003; Chamberlain et al. 2003). Females hunt more frequently than males, and they concentrate their hunting in one of several areas within their home ranges. These areas are typically within one mile of a protected resting place, such as a ledge or cave. After hunting in one area for a few days, the female moves to a new location (Anderson 1987a; Wassmer et al. 1988). As a result, the same areas are used repeatedly. The function of the female bobcat's home range is to provide enough prey and denning sites for raising kittens, even in years of low prey numbers. This is why females seem less tolerant of other females in their home ranges, but males are allowed. However, females seem more tolerant of daughters that take up residence in adjacent and sometimes overlapping home ranges. This tendency of females to stay close to their natal home range is called philopatry and it results in the formation of clusters of related females (Sunquist and Sunquist 2003). This relatedness among resident females could influence the degree of home range overlap (Chamberlain and Leopold 2001). In Mississippi, female bobcat home ranges decreased in size over time, suggesting that size was a function of increased hunting skills, familiarity with resource distribution, and changes in social pressure and habitat quality (Conner et al. 1999).

Back on the TWMA in Mississippi, Benson and colleagues (2004) documented a home range shift and abandonment by a resident female (no. 21) after another female (no. 22) moved into her home range. They observed female 22 establish a home range in essentially the same location as female 21. Female 21 responded by shifting her home range to the fringes of her former range, then finally abandoning it to establish a new home range to the east. Whether this was a mother accommodating an offspring for indirect genetic benefits or the result of some type of dominance hierarchy and or aggressive encounter between the females is unknown. The investigators pointed out, "Regardless of whether the home range transfer was voluntary, it is clearly in conflict with notions that bobcat home ranges are held for life and that same sex conspecifics do not contest occupied home ranges."

Males move about their home ranges more widely and constantly, and they scent mark along saddles, ridge lines, travelways, and so on. In South Carolina, female bobcats occupied definite core areas, whereas males moved in a linear fashion over a much wider area and did not remain in core areas (Fendley and Buie

1986). Males seldom, except during winter, returned to previously used resting places. They moved farther and faster than females, especially at night, when hunting and investigating scent marks, especially during the breeding season (Woolf and Nielsen 2002; Chamberlain et al. 2003). Murphy (personal communication) emphasized that, by maintaining home ranges that exclude other breeding males but encompass several females, males use exclusivity to increase their reproductive success.

Prey numbers and the amount of stalking cover in bobcat habitat obviously influence the density of the bobcat population. Bobcat density in turn influences home range size and the degree of overlap in an area. The smaller the home range, the higher the bobcat density. Lembeck (1978) recorded some of the highest bobcat densities, 1.27 to 1.53 animals per square kilometer (0.5–0.6 per square mile), and some of the smallest home range sizes, 0.6 to 4.4 km^2 (0.2–1.7 square miles) for females and 0.88 to 6.4 km^2 (0.3–2.5 square miles) for males, in the chaparral vegetation of southern California near San Diego. Male home ranges showed seasonal overlap with those of other males, ranging from 28.4% during July-August to 59.7% during November-December. This is contrary to what Bailey (1974) found in Idaho, where only 2% of the combined areas of four male home ranges overlapped. Female home ranges in Lembeck's (1986) study area showed no overlap at all. Further east, in the oak-pine forest of the Ozark Mountains, Hamilton (1982) documented low densities of 0.064 to 0.097 bobcats per square kilometer (0.024–0.038 per square mile) and large home ranges of 30 to 108 km^2 (12–42 square miles) for males and 6.2 to 31 km^2 (2.4–12 square miles) for females. Male home ranges overlapped an average of 22%, but the female overlap was only 7%. Lembeck's study population was unharvested, while Hamilton's (1982) was harvested, which could have been a contributing factor to the difference in densities.

The matrix of adjacent and overlapping home ranges shown in Figure 4.1 gives the impression of uniformity and stability. In the real world of bobcat society, the location of a home range depends on the stability of the environment. Dramatic home range shifts can occur in the face of crashes in prey numbers (Bailey 1981; Knick 1990) or the death of a resident bobcat due to disease or hunting and trapping (Miller 1980). Home range size can even change with the seasons. Males expand their home ranges during the breeding season to mate with as many females as possible, whereas females constrict their home ranges after giving birth to remain close to their kittens (Anderson 1987; Sandell 1989). However, Nielsen and Woolf (2001b) found no change in home-range size between seasons in southern Illinois, and seasonal home-range shifts were minor. They suggested that either it was best to remain in the same area all year round for optimal use of resources or territorial behavior hindered seasonal shifts.

Change in vegetation structure can also affect home range size. Researchers studying bobcats on the Savannah River Plant in South Carolina found that home range size increased from the mid-1960s to the late 1970s, as old agricultural fields were transformed into uniform pine plantations. These homogenous stands of trees provided unfavorable habitat for eastern cottontails and cotton rats, so their numbers declined. Bobcats responded by expanding their home ranges, because they needed to hunt over a larger area to find adequate prey (Provost et al. 1973; Buie et al. 1979; Jenkins et al. 1979). Morse (personal communication) observed a similar pattern in her Vermont study. During a decline in the snowshoe hare population from 1976 to 1996, resident bobcats needed more habitat to survive.

Although boundaries around the home ranges shown in Figure 4.1 are clearly delineated, it is important to understand that home ranges are not necessarily continuous areas. Ewer (1973) pointed out that a home range may consist of feeding and resting places connected by a series of pathways. Bailey (1974) confirmed this description in his study of Idaho bobcats. He explained that female home ranges are essentially a collection of temporary dens and hunting areas that are routinely marked and repeatedly used. This allows different bobcats to use common areas at different times (temporal spacing). What a human observer perceives as a violation of a territorial boundary may just be a bobcat neighbor passing through. As further evidence of this home range flexibility, bobcats do not use all parts of their home range equally. At the Savannah River Plant in South Carolina, biologists found that bobcats most often hunted in bottomland hardwoods, even though they represented only 17% of the total home range. They avoided mature pine plantations, which made up 64% of the area, because their main prey were mostly found in bottomland hardwoods (Heller and Fendley 1986).

Bailey (1974) believed that bobcat social organization revolves around the characteristics of their prey:

> If the prey is uniformly distributed and sedentary, competition for food could be reduced by having exclusive areas. If the prey becomes localized or is highly mobile, bobcats would have to follow their prey and exclusive areas would be of little survival value. Similarly, after rabbit populations crash, small localized concentrations of jackrabbits could be found quickly and perhaps utilized more efficiently if bobcats wandered beyond their normal ranges in search of prey. In the process, their home ranges would gradually become larger and exhibit more overlap. Some ranges might eventually be abandoned. In such fluctuating environments, territoriality among bobcats may only occur during those periods when prey is widespread and abundant.

Thirty years after Bailey's work in Idaho and in the wake of hundreds of other published studies, there remains much to be learned about the bobcats' land tenure system. Sunquist and Sunquist (2002) pointed out that bobcats use a variety of habitats with a variety of population and prey densities, and many of these study populations are harvested at some level. Most studies are short-term, rarely lasting the entire life of the felid, and lack genetic information on the subjects. All of these factors conspire to make generalizations difficult. They suggested, "The widely varying land tenure systems that have shown up in bobcat studies ought, perhaps, to be regarded simply as a series of snapshots of an adaptable predator living under a variety of social and environmental conditions. Only a study of an unharvested population in which individuals are known and followed over their lifetimes will reveal the whole picture."

Bobcat Society

Bobcats spend most of their lives alone. Interactions with other bobcats are brief and infrequent. The only associations of length are between females and their kittens and between adult males and females during the breeding season (Anderson and Lovallo 2003). But adult bobcats are more than solitary and territorial felines that get together only to mate. Kitchener (1991:155) explained that the social life of wild cats is far more sophisticated:

> Thus, far from having a chaotic, random system of home ranges driven by the need for 'solitary' cats to avoid each other at all costs, most wild cats maintain a predictable system of land tenure, which promotes social stability and maximizes the reproductive success of both males and females. Males mate with more than one female to maximize the number of progeny they sire, and females are defended from intruding males who might kill their young. Far from being strangers, neighboring cats probably know each other very well from their own distinctive smells.

Solitary or not, within a population not all bobcats are created equal. This feline social hierarchy consists of five classes of animals: resident adult males, resident adult females, transient males, transient females, and dependent kittens of resident females. Resident adults maintain established home ranges and do most of the breeding in a population. Transients are usually subadults moving through the home ranges of residents in search of a vacant home range of their own (Sunquist and Sunquist 2002), but they can also be older bobcats that are shifting home ranges. Female transients tend to delay breeding until they find and occupy a home range. Kittens still rely on their mother to hunt for them (Anderson and Lovallo 2003).

There are usually an equal number of males and females at birth (Anderson 1987; Stys and Leopold 1993; Anderson and Lovallo 2003). Sex ratios (male:females) in most adult bobcat populations also approximate 1:1 (Lariviere and Walton 1997), but they have been reported to be 0.83:1 to 1.25:1 (n = 1,238) in Washington (Knick et al. 1985), 0.87:1 (n = 411) in Oklahoma (Rolley 1985), and 1.08:1 (n = 605) in Nova Scotia (Parker and Smith 1983). Harvest records consistently show that males are killed more frequently in the younger age groups, whereas females are taken more often in the older age groups (Crowe and Strickland 1975; Fritts and Sealander 1978b; Parker and Smith 1983). In his discussion of bobcat population modeling and analysis, Gilbert (1979) suggested that sex ratios may reflect the intensity of harvest. He expected lightly and moderately harvested populations to show mostly males, but greater harvest pressure would result in a more even sex ratio. Knick et al. (1985) found that the proportion of males in a sample from western Washington increased as the harvest progressed. They suggested that, as the breeding season approached, males moved more frequently between females' home ranges to assess their breeding status and thereby made themselves more vulnerable to trapping. During the same study, the sex ratios of hunted versus trapped bobcats were compared, and little or no difference was found. Nielsen (personal communication) cautioned, "Varying sex ratios are frequently not indicative of the true population, but are rather biased by our measurement techniques (i.e., harvest returns)." McCord and Cardoza (1982) were skeptical of sex ratio data from harvests because of frequent misidentification of sex by field personnel. They also believed that the theory that male bobcats are more vulnerable than females due to their larger home ranges or more intense breeding season activity is suspect.

Studies in California indicate that bobcat population density can dramatically alter sex ratios. Lembeck and Gould's (1979) work with an unexploited population of bobcats near San Diego showed a sex ratio of 2:1 (male/female) at the highest population density but only 0.86:1 at the lowest density. In the Mojave Desert, Zezulak and Schwab (1979) found seven adult males for every female. They speculated that more males survived when competition for food was intense and that the unbalanced sex ratio would be compensated for by fewer births, more deaths, and greater emigration, until population density and competition were reduced.

The age distribution of harvested bobcat populations has been examined in a number of studies, and kittens have been found to be underrepresented; yearlings usually make up a greater proportion of the sample than kittens (Bailey 1979; Brittell et al. 1979; Parker and Smith 1983). It is unknown whether this disparity is due to differences in capture vulnerability or differences in reporting rates of hunters and trappers (Anderson and Lovallo 2003). According to Obbard (1987), pelts from juvenile bobcats are commercially valuable, and pelts of juvenile Canada lynx are more valuable than those of adults because their fur is finer and silkier. In Texas, Blankenship and Swank (1979) found that the proportion of kittens in the harvest increased from 6.7% in November to 31% in February. A similar increase was observed on Cape Breton Island, Nova Scotia, where the proportion of kittens taken went from a little over 10% in November to more than half the sample by March (Parker and Smith 1983). Kittens probably grow more vulnerable to harvest due to a combination of independence from the protection of their mothers, increased movement as they begin to disperse, unfamiliarity with areas they are traversing, and increased vulnerability after their mother is removed by trapping (Anderson 1987; Anderson and Lovallo 2003).

Older bobcats dominate unexploited bobcat populations, but there is a larger percentage of younger animals in populations that are hunted and trapped. The proportion of younger bobcats (<2 years old) depends on the intensity of the harvest. This may be a result of increased reproduction, more deaths among adults, or both (Anderson and Lovallo 2003). Lembeck and Gould (1979) examined the dynamics of harvested and unharvested bobcat populations in similar habitat in

California. They found that 16% of the bobcats in the unharvested population were younger than 2 years old, compared with 43% of the harvested group. In South Dakota, in an area where bobcats existed in low densities and were subjected to intense harvest, 1- and 2-year-olds made up almost 76% of the population (Fredrickson and Rice 1979).

"Only in a population of wild cats which are subject to heavy human exploitation are transients going to find it easy to establish a new home range," wrote Kitchener (1991:161), "because the stability of the land tenure system and potential long life of most species of wild cat probably provide few openings except in marginal habitats." But a bobcat cannot expect to eat regularly or mate until it has claimed its own home range. Transients are also more vulnerable to predation and attack from residents, which can increase mortality. How the cats "test" a population for vacated home ranges is poorly understood. Smell probably plays an important role in a transient's ability to assess the presence or absence of a resident. It is generally believed that a transient either finds a vacant home range or displaces an older resident. If a vacant home range is found, the young male or female will establish its place in the population. If the population density is so high that no vacant home ranges exist, the transient moves on.

Bailey (1974) observed in Idaho that when resident females died, either the adjacent female resident expanded her range to encompass the new area or a transient female took over the vacant area. In Alabama, Miller and Speake (1979) noted that, after the deaths of two resident males, one vacant home range was occupied within two days by a young male, and the other was taken over by the adjacent resident male expanding his home range. Hamilton (1982) found that all home range vacancies in his Missouri study area were resettled by transients within two to three months. Apps (personal communication) believed that male bobcat dispersal in British Columbia was probably not density dependent. That is, juvenile males might simply be in a transient mode, regardless of home range vacancy, until the onset of sexual maturity. However, bobcats and pumas exhibit similar social ecology. Maehr and his colleagues (2002) examined Florida panther dispersal in south Florida and made a compelling argument that dispersal distances among males were density dependent. Evidence suggests that the situation may be different for females; female dispersal may in fact relate to home range vacancy. However, it cannot be assumed that trapping and hunting exploits only established residents, while transients remain invisible, waiting to take over. Certain kinds of hunting, such as predator calling, may select for younger, less experienced animals; on the other hand, experienced trappers may well select for larger, resident bobcats.

The role of transients in populations is important, because they are the primary source of replacements for resident bobcats who die as a result of hunting, trapping, old age, or accidents. Transients also ensure genetic mixing between populations, and they appear to be a major factor in the recovery of exploited populations or even the rescue of insular populations.

Experts speculate that land tenure and mutual avoidance allow bobcats to maintain home ranges and live together in a number of ways that are beneficial to the bobcat population as a whole. The greatest advantage is that it partitions food and habitat resources by limiting bobcat density. Such an arrangement is less stressful than exclusive territoriality. Bobcats do not have to expend valuable energy patrolling territorial boundaries to exclude competing felids. Mutual avoidance and land tenure are also thought to reduce fighting and possible injury (Hornocker and Bailey 1986). "However, strife among males has been documented among numerous felids (i.e., African lions, cougars), particularly over access to females," said Koehler (personal communication). "Strife is the 'ultimate' reinforcement for social organization in felids."

Fighting occurs among bobcats, usually between males, but it is difficult to detect. While snow-tracking bobcats in February during an ecological study in Michigan, Erickson (1955) observed an area in the snow where one large and two smaller bobcats engaged in a severe fight, leaving the two smaller bobcats badly bleeding. In the warmer climes of South Carolina, Provost et al. (1973) reported that an adult male chased a younger male up a tree. The two growled and spat at each other until the altercation was interrupted by the approaching researchers, and the adult male then fled. Hamilton (1982) watched an adult and juvenile hissing and screaming at each other for more than two minutes in Missouri. The confrontation ended without violence when the adult male turned and walked away. Two months later, he observed a "vicious battle" between two adult males. While studying dispersing bobcats from northeastern Kansas, Kalmer and colleagues (2000) observed an aggressive encounter in mid-December between an adult female and a male offspring that had become independent 11 months earlier. The adult female growled, hissed, screamed, and then lunged at the male, causing it to retreat.

Only 2 of 86 captured bobcats in an Illinois study had wounds attributed to fighting with other bobcats. Both were adult males, and one had wounds serious enough that they were cleaned and sutured by a veterinarian before the cat was released (Woolf and Nielsen 2002). Most fighting appears to take place during the breeding season, when spermatogenesis, and presumably testosterone levels, are at their peak (Anderson 1987). Because bobcats are polygynous and multiple male home ranges may overlap that of a single female, it is not surprising that competition for matings occurs. However, the general lack of fighting among females, combined with evidence that females maintain home ranges exclusive of each other, suggests that female bobcats engage in strong, sex-specific territorial marking (Anderson and Lovallo 2003). Benson and his colleagues (2004) documented that a resident male bobcat killed another male that intruded into his home range in Mississippi. It was unknown whether the intruder was a transient or resident. The resident male had shifted to the home range only six weeks before it killed the intruder, so it is possible that, because neither male had established prior residence, a fight ensued for the vacant home range. It is also possible that the resident male detected the intruder in his home range, judged him a weaker opponent of lesser age and size, and killed him to prevent any future intrusions into his newly established home range. The researchers emphasized, "Regardless of the circumstances that led to the killing, bobcat social organization appears to be less peaceful than previously suggested" (Benson et al. 2004:986).

There are times when bobcats demonstrate exceptional tolerance of each other. The most famous incident took place during one particularly harsh Idaho winter. A combination of severe weather and low rabbit populations forced four bobcats to take shelter in a common rock pile. The two males and two females seemed to get along for almost two weeks, while high winds, deep snow, and subzero temperatures restricted their movements. They were occasionally seen sunning themselves within three to four yards of each other, but no threatening behavior nor fighting was seen (Bailey 1974).

Bobcats on the Move

"There are certain things in Nature in which beauty and utility, artistic and technical perfection, combine in some incomprehensible way: the web of a spider, the wing of a dragon-fly, the superbly streamlined body of the porpoise, and the movements of a cat" (Konrad Lorenz, quoted in Seidensticker and Lumpkin 1991:11). These words, written by famed animal behaviorist Konrad Lorenz, evoke the pervasive fascination humans have with felines. It is how they move. Cats are stealthy, efficient, purposeful, yet mysterious. It is the way they move that has led to such descriptive names as ghost cat, shadow of the forest, and silent death. It is how bobcats move in the more prosaic world of their home ranges that biologists endeavor to understand.

Male and female bobcats appear to differ in both the distance and the speed at which they travel on a daily basis. Biologists calculate these average daily movements from the differences in daily fixes from radio-collar signals. For instance, male bobcats in eastern Tennessee covered a daily average of 4.5 km (2.7 miles), whereas females moved only 1.2 km (0.72 miles) (Kitchings and Story 1984). But these measurements represent only the straight-line distance between locations on a map and do not reflect the actual distance covered. When a bobcat is hunting, it traverses a zigzag course through its home range. An entire day of searching for prey probably brings the bobcat only a few linear miles from its starting point.

In the bottomland hardwoods of southern Louisiana, males moved at a rate of 364 to 455 m/hr (400–500 yards/hr), whereas females covered less ground at 191 to 223 m/hr (210–245 yards/hr) (Hall and Newsom 1978). In Idaho, Bailey (1974) found that males wandered only 1.61 km (1 mile) and females 1.21 km (0.75 mile) each day. He cited this difference as additional evidence that females hunt their smaller home ranges more intensively than males do in their larger home ranges.

Females followed the pattern of concentrating their hunting effort in one location for a few days, whereas males moved more widely about their home ranges. Bailey (1974) also noted that both sexes traveled distances greater than one mile more frequently during the spring and summer than during the fall and winter. Recent work in central Mississippi revealed that males moved through their home ranges at faster rates (376 m/hr [410 yards/hr]) than females did (332 m/hr [362 yards/hour]), and both sexes moved fastest (385 m/hr [420 yards/hr]) at night. They also moved at greater rates during winter (373 m/hr [407 yards/hr]) than in other seasons (Chamberlain et al. 2003). During their study in southern Illinois, Woolf and Nielsen (2002:18–19) monitored bobcats in spring (March-May), summer (June-August), and fall (September-November) during two tracking periods (1600–0100 [4:00 pm to 1:00 am] and 0100–1000 [1:00 am to 10:00 am]), which were the periods of highest bobcat activity. Males traveled farther than females during both time periods and in all three seasons. Distances varied, with males covering from 0.4 to 12.5 km (0.25–7.75 mi) and females covering 0.8 to 7.1 km (0.5–4.4 mi). Males traveled farthest during the spring, probably in search of mates. Males also moved faster (601 m/hr [655 yards/hr]) than females did (300 m/hr [327 yards/hr]). Woolf and Nielsen (2002) noted that Illinois bobcats followed stream valleys and associated ridges as travel routes. They moved through woods or along wooded edges and rarely crossed open areas, but when necessary they did so quickly. They also observed, "Males traveled farther and faster than females when in movement paths, and spent more time (43% were >2.5 hours duration) in the movement paths than females (16% were 2.5 hours duration)."

As discussed in Chapter 2, bobcats are considered to be crepuscular, and both sexes exhibit similar patterns of activity that peak in the few hours before and after sunset and sunrise. These peaks occur at 1800 to 2400 and 0400 to 1000 (Buie et al. 1979; Miller and Speake 1979; Lariviere and Walton 1997). These periods coincided with the peak activity of lagomorphs, their primary prey (Anderson and Lovallo 2003). As usual, there are exceptions to this pattern. Some studies have found the cats to be primarily nocturnal, and others have reported that they are active throughout the day, or that they are arrhythmic (Sunquist and Sunquist 2002). In the Mojave Desert of California, Zezulak and Schwab (1980) noted seasonal differences in bobcat activity between winter and spring. During winter, the peak activity periods were from 0400 to 1000 and 1600 to 2200, whereas the bobcats became more nocturnal (1800 to 0600) in the spring. The lower activity in the spring appeared to be related to warm temperatures, because bobcat activity decreased when temperatures were greater than 26°C (80°F). It was unclear whether the reduced activity was due to increased temperature or reduced prey activity. They also found that the bobcats were active about 12 hours per day throughout the year. South Carolina bobcats increased their daylight movements during the winter, and males used their home ranges more extensively by traveling greater distances during 24-hour periods while maintaining the same home range size (Buie et al. 1979). In Oklahoma, Rolley (1983) found contrasting behavior. The daylight movements of males and females and the 24-hour movements of males were least during fall and winter.

It was long thought that bobcats follow a regular and predictable circuit around their home range. This assumption stemmed partly from observations of trappers in the field, from observations of domestic cats, or even from vague attempts to apply human behavior to bobcats. Although radiotelemetry monitoring indicates that bobcats concentrate their hunting efforts at various locations within their home range, bobcats are not known to pass a fixed point at set intervals. As a stalking predator that depends on the element of surprise to capture prey, regularity of movement would seem to handicap the bobcat's ability to survive. Koehler (personal communication) disagreed: "Trappers and hunters are able to capture and kill bobcats at 'trap sites' over generations of bobcat litters. There must be some 'fixed' travel pattern or hunting use in their home areas." Dave Maehr (University of Kentucky, personal communication) stated that the travel pattern probably depends on the temporal scale of measurement. At weekly or monthly intervals, male movement may appear regular and predictable. At a daily scale, movement probably appears irregular. This is yet another piece of the bobcat puzzle that needs further investigation.

Bobcats are not always on the move. In fact, like most other species of cats, the bobcat's primary activity is inactivity—mostly resting and sleeping. Mellen (1991:75) said that the lifestyle of cats is best described as "one of inactivity punctuated by forays in search of food." Whether the domestic tabby or the untamed tiger, cats tend to sleep unless hunger drives them to hunt. When a cat is asleep, it runs through several short sleep cycles, occasionally snapping awake to investigate a sound or flash of movement, then returning to its slumber if nothing captures its attention. This is the origin of the term *cat nap* (Sunquist 1987). According to Morse (personal communication), a bobcat's five favorite activities are resting with its eyes open, resting with its eyes closed, lolling about, napping, and sleeping.

Deep snow and cold can significantly limit the movement of bobcats. Accumulations greater than 13 to 15 cm (5–6 inches) restricted bobcat mobility in Maine (Litvaitis et al. 1986a) and in Massachusetts (McCord 1974a), and in Missouri, Hamilton (1982) observed increased use of protected rock ledges and small caves during and after winter storms. Bobcats avoid deep snow by staying under forest canopies that either block the snow from reaching the ground or reduce its depth. They travel in trails left by other animals, on logs, on plowed roads, even on snowmobile trails. Roads and trails are avoided because they tend to not be sheltered by trees and shrubs and therefore allow deeper accumulations of snow. These conditions force the bobcat to change its travel routes and choice of habitats used (Marston 1942; McCord 1974a; McCord and Cardoza 1982; Litvaitis et al. 1986a). On the positive side, deep snow also makes it easier for bobcats to catch and kill deer (McCord 1974a; Petraborg and Gunvalson 1962).

"Deep and fluffy snow drives the bobcat's energy needs through the roof," said Apps, (personal communication) who has spent extended periods observing the cat in the severe winter conditions of the East Kootenay Mountains of British Columbia. "Occasionally we will get chinooks [a warm, moist southwest wind], which puts a crust on the snow and makes it easier for bobcats to walk on the surface." But it is the combination of deep snow and bitter cold that can be most deadly. "It can be very cold up here, one to two months of -30°C (-22°F)," explained Apps. "Under such circumstances bobcats simply hunker down and don't move. Starvation among females and juveniles is high under such conditions." Morse (personal communication) told of one cold winter in bobcat heaven-on-earth in Vermont when the mercury dropped to -52°F. It is most likely this combination of deep snow and extremely cold temperatures that limits the northern extent of the bobcat's range (McCord and Cordoza 1982; Parker et al. 1983; Rolley 1987; Sunquist and Sunquist 2002).

Bobcats share the landscape with a variety of other predators and therefore must compete for resources, especially prey. This competition takes two different forms. Exploitative competition occurs when different species use a common resource that is in short supply. Interference competition occurs when a species acts aggressively toward another and denies it access to a resource. Both forms can influence the distribution and population dynamics of bobcats (Anderson and Lovallo 2003).

Coyotes (*C. latrans*) are a major competitor of bobcats. They both use the same habitats and prey heavily on lagomorphs. Buskirk and colleagues (2000) pointed out that coyotes have numerous ecological advantages over bobcats due to their larger size, more diverse diet, wider habitat tolerance, higher reproductive rate, wider behavioral plasticity, and higher human tolerance. There is growing evidence that coyotes can greatly influence bobcat population size through either exploitative or interference competition. Robinson (1961) examined predator control records from New Mexico, Colorado, and Wyoming, collected at 10-year intervals from 1940 to 1960, and identified a decline in coyote numbers, whereas the numbers of bobcats, skunks, raccoons, badgers, and swift foxes generally increased. Nunley (1978) searched annual U.S. Fish and Wildlife Service Animal Damage Control trapping records from 1916 to 1976 to estimate relative bobcat and coyote abundance in the western United States over time. He found that bobcat, skunk, fox, and badger harvests declined as the coyote harvest increased. Hass (1989) described inverse relationship between population levels of coyotes and bobcat indices over 62 years (1922–1984) on the National Bison Range in Montana. Coyotes were killed by refuge personnel by trapping, poisoning (Compound 1080), and opportunistic shooting to protect transplanted bighorn sheep. In 1947, an active poisoning campaign began in areas surrounding the refuge. As a result, coyote numbers dropped, while bobcat and bighorn numbers increased. When the coyote poisoning program on the refuge was stopped in 1966, coyote numbers rose, bobcat numbers decreased, and ewe/lamb ratios decreased. A similar pattern was identified by Litvaitis and Harrison (1989) in Maine: A sudden drop in bobcat harvest between 1974 and 1985 occurred at the same time as a dramatic increase in coyote harvest. During a 3-year controlled experiment in western Texas, Henke and Bryant (1999) reduced the coyote population in an area with bobcats;

this resulted in an increase in rodent density and biomass, along with an increase in the relative densities of bobcats, badgers, and gray foxes.

Wildlife biologists have always been curious about the nature and degree of competition between bobcats and coyotes. Initially, it was thought that the two species competed directly for both habitat and prey. More recent studies have discovered that when the two predators exist in the same landscape they generally share available resources with little conflict, an arrangement known as niche partitioning. Studies in Arizona (Small 1971) and Colorado (Makar 1980) showed that, despite significant overlap in habitat, there was little overlap in prey, indicating little competition for resources. Research in Maine (Major 1983) found no evidence of competition between coyotes and bobcats. However, the presence or absence of competition between these two animals in some areas may partly depend on the season, adequate refuge areas for bobcat natal dens, and the abundance of prey. Witmer and DeCalesta (1986) used scat analysis and radiotelemetry in Oregon to show that there was a 92% dietary overlap between bobcats and coyotes. Major and Sherburne (1987) applied the same techniques in Maine to show a 68% overlap. In both locations, bobcats and coyotes also used similar habitat and had simultaneously overlapping home ranges. Neither study found any evidence of aggression or avoidance between the two species. Witmer and DeCalesta (1986) concluded that abundant prey minimized competition. Major and Sherburne (1987) agreed that abundant prey was a factor, but they also believed that evolutionary and taxonomic separation prevented direct competition between the two species. A subsequent food habits study conducted in the same area by Dibello et al. (1990) found extensive overlap of hare in the diets of bobcats, coyotes, and red foxes, leading them to the conclusion that some level of exploitative competition was occurring.

Maine was the setting for yet another study, where Litvaitis and Harrison (1989) used a different research design that more definitively showed exploitative competition between bobcats and coyotes. They combined their data on high levels of dietary, temporal, and spatial overlap of bobcats and coyotes with harvest data for both species over the previous 10 years. What they found suggested a significant bobcat decline in response to exploitative competition by the increasing coyote population, especially during winter and spring. Across the country, in the Santa Monica Mountains of California, Fedriani et al. (2000) found high seasonal food overlap among bobcats, coyotes, and gray foxes. Coyotes were the dominant predator, using more foods and more habitats and being more abundant than the other two species. Coyotes also killed two adult bobcats, behavioral evidence of interference competition. There are numerous documented reports of coyotes preying on bobcats, indicating that interference competition is present in some ecosystems (Anderson 1987; Litvaitis and Harrison 1989; Fedriani et al. 2000).

Morse (personal communication) agreed that the relationship between bobcats and coyotes is indeed complex, especially in northern New England:

Changes in climate and landscape may never allow us to adequately sort out the subtleties of bobcat/coyote competition, because the habitat is always changing. Bobcats are generalist predators (unlike the Canada lynx) and have increased their numbers corresponding to a favorable abundance and diversity of prey, plus an increasing amount of security and cover in their habitat. Today, as we see in much of northern New England, some of these habitat values are diminishing as forest cover matures [ecological succession progresses] and as coyotes expand where they didn't exist before. Tough winters are a lethal bottleneck, especially on the edge of bobcat habitat. Omnivorous carnivores and scavengers will survive more readily than juvenile bobcats.

Maehr (1997) compared the ecology of bobcat, black bear, and Florida panther in south Florida. All three species preferred upland forests, but they consumed different foods and used the landscape in ways that resulted in ecological separation. Bobcats and panthers were primarily crepuscular, and black bears were predominantly diurnal. Panthers showed no seasonal variation in their use of food and space, whereas black bears exhibited extreme seasonal responses. Bobcats exhibited no seasonal variation in home range use and only moderate cyclicity in diet and possibly reproduction. Food habits separated these species more effectively than any other comparison. Scat analyses showed that panthers preyed almost exclusively on white-tailed deer, whereas bobcats were small-prey specialists but under the right conditions would kill white-tailed deer. Black bears and bobcats were more tolerant than panthers of anthropogenic influences in an increasingly fragmented landscape. Another factor threatening this carnivore community was the range expansion of the coyote into south Florida. The coyote has exhibited interference competition with bobcats, black bears, and pumas in other parts of North America. The diet of the coyote in Florida overlaps that of these three carnivores by at least 34%, and by as much as 64% in the case of bobcats.

How bobcats and foxes interact is yet another relationship that has been little studied. Major and Sherburne (1987) studied the relationships among coyotes, bobcats, and red foxes in western Maine but found no evidence of competition between the latter two. Riley (2001) studied the habitat use and interactions of bobcats and gray foxes in the Golden Gate National Recreation Area, north of San Francisco. One interesting finding of Riley's work was that both bobcats and gray foxes seemed to thrive in close proximity to urban areas, as long as there was sufficient habitat, prey, and "remoteness" in the adjacent wildlands they inhabited. This appeared to be true in habitats of greatest productivity, not necessarily all places.

Because some bobcats exist close to urban, suburban, and agricultural areas, encounters with domestic dogs are inevitable. Dogs killed 20% (n = 6) of the bobcats in Lembeck's (1978) study near San Diego. Although bobcats generally avoid dogs, interactions with domestic cats can be more varied. Riley (personal communication) witnessed a nonviolent encounter between a domestic cat and a bobcat near his study area. The housecat crouched and appeared frightened, but the bobcat took no aggressive action. Conversely, Apps (personal communication) reported one case in British Columbia of a bobcat eating a domestic cat. Survival is tough for Canadian bobcats, and perhaps if they hope to eat regularly they cannot aVord to be fussy about the menu.

The distributions of bobcats and fishers (*Martes pennanti*) are separate (allopatric) over much of their geographic ranges, but they overlap in the upper Great Lakes region. Gilbert and Keith (2001) examined spatial and dietary overlap between the two species in northern Wisconsin. They concluded that competition was relatively weak but suggested that, in areas where fishers were abundant, bobcat kitten mortality might increase and subsequent reduction in bobcat population growth might result.

Buskirk and associates. (2000) suggested that both bobcats and Canada lynx may benefit from the presence of wolves (*Canis lupus*). Wolves are fierce competitors with coyotes, and they reduce coyote populations where they coexist with bobcat and lynx. Wolves also do not prey heavily on rabbits and hares, so they actually reduce food competition with bobcat and lynx by lowering coyote numbers. These authors suggested that expanding wolf populations should provide an opportunity to test the hypothesis.

I have vivid memories of the shredded bobcat carcass left behind by a puma in the Huachuca Mountains of southern Arizona. Koehler and Hornocker (1991) examined the seasonal resource use of pumas, bobcats, and coyotes in Idaho's Frank Church–River of No Return Wilderness and found that pumas accounted for five of eight bobcat deaths and three of seven coyote deaths. They further emphasized that both the bobcats and the coyotes were killed near puma feeding sites and left intact, suggesting that they were killed by pumas defending or usurping a food cache. Young (1978) reported pumas preying on bobcats in Nevada, Utah, and New Brunswick. This is, of course, the ultimate form of interference competition.

It is the bobcat's relationship with its more northern neighbor, the Canada lynx, that most fascinates biologists. The two species are similar ecologically, especially in their feeding habits, but they are rarely sympatric (occupying the same geographic area). This is consistent with Gause's competitive exclusion principle, which posits that ecologically similar species cannot exist in the same area at the same time (Anderson and Lovallo 2003). One characteristic that seems to contribute to the geographic separation is the lynx's larger feet. The lynx has feet with twice the surface area of the bobcat's. These built-in snowshoes are as big as a 100-pound cougar's paws, and they make the lynx ideally suited for pursuing snowshoe hares across the deep snow, although bobcats dominate in all other areas. Smith (1984) studied bobcats in the mountains of western Montana in winter and found that their home ranges were at significantly lower elevations than the lynx home ranges, but there was no altitudinal segregation during fall and spring. As described earlier, bobcats are not as well adapted as lynxes for coping with deep snow and must expend much more energy. "In northern Washington, where I have tracked both lynx and bobcats, lynx stay up in the mountains above 5,000 feet when winter arrives, while bobcats move to lower elevations, where snow is not so deep," explained Koehler (personal communication). "When the snow leaves in late spring, bobcats again hunt the mountaintops where the lynx roam." Probably the classic example of bobcat dominance over lynx took place in Nova Scotia. In the mid-1950s, bobcats moved onto Cape Breton Island, probably via a newly built causeway from the mainland. Until then, lynx were common over much of the island. The bobcats, however, soon laid claim to the lower elevations where snow was not so deep, and the lynx retreated to the higher plateaus (Parker et al. 1983).

As part of their research on Cape Breton Island, Parker et al. (1983) tested the relative supporting capacity of lynx and bobcat paws in snow. They found that lynx paws, because of their greater surface area, supported approximately twice the weight of bobcat paws. Buskirk et al. (2000) calculated the average foot loading of both species and found that bobcats exert almost four time the weight on each foot than lynx. This critical adaptation gives the lynx a decided advantage in capturing their primary prey, snowshoe hare, in deep snow. It also helps explain how deep snow limits the northern distribution of the bobcat and creates an almost allopatric distribution of the two species (Quinn and Parker 1987; Anderson and Lovallo 2003).

Adult Canada lynx are slightly larger than bobcats, but in areas where both species are present, the bobcat is frequently larger. This may explain the bobcats' dominance in such circumstances (Anderson and Lovallo 2003). On Cape Breton Island, Parker et al. (1983) found that adult male bobcats were 40% heavier than adult male lynx. In Montana, Buskirk et al. (2000) found that the largest male bobcat outweighed the largest male lynx by 2 to 4 kg (4.4–8.8 pounds). The difference in weight suggests that interference competition would favor the bobcat, but exploitative competition for a common prey, the snowshoe hare, is also possible (Anderson and Lovallo 2003).

Experts speculate that bobcats may be more aggressive than the more docile lynx, a factor that could contribute further to the two felines' avoidance of each other. But few bobcat-lynx encounters have been observed in the wild. During a recent Canada lynx reintroduction effort in southwestern Colorado, Tanya Shenk (Colorado Division of Wildlife, personal communication) reported circumstantial evidence suggesting that a bobcat killed a lynx. There were numerous bobcat tracks around the lynx carcass, which had definitely been cached by a bobcat. Only the head and one foot remained. The lynx was aged through tooth analysis and found to be more than 10 years old. There was also circumstantial evidence that three lynx had been killed by pumas.

In the summer of 2003, U.S. Forest Service scientists at the Rocky Mountain Research Station's genetics laboratory in Missoula, Montana, discovered through DNA analysis the first evidence of hybridization between the bobcat and the Canada lynx in the wild. Tissue and hair samples from 19 cats believed to be Canada lynx were collected on the Superior National Forest in northeastern Minnesota. Two of the cats had external physical characteristics resembling both species. DNA analysis revealed three hybrids. All three were from male bobcats mating with female lynx (U.S. Fish and Wildlife Service [USFWS] 2003a). Later the same summer, DNA tests conducted in the same laboratory on 29 cats from Maine identified two hybrids—one male and one female. Again, both were revealed to be offspring of a female lynx and a male bobcat (USFWS 2003b). Dr. Michael Schwartz, the scientist who heads the genetics laboratory where the hybrid test was designed, along with his colleagues, emphasized that "hybridization may be an under-appreciated factor limiting the distribution and recovery of lynx" (Schwartz et al. 2004). They warned that hybridization also presents two possible legal implications. Bobcat trapping is currently legal in counties where lynx are present, but it is illegal to trap lynx anywhere in the conterminous United States. The USFWS has no official hybrid policy, so it is unclear whether the bobcat-lynx hybrid is protected under the Endangered Species Act. If the hybrids are protected, bobcat trapping in areas where lynx are present is problematic, because both lynx and lynx-hybrids may be incidentally killed. Moreover, threats to lynx recovery need to be identified. "Any factors that favor bobcats in lynx habitat may lead to the production of hybrids and thus be potentially harmful to lynx recovery" (Schwartz et al. 2004).

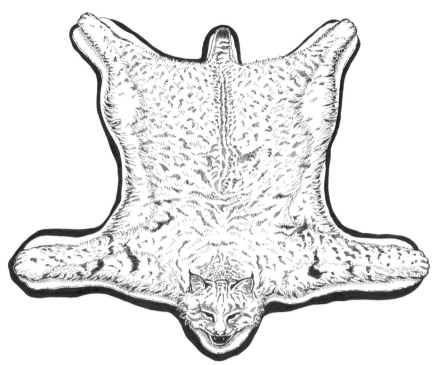

5 From Predator to Pelt

Dave Fjelline was born 150 years too late. His wiry build, weathered face, and full beard make him seem better suited for sharing a campfire with Jedediah Smith or John Colter. Dave is a man at home in the outdoors, and he makes his living as a professional trapper and houndsman. Employed by Placer County, a 1,500-square-mile area in northern California that extends from the agricultural Central Valley to the high Sierra Nevada, Fjelline is responsible for catching and killing wildlife that cause damage to private property.

"Most of my daily control work now is coyote and beaver," he says, feeding chunks of wood into a pot-bellied stove. "Coyote because of attacks on sheep, and beaver because of the damage they cause to irrigation levees and mitigation sites. Beaver are the biggest pest. They are the largest contributor to financial loss in Placer County. In addition to the levee damage, they girdle fruit trees. Just today I looked at one 300-year-old blue oak tree that had been girdled by a beaver."

Turning to a refrigerator, he extracts two sodas, offers one to me, then settles into a chair behind his desk and begins pulling off his heavy boots. He has been in the field all day. "Bobcats occasionally take chickens, ducks, and geese. I probably get one bobcat complaint a month, and it usually can be solved with a nonlethal approach. Such as putting a top on the chicken coop." He explains that when he is forced to trap the *feline, he may use bobcat urine as a lure, sprayed on a bush high above the set. Some trappers use curiosity lures such as the top of a tin can, a feather, or even a strip of white cloth.*

We are sitting in Dave's workshop and office, just across the driveway from his house. Covered in dark wood paneling, one end of the room doubles as tack shed. There are mule pack frames, bridles, saddles, rope, panniers, and an historic collection of bridle bits. In one corner sits an industrial sewing machine for leather repair. Another corner is filled with an impressive stack of ammunition and reloading equipment. Several shotguns and rifles are leaned against a table. Snowshoes hang from one wall, a buffalo skull from another. A stuffed mountain lion stands silently on the floor below. Two easy chairs face the stove, which is starting to warm the room. Dave's desk is buried deep in books and paper, and the wall behind him is covered with photographs. On a shelf above his head is a neat row of about a dozen mountain lion skulls.

In addition to being a trapper, Dave is an expert houndsman. He uses specially bred hounds to track and tree mountain lions and bobcats. He explains that a good trailing hound, as he calls them, is the result of bloodlines bred for generations. His four hounds are a mix of French blue tick and red tick and are kept in kennels behind the workshop." I've been running hounds since 1966, both for hunting and companionship. In the early 1980s, I started doing contract work for the California Department of Fish and Game, tracking and treeing mountain lions for researchers." While he admits lions are impressive, Dave has even greater respect for the wily bobcat.

"Bobcats are very challenging to hunt. Their track is harder to follow than a mountain lion's. Being smaller than a lion they can twist and wind their way through heavier cover. Their scent is harder to follow, they're harder to tree and harder to see, even while up in a tree. And females are harder to catch than males. Bobcats are more of a puzzle, more of a test of skill, than hunting a lion. When the price of pelts was high [back in the late 1970s and early 1980s], everyone became a bobcat trapper," he chuckled. "A large male bobcat pelt would go for $225 to $300."

Dave tells me of a friend and his wife who trap a lot of bobcats east of the Sierra Nevada Mountains, out of the small town of Olancha. "They're professionals," he says with satisfaction. "They scout an area real good and read the sign [tracks and scrapes] to get an idea how many bobcats are there. Then they only harvest as many as the area can support."

After our chat, Dave invites me to join him for a late dinner. While standing in the doorway between his kitchen and living room, I notice two large bobcat pelts draped over the back of a couch. I run my hand over the soft fur. They are beautiful. "If I had to make a choice of what to hunt for the rest of my life—bobcat or lion—I'd choose the bobcat hands down," says Dave seating himself at the kitchen table. "Hunting bobcats tests you and the hounds more than a lion. I'd do it for pure enjoyment."

■

Native Cultures and Furbearers

Native Americans hunted and trapped furbearing animals for food and warm clothing in North America for more than 11,000 years. The prominence of hunting and trapping in a culture was largely determined by geography and climate—the harsher the landscape and the colder the temperatures, the greater the dependence on wild animals. The Inuit and Yuit peoples of the Alaskan and Canadian Arctic lived in a cold region devoid of much vegetation and depended almost exclusively on land and sea mammals to feed and clothe themselves. The Iroquoian-speaking peoples of the upper St. Lawrence River and lower Great Lakes and many tribes of the American Southwest were primarily farmers who took advantage of their relatively warmer climates to grow corn, beans, squash, sunflowers, and tobacco. According to archaeologist J.V. Wright, even these agricultural societies hunted and fished to clothe themselves with animal skins and augment their carbohydrate diet with animal protein. Wright also pointed out that most of the furbearing animals we value today were relatively unimportant to prehistoric hunting peoples. They placed far more importance on major food animals such as ungulates (hoofed animals such as deer, elk, caribou, and buffalo), cetaceans (whales and porpoises), pinnipeds (walruses and seals), and, depending on location and season, fish, mollusks, and birds (Wright 1987).

Although many cultures produced skilled hunters, successfully employing the bow and arrow, lance, atlatl, and throwing stick, trapping represented a technical advance over hunting. North American Indians used a variety of snares and deadfalls to catch and kill both small and large furbearers, as well as birds. Again, geography and climate played a role in the frequency with which traps were used. Canadian trapping expert Milan Novak explained that native cultures living in warmer climates or along seashores where food was plentiful used fewer traps than did tribes living in harsh, cold northern environments where food was often scarce. The Seri of Mexico, who lived in a warm desert climate on the edge of the sea, from which they caught the bulk of their food, had no known animal traps. Conversely, the Nabesna of east-central Alaska lived in a harsh environment and used a variety of snares, nets, and deadfall traps to capture moose, snowshoe hare, muskrats, foxes, and Canada lynx (Novak 1987).

The design of early traps was as diverse as the animals caught. The Seneca used spring pole snares to catch mink, striped skunk, groundhogs, rabbits, and ruffed grouse. The Iroquois employed an ingenious rabbit snare that was triggered only after the animal chewed through a salt-soaked string. The Nootka of British

Columbia used deadfalls to capture bears, deer, mink, martens, beavers, marmots, and raccoons. The Navajo used large stone deadfalls to trap coyotes, foxes, and bobcats (Novak 1987).

Once captured and killed, the furbearer's flesh was usually eaten, and its pelt was put to a variety of uses. Canadian anthropologist Harold F. McGee, Jr., explained that, among California natives, the most prestigious cloaks were made of sea otter skins, but bobcat, deer, river otter, and other furs were also used. The Shoshone of the Great Basin placed little value on the fur of carnivorous animals. Wolves, mountain lions, and bobcats were taken with great difficulty and rarely eaten. Their fur was also of little importance, with the exception of the bobcat's, which was prized for quivers (McGee 1987). Stanley Young told how tribes along the lower Columbia River prized bobcat pelts for making robes, and how the Plains tribes fashioned the bobcat's skin into quivers with the tail and extended claws hanging below (Young 1978). The Athapaskan- and Algonquian-speaking peoples of the Alaskan and Canadian Subarctic actively hunted and trapped moose, caribou, bears, beavers, muskrats, snowshoe hares, porcupines, lynx, bobcats, and other small mammals, which were converted into moccasins, leggings, breechcloths, shirts, robes, and dresses of various cuts. In the Southeast, a variety of cloaks, shawls, and blankets were worn during the winter or for ceremonies. These were most often made of squirrels, muskrats, raccoons, rabbits, weasels, bobcats, otters, skunks, and occasionally bears and mountain lions. Some groups stuck the claws of squirrels, bobcats, and other animals into holes in their ears for decoration (McGee 1987).

The relationship between native cultures and wildlife was more than utilitarian; it was deeply spiritual. Native cultures believed (and still do today) that all living and nonliving things—plants, animals, rocks, stars—were imbued with a type of force or power. Wright explained that all natural phenomena were interpreted in spiritual terms and regarded as having life, and therefore power. This power varied depending on the animal. The bear or mountain lion carried much greater power than the deer mouse or pocket gopher. Because this force was capable of good or evil, it was in the native peoples' self-interest to ward off evil or to seek assistance from the powers surrounding them. Naturally, the spirits controlling the food supply required special attention. Native peoples were concerned with how the "living" phenomena around them affected their welfare and how they could manipulate these mysterious powers to their benefit (Wright 1987; Martin 1978).

Spiritual power was enhanced or controlled through numerous rituals and taboos. For instance, esteem for the bear was universal among native peoples throughout the boreal forests of North America. Elaborate bear ceremonies included hunting the bear in the spring while it was still hibernating and killing it in or near its den; addressing it with honorific titles when dead or alive; making a conciliatory speech to the animal, either before or after killing it and sometimes both, in which the hunter apologizes for the necessity of his act; treating the carcass respectfully and disposing of those parts not used (especially the skull) while adhering to certain customs. By showing the proper respect for his prey, the hunter appeases the spiritual controller, or keeper, of the bears and ensures that it will continue to furnish game to the hunter (Wright 1987; Martin 1978).

According to ethnozoologist Steve Pavlik, the Navajo, in the past as today, believed that their creation was the result of a series of "emergences" from one world to the next. The Seventh World of the Navajo was described as the home of the Cat People, meaning the bobcat, the mountain lion, and possibly the Canada lynx. The Cat People were anthropomorphic beings or deities who could talk and behave like people and who possessed supernatural powers. In time, many of these beings transformed into the animal forms we recognize today (Pavlik 2000).

The bobcat, puma, and Canada lynx carried significant spiritual power, probably because of their skill as hunters. All three cats appear to have been widely consumed as food, and their fur was also used by native peoples. Bobcats and lynx were trapped in snares and sometimes in deadfalls, and rituals were involved with the killing of each (McGee 1987).

The Navajo trapped and hunted bobcats for their body parts and occasionally for their meat. The most common method used to kill bobcats was stone deadfall traps. Sometimes they were tracked and killed in deep snow or treed by dogs and shot (Hill 1938). If the bobcat was fat, the animal was eaten. The Navajo reportedly made sausage of the meat, which was stuffed into casings made from the skin (Hill 1938; Johnson 1977). However, the primary reason for killing bobcats was to acquire their skins and claws. Skins were used to make caps, mittens, scarves, and arrow cases (Kluckhohn et al. 1971), and claws were used to decorate clothing or in certain ceremonial items. Bobcat sinew was employed as string to sew the medicine bag, or *jish*, used in some Navajo ceremonies (Frisbie 1987). Pelts were also fashioned into bandoleers or wristlets used by medicine men performing various healing ceremonies (Wyman and Bailey 1943). Bobcat gall was ground and added to herbal powder to ward off witchcraft. Bobcat fat was added to the fat of other animals to create a lotion that was smeared over a patient in ceremonies to exorcise evil caused by ghosts and witches. The Navajo also believed that bobcats possessed the ability to "witch" people. They did this with their whiskers, which were said to have power (Pavlik 2000).

Belief in the bobcat's unusual powers was not restricted to native cultures. Stanley Young found that early European settlers brought many superstitions to the New World, probably associated with the European lynx, which later became associated with the North American bobcat. One Mexican peasant stated that the bobcat had such keen eyesight that it could see through blocks of wood, trees, stone, or boulders, all of which aided it in hunting rabbit and other prey. Others believed that bobcat urine turned to precious stone, and that was why the animal always covered the spot where it urinated, so that no human could find it. Various parts of the bobcat were believed to have medicinal value. Early Guatemalans held bobcat testicles against the stomach to ease pain associated with pregnancy. The cat's tenderloin was eaten to cure headaches, and its paws were thought to suppress abdominal cramps. The fur was used as a poultice for open cuts and wounds, and the feces were applied to pimples, boils, and carbuncles as a healing salve (Young 1978).

Still, the cosmology of native cultures, particularly their relationship with animals, was alien to European cultures. Where native cultures saw wildlife as a community to which they belonged, Europeans saw wildlife as a commodity to be exploited. In their exhaustive study of furbearer harvests in North America, Martyn E. Obbard and his colleagues (1987:1007) observed, "Once humans began hunting and trapping for commercial purposes, a significant change occurred: market demand replaced individual need in controlling the size of the harvest. This shift held serious consequences for the survival of several animal species because the forces of the market system, more so than those of individual need, had the potential to cause a major decline in populations or even the extinction of a species." It was to have serious consequences for the survival of many native cultures as well.

The Commercial Fur Trade

It was beaver, not bobcat, that initially brought early European fur traders to North America. The popularity of felt hats in Europe from 1550 to 1850 was the primary market force driving the search for pelts, and beaver felt was the most prized of all (Ray 1987). Matthiessen (1987:79) recounted, "Exploited for its rich, dense fur from the outset, this largest of the American rodents commenced its decline as early as 1638, when to its misfortune the compulsory use of it in the manufacture of hats was decreed by King Charles II." But trappers also actively sought otter, muskrat, marten, bear, fox, lynx, fisher, mink, and wolf. Supplementing these were the hides of moose, white-tailed deer, pronghorn, elk, bison, and caribou. While European and American traders struggled for control of the expanding land-based fur trade in the East, the Russians were establishing a maritime trade on the West Coast. Working from ships, they aggressively exploited populations of sea otters and fur seals found in the coastal waters from Alaska to California (Obbard et al. 1987). Thus was launched a coast-to-coast assault on North American furbearers (and other wildlife) that was to last 400 years.

The French were pioneers in the fur trade, trapping throughout Nova Scotia, the Gaspé Peninsula, and the upper St. Lawrence River region from 1581 to 1763. French explorer Champlain established the first fur-trading post in Quebec in 1608. But increasing competition with Dutch and English traders led to friction over territory, commerce, and the fur trade, resulting in the French and Indian War (or Anglo-French War), which lasted from 1754 to 1760. Under the terms of the Treaty of Paris (1763), France surrendered all Canadian possessions and all French territory east of the Mississippi River. British, Dutch, and American traders then dominated the fur trade (Obbard et al. 1987).

The seeds of the American fur trade were planted in 1606, when King James I of England issued charters to the Virginia Company of London for territory in present-day Virginia, and to the Plymouth Company for land in what is now New England. Merchants with the two companies intended to establish trading posts, bartering manufactured goods for whatever they needed from the Indians. These charters laid the foundation for the early colonial states (Obbard et al. 1987). Matthiessen (1987:55) recounted, "When the *Mayflower* rounded Cape Cod in 1620, tobacco had already been grown and exported from Jamestown, and a Virginia price list of 1612 indicates an extensive fur trade. Mink, marten, otter, and wildcat brought up to ten shillings apiece, and prime beaver were worth seven."

Fur trapping became the most important commercial activity in the colonies, exceeding commerce in timber and fish. An estimated 12 million pelts of all species of furbearers were taken during the 1700s. Determining the number of bobcats killed during this period is difficult because, prior to the 20th century, harvest records for most companies (except the Hudson's Bay Company) did not distinguish between lynx and bobcat pelts. Harvest records listed the two furbearers separately only after 1900. Hudson's Bay Company trappers began to kill bobcats and Canada lynx in the decade 1700–1709. The total number of bobcats and Canada lynx killed for the commercial fur trade during the 18th century was approximately 750,000 (Obbard et al. 1987).

It was the Louisiana Purchase in 1803 and the subsequent Lewis and Clark expedition that contributed most significantly to the expansion of trapping in the United States. This historical transaction between Napoleon and Thomas Jefferson doubled the new country's size, opened a vast region for settlement, and made tremendous wildlife resources available to American trappers (Ray 1987). Stanley Young (1978) described how the Indian tribes of the lower Columbia River prized bobcat skins for making robes. Lewis and Clark reported that four skins were required to make such a robe. Besides opening the West, the Louisiana Purchase made New Orleans a valuable shipping port for the fur trade (Ray 1987).

Probably the most successful fur-trading company in history was the Hudson's Bay Company. In May of 1670, King Charles II of England granted the Hudson's Bay Company exclusive trading rights to all territory drained by waters flowing into Hudson Bay. Called Rupert's Land, this vast territory encompassed 3.9 million km² (1.5 million square miles) and extended from Quebec to Alberta and the Northwest Territories (Obbard et al. 1987; Ray 1987). A system of trading posts was established at the outlets of major rivers flowing into Hudson Bay and James Bay, while the more inland trade was carried out by Indian trappers and middlemen, mostly the Cree and Assiniboine. Over the next 200 years, native and European hunters and trappers employed by the Hudson's Bay Company killed and skinned hundreds of millions of furbearers throughout Canada and the Great Lakes area. According to Matthiessen, in November 1743 alone, the Hudson's Bay Company sold 26,750 beaver pelts, 14,730 martens, and 1,850 wolves. During the same year, the furs of 127,080 beavers, 30,325 martens, 1,267 wolves, 12,428 otters and fishers, 110,000 raccoons, and 16,512 bears were received in the French port of Rochelle (Matthiessen 1987). Its profits allowed the Hudson's Bay Company to grow into North America's oldest multinational resource and trading company. But in 1857 the Canadian government petitioned the British government to break the Hudson's Bay Company's monopoly, and in 1870 the company ceded control to the Canadian government (Obbard et al. 1987).

In the late 1700s and early 1800s, the primary rival of the Hudson's Bay Company for pelts was the North West Company. Formed by a loose group of Montreal merchants, the North West Company challenged the Hudson's Bay Company by aggressively seeking out furs from natives on their home territory. The Nor'Westers, as they came to be called, traded throughout Rupert's Land west to the Pacific Ocean and along the St. Lawrence River and the area surrounding the Great Lakes, including American territory south of the Great Lakes. Throughout its controversial existence, the North West Company dominated the fur trade. In 1795, the Nor' Westers accounted for 79% of the fur trade in Canada, whereas the Hudson's Bay Company controlled only 14%, with independent traders making up the remaining 7%. When conflict between the two companies led to bloodshed in 1819, the British government stepped in, and the North West Company merged with the Hudson's Bay Company in 1821 (Obbard et al. 1987).

The steel leghold trap (see Figure 5.1) was the popular choice of most trappers, and it still is today. The leghold trap is spring-powered, featuring two metal jaws that clamp shut on an animal's leg when the it steps on a weight-sensitive trigger. Iron traps of various designs were used in North America as early as 1633 to capture and kill furbearers (Novak 1987) Eventually, steel traps replaced iron traps, snares, and deadfalls. In 1823, Sewell Newhouse revolutionized trapping with his invention of the tooth-jawed leghold trap. Newhouse's fame and reputation spread, and soon his business was taken over by the Oneida Community, which set up a machine shop in 1855 with the Hudson's Bay Company as a major customer. Between 1859 and 1867, the Oneida Community manufactured 750,000 leghold traps in eight sizes. This was eventually expanded to 25 different sizes, from No. 0 (3.5 inches across) to the No. 6 Great Bear trap, which weighed 42 pounds and had a jaw spread of 16 inches. Steel traps were rare until after 1850, but by 1900 half the trappers in the United States did not know how to use deadfalls or snares (Novak 1987).

Although there were many attempts to design better traps, Novak pointed out that none of the new traps ever became as popular as the leghold trap. As an example, in 1910 the Oneida Company manufactured 6,812,000 leghold traps and shipped them around the world. From 1911 to 1920, they sold an average of 5.4 million traps annually, 8% of them to Canada. It is estimated that 350 million steel traps have been made to date by more than 100 shops and factories in the United States (Gerstell 1985). Most of these traps were manufactured by the Oneida line of companies, which today is the Woodstream Corporation, the largest trap manufacturer in the world (Novak 1987). But the growth of the animal welfare

Figure 5.1
Steel leghold trap.

movement in the late 1800s led to the elimination of tooth-jawed leghold traps (Novak 1987), which are no longer produced, and their use is not allowed in any state except Maine. The most significant change in trap design was Frank Conibear's killing trap, which was developed in 1929 but not produced until 1957 (Novak 1987). This scissor-like device is spring-activated to snap closed with tremendous force once it is triggered, breaking the neck and back of the animal (see Figure 5.2.)

Furbearers were generally viewed as a limitless resource by most trappers of this era, and restraint was rarely practiced. Martin related that 20 trappers took 5,000 beaver in 212 traps during the 1823–1824 season in Montana's Bitterroot

Figure 5.2
Body-gripping trap.

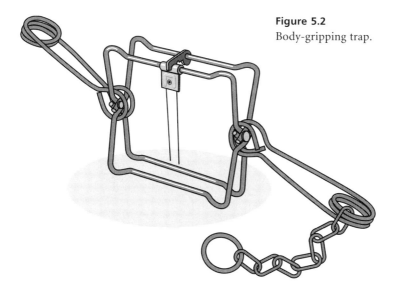

Mountains, and James O. Pattie took 250 beaver in two weeks on Arizona's San Francisco River (Martin 1978). Viewed from the perspective of a lifetime of hunting, the carnage is even more grim. Newhouse (1893:63) reported that 64-year-old John Hutchins of Manlius, New York, boasted in 1865 that he had "caught in traps, or otherwise destroyed . . . 100 moose; 1,000 deer; 10 caribou; 100 bears; 50 wolves; 500 foxes; 100 raccoons; 25 wild cats; 100 lynx; 150 otter; 600 beaver; 400 fishers; mink and marten by the thousands; muskrats by the tens of thousands." Such slaughter would eventually lead to regulation of harvest by the states, but not until the next century.

The 1830s brought a collapse in the beaver fur market, caused by a growing preference for hats made from Oriental silk, overtrapping of beaver, and loss of beaver habitat due to forest clearance and the expansion of farming. These factors brought to an end a 300-year period in which pursuit of beaver was the driving force behind the expansion of the fur trade. Raccoon and muskrat became the most valuable furs in American domestic trade and export from the 1840s until the end of the Civil War. The American fur trade continued to grow after the Civil War, with the pelts of mink, skunk, and fur seal figuring most prominently. Britain was the primary fur export market, and exports of mink increased tenfold between 1860 and 1880 (Ray 1987).

Harvest pressure on the bobcat and Canada lynx increased throughout the 1800s:

> Beginning in the 1820s the annual harvest began to rise; in the 1830s, 1840s, 1860s, and 1880s the average annual harvest was 25,000–33,000 pelts. Major harvest by American companies began in the 1760s and soon greatly exceeded the Hudson's Bay Company's harvest. By the 1830s, harvest by American companies had begun to decline and after this period the Hudson's Bay Company's harvest was generally two to Wve times greater than that taken by American companies. The North West Company's harvest began in the 1780s at a level equal to that of the American companies and at a value at least Wve times greater than that of the Hudson's Bay Company. Harvest values remained more than 2.5 times greater than that of the Hudson's Bay Company until the 1820s. (Obbard et al. 1987:1025)

The result? It is estimated that approximately 2,655,000 bobcats and Canada lynx were killed for the commercial fur trade during the 19th century (Obbard et al. 1987).

Competition between American and Canadian furriers increased throughout the latter part of the 19th century as the fur market in North America continued to grow and develop. In 1870 there were only 200 furriers in the United States, with a gross product of $8.9 million. By 1900 there were more than 1,000 furriers, with a gross product of more than $55 million. During this time, the United States ceased to be a net fur exporter, and by 1900 the country was importing three times as many furs as it was exporting. St. Louis and New York vied with each other to dominate the fur-auction business. American buyers and agents traveled through-out the Canadian North and were increasingly successful in taking business from the once-dominant Hudson's Bay Company (Ray 1987).

An anti-trapping movement began during the Roaring Twenties and was led, in part, by fox and raccoon hunting organizations angered by accidental trapping of their hunting dogs, as well as competition with trappers for fox and raccoon. Declines in wildlife populations became apparent during a boom in the fur in-dustry. Commercial trapping already had depleted mink, marten, fisher, otter, and beaver populations throughout most of North America. Damage was exacerbated even further by extensive loss of habitat. Many of the furs popular in the 1920s—fox, opossum, skunk, muskrat, squirrel, and raccoon—were relatively inexpen-sive and affordable to the less affluent. But the growing humane movement also was on the offensive against trapping. The Anti-Steel Trap League, founded in 1925, was one of the first organizations to focus specifically on the trapping of wild ani-mals. Decisive, if fleeting, state legislative victories were won against trapping during the late 1920s and early 1930s. Bills banning or restricting the leghold trap and other trapping practices were passed in South Carolina, Georgia, Massachu-setts, New York, and Kentucky. These laws were repealed during the Depression, because of compelling arguments about the need for food and a supplemental, if meager, income. Fur prices fell, but, surprisingly, sales remained high. Two mil-lion garments were produced in 1936, mostly small fur pieces such as stoles and capes (Defenders of Wildlife 1984).

After World War II, fluctuating demand for furs, combined with increasing attacks on the cruelty of trapping, began to affect the fur industry. Defenders of Furbearers, founded in 1947 and later renamed Defenders of Wildlife, was a major force in educating the public about trapping. A growing concern for wildlife also discouraged the wearing of furs. Even the popularity of new ranch-bred mink couldn't stem changing attitudes (Defenders of Wildlife 1984). As a result, fur sales slumped to an all-time low during the 1950s. Still, it is estimated that during the first 60 years of the 20th century almost 400,000 bobcats were killed for the com-mercial fur trade (Obbard et al. 1987).

The paradox of the 1960s is that, while this decade saw increased environmen-tal awareness, improvements in wildlife science, and increased concern for ani-mal rights, it was also a time of dramatic increase in bobcat harvests. The combined harvest of lynx and bobcat did not approach the peak of the 1800s until the 1960s:

[During the 1960s] the average combined lynx and bobcat harvest was about 46,000 pelts per year. This harvest rose sharply in the 1970s (>83,000) and 1980s (nearly 114,000) as a result of a great increase in the annual harvest of bobcats in the United States (from about 10,000 in the 1950s and 1960s to 44,000 in the 1970s to about 76,000 in the 1980s). In the 1970s and 1980s the North American harvest of bobcats was about 1.4 and 2.3 times greater than that of the lynx harvest for those decades respectively. Throughout the 20th century the U.S. harvest of bobcats greatly exceeded the Canadian harvest of bobcats, varying between 72% of the total harvest in the 1930s and 97% of the total harvest in the 1980s. (Obbard et al. 1987:1025)

From 1977 to 1984, an average of 94,000 bobcats were harvested annually from the United States and Canada (Funderburk 1986). Many state and federal biologists insist that there is no evidence of a concurrent decline in bobcat numbers during this period. However, no studies were conducted to isolate the impact of these years of high harvest. In their review of bobcat status and management from the 1970s through the 1990s, Woolf and Hubert (1998) analyzed harvest data and concluded that bobcat populations probably were not reduced but remained stable during these high-harvest years. Rolley (1985) examined the dynamics of an exploited bobcat population in the Ouachita National Forest of southeastern Oklahoma from 1977 to 1981. Although not providing conclusive proof, he suggested that high harvests both increased adult bobcat death rates and were associated with a period of population decline. His follow-up conversations with Oklahoma's furbearer biologists indicated that harvests declined in the 1980s, and bobcat populations subsequently increased (Robert Rolley, Wisconsin Department of Natural Resources, personal communication).

Today, commerce still drives the killing of furbearers. Although pelt prices fluctuate, harvests remain high. Before the 20th century, peak annual harvests occurred in the 1870s (4.5 million animals) and 1880s (4.9 million animals). After 1900, the peak harvest occurred in the 1940s, with an impressive 23.7 million animals killed. During the 1980s, half a million trappers annually took about 19 million pelts of more than 30 species in North America (Obbard et al. 1987).

According to the Office of Management Authority of the U.S. Fish and Wildlife Service (USFWS), the number of bobcat pelts tagged for annual export averaged about 77,000 from 1978 to 1987, then dropped off dramatically to an average of 24,000 between 1988 and 1994 (USFWS 2004c). The bottom fell out of the commercial fur market in the fall of 1987. On October 19 of that year, wild fur markets crashed, as did the rest of the stock market in the now famous "Black Monday." The Dow Jones Industrial Average fell from 2,246 to 1,738, losing 22.6% of its total value (Stock Market Crash 2005). Hundreds of commercial furriers went out of business in both the United States and Europe.

C. Horton (USFWS, personal communication) explained that there is a direct correlation between fur harvest pressure and price (demand). "When prices paid for bobcat pelts are high, bobcat harvest increases; when the price paid for bobcat pelts is low, the harvest also decreases. For example, Nevada bobcat prices have increased from an average of $84 in 1999–2000 to $253 in 2003–2004. Adjusted for inflation, bobcat prices were over $700 in 1979–1980, and fell steadily until the mid-1990s. Fashion trends, anti-trapping activity, and availability of new markets (Asia, former Soviet republics, etc.) have all had major impacts on price fluctuations."

The Fur Information Council of America reported that fur sales for 2003 were the highest since 1991. In 2003, U.S. retailers reported fur sales of $1.8 billion, an increase of 7.5% from 2002 and up 80% from 1991 (Fur Information Council of America 2005).

Bobcat harvest in the United States increased by 54% from 1992–1993 (21,168 animals) to 2002–2003 (39,005 animals) (see Figure 5.3). During the same period exported pelts from the United States climbed from approximately 21,735 to 30,400 (see Figure 6.2 in Chapter 6), while Canadian exports went from 7,782 to 16,377 (see Figure 6.3 in Chapter 6). A bobcat pelt that brought $50 in Utah in 2001 was worth $250 in 2003 (Utah Division of Wildlife Resources 2003). Bobcat pelts in Montana went for $106 in 2000–2001 and $203 in 2003 (Montana Fish, Wildlife and Parks 2003). North Dakota bobcat fur commanded $257 in 2003 (North Dakota Game and Fish Department 2004). Disparities between harvest and export numbers are caused by several factors. Harvest and export numbers may actually be higher, because data were not provided for every state that allowed the take of bobcat. It should also be noted that not all harvested pelts are exported; some are

Figure 5.3

U.S. bobcat harvest (1970–2003) and fur value (1974–1998).*

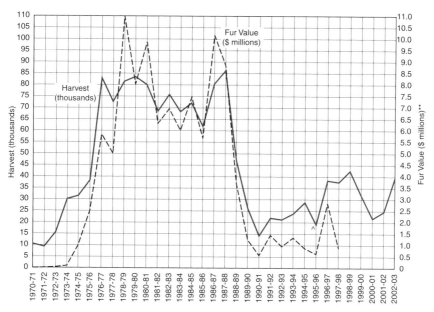

* International Association of Fish and Wildlife Agencies (IAFWA) and state wildlife agencies. Does not include bobcats taken by USDA Wildlife Services Program.
** The total value of pelts is based on a weighed average by region. Pelts from the west and northeast typically are of better quality than those from the midwest and southeast.
^ Does not include harvest numbers from Texas.

kept for domestic use. Additionally, not all tagged pelts are exported the same year they are harvested; some are retained in storage.

Although most European immigrants viewed furbearers as important sources of revenue, predators were also scorned. Bears, wolves, mountain lions, and bobcats were feared as threats to domestic livestock and competitors for game. Many of these people came from countries that were heavily settled and relatively free of predators. Their simplistic thinking separated animals into two categories: beneficial (edible wild game and livestock) and vermin (all other mammals and birds). There was no place for predators in such a world.

Predator Control

As colonization spread west, the great hardwood forests of the Northeast were cleared and subdivided, replaced by an ever-increasing number of townships and farmsteads, effectively destroying substantial wildlife habitat. Large predators were quickly eliminated. By 1900, the puma was effectively exterminated east of the Mississippi (Hansen 1992), but the smaller bobcat adapted and retreated farther into the shadows. Thousands of farms and ranches sprang up in what had previously been wilderness. Cattle, sheep, goats, and chickens were increasingly available and easy to kill. The bobcat's occasional nighttime forays into a barnyard or chicken coop and its taste for venison quickly earned it the scorn of settlers—and they declared war.

Their first step was to establish bounties. In 1727, Massachusetts paid a bounty of 20 shillings for every adult bobcat. By 1903 the bounty was $3, and by 1951 it was as high as $10 per animal. Pennsylvania's bobcat bounty began in 1819 at $1 for an adult and 25 cents for young, reached $15 per bobcat in 1923, and declined until 1937, when the bounty was removed (Young 1978). Such bounty programs proved to be largely arbitrary and ineffective, and they even contributed to fraud. Young cited numerous incidents of individuals collecting multiple bounties for the same pelt. Lax enforcement frequently encouraged such behavior. Young believed that "the bounty as a measure of [predator] control not only creates opportunities for fraud, but is usually ineffective, and a waste of funds that might be better used toward improvement of game management" (Young 1978:128). Most states began to eliminate bounty programs in the 1960s and 1970s, and the bobcat was reclassified as a game animal or furbearer, with hunting and trapping regulated through designated seasons and restrictions on the methods of take.

The U.S. government entered the business of killing wild animals in 1915, when western stockmen pressured Congress to appropriate $125,000 to wipe out wolves and coyotes and supposedly save beef for our troops and allies in World War I (U.S. Department of Agriculture [USDA] 1997; U.S. General Accounting Office 2001). The U.S. Biological Survey, the predecessor of the USFWS, was charged with the responsibility of hiring hunters and trappers to do the job. But it was the passage of the Animal Damage Control Act of 1931 that gave birth to the Animal Damage Control (ADC) program and provided the primary statutory authority under which the current federal predator control program operates (USDA 1997; U.S. General Accounting Office 2001). It granted the Secretary of Agriculture broad discretion to "promulgate the best methods of eradication [and] suppression . . . of mountain lions, wolves, coyotes, bobcats, prairie dogs, gophers, ground squirrels, jackrabbits, and other animals injurious to agriculture." This law remained intact until 2000, despite passage of the Endangered Species Act of 1973, which made illegal the eradication of any species (Defenders of Wildlife 1984).

Between 1937 and 1970, federal employees of the ADC program killed 477,194 bobcats, 7,255 cougars, 23,830 bears, 50,283 red wolves, 1,744 gray wolves, 2,823,000 coyotes, and millions of other animals. After 1970, control focused on cougars, coyotes, and bobcats, because the grizzly bear and the wolf were placed on the endangered species list (Cain 1972; Defenders of Wildlife 1984).

The Federal ADC program operated throughout the 1930s, 1940s, and 1950s in relative obscurity with little public opposition. However, growing environmental awareness in the 1960s brought the ADC program under closer scrutiny. The use of poisons to kill predators was particularly criticized. Three separate investigations, commissioned under three different administrations, were all critical of the ADC. In 1972, lawsuits from animal welfare organizations helped spur an investigation that eventually led President Nixon to ban the use of poison for predator control by Federal agencies or on Federal lands. The ADC Policy Study Committee, appointed by Secretary of Interior Cecil Andrus in 1978, found insufficient documentation to justify the program's existence. Andrus issued a policy that

Figure 5.4

Bobcats killed by Animal Damage Control to reduce attacks on livestock, 1937–1970. (Cain 1972; Defenders of Wildlife 1984:45.)

stopped the practice of denning (the finding and killing predator young in their dens) and stopped research on the poison Compound 1080 (USDA 1997; U.S. General Accounting Office 2001).

With each new report and set of recommendations, through all the criticism and controversy, ADC continually reorganized, but their role remained the same: they killed wildlife that attacked livestock or damaged crops. But ADC also had, and still has, powerful and influential supporters. The program's political fortunes changed most dramatically in 1980 with the election of Ronald Reagan and the subsequent appointment of Secretary of the Interior James Watt. Watt quickly rescinded Andrus's ban on denning, and Reagan revoked Nixon's ban on the use of poisons. The most influential change took place in 1986, when Congress transferred all ADC personnel, equipment, and funding from the Fish and Wildlife Service of the U.S. Department of Interior to the USDA's Animal Plant and Health Inspection Service (APHIS). With the transfer to USDA, the ADC program rebounded, and in 1988 agents killed 1,220 bobcats, 237 cougars, 236 black bears, 80 gray wolves, 7,158 foxes, and 86,502 coyotes (USDA 1997; U.S. General Accounting Office 2001).

As further evidence of shifting political winds, ADC was renamed Wildlife Services in August 1997. "The new title is more indicative of what we do," claimed Rick Wadleigh (personal communication), ADC's former national environmental compliance manager. Perhaps not indicative, but certainly ironic.

With a budget of $98 million in fiscal year (FY) 2003 (30 September 2003–1 October 2004), Wildlife Services' 1,216 employees responded to complaints of wildlife damage on both private and public lands by providing technical advice or through direct control (Wildlife Services 2005). Direct control usually means capturing and killing the offending animal. Additionally, Wildlife Service's activities have grown more diverse since the 1930s and now include the following

- Killing predators that attack livestock (cattle, sheep, goats, and poultry). Increasingly, nonlethal methods are used, such as changing animal husbandry techniques or erecting predator-proof fences.
- Working with airports to prevent collisions between wildlife and aircraft. This includes bird strikes and deer wandering onto runways.
- Protecting grain crops from blackbird and starling damage by using frightening devices, structural or habitat modification, or direct removal.
- Removing predators that attack threatened and endangered species such as the western snowy plover, San Clemente loggerhead shrike, and salt-marsh harvest mouse.
- Protecting public safety by removing wildlife carrying rabies, plague, and tuberculosis.
- Vaccinating wildlife against rabies to reduce public health threat.

Wildlife Services also administers the National Wildlife Research Center (NWRC) in Fort Collins, Colorado. This sprawling 43–acre facility employs 160 scientists, technicians, and support personnel devoted to conducting research to resolve problems caused by the interaction of wild animals and society. In addition to NWRC, there are ten field stations located throughout the United States. Originally called the Eradication Methods Laboratory, with emphasis on development of traps and poisons to control predators and rodents (U.S. General Accounting Office 2001), the modern NWRC currently has research projects underway that include development and evaluation of new techniques for solving predator depredation problems, ecology of coyote depredation, reduction of mammal damage to forest resources, management of wildlife that pose hazards to aviation, and registration of vertebrate pesticides for use as wildlife damage control agents (NWRC 2004).

Sheep are the most frequent victims of predation. According to the USDA's National Agricultural Statistics Service (NASS), predators killed a total of 224,200 sheep and lambs during 2004 in the United States. This represents 37.3% of the total losses from all causes and a loss of $18.3 million to farmers and ranchers. Coyotes were the most problematic predator, accounting for 135,600 (60.5%) of the total losses, followed by dogs with 29,800 (13.3%), pumas with 12,700 (5.7%), bears with 8,500 (3.8%), eagles with 6,300 (2.8%) and foxes with 4,200 (1.9%). Bobcats killed 11,100 sheep and lambs, or 4.9% of the total, for a loss of $814,000 (NASS 2004).

During the same year (2004), a total of 415,000 goats and kids died. Diseases and other known causes accounted for 180,000 deaths, or 43.5% of the total, and $18,540,000 in losses. Another 80,200 or 19.3% died from unknown causes, with $8,261,000 in losses. Predators killed 155,000 animals (37.3%), for an estimated loss of $15,965,000. No information was provided on how many goats were killed by each species of predator (NASS 2004).

Data on cattle and calf losses from predators were not available for 2004 from NASS, but an examination of figures from 2000 showed that 147,000 head were lost, with a total value of $51 million. Again, coyotes caused the majority of cattle and calf losses to predators, accounting for 95,000 (64.6%) of the total, at a cost of $31,754,000. Dogs were second with 26,000 (17.7%), and bobcats were lumped together with pumas and Canada lynx in third place, with 11,000 head lost (7.5%) at a cost of $4,334,000. Because bobcats were included with pumas and Canada lynx, it is not possible to precisely assess their impact on cattle and calves (NASS 2000).

As sobering as these numbers appear, the NASS reports contain a cautionary note on the reliability of livestock loss estimates. Survey procedures are described as random samples of U.S. producers to provide data for the estimates. "Survey procedures ensured that all sheep producers, regardless of size, had a chance to be included in the survey. Large producers were sampled more heavily than small operations. About 22,000 operators were contacted during the first half of January by mail, telephone and face-to-face personal interviews" (NASS 2005:15). Cattle and calf losses were estimated in a similar fashion. Two factors immediately cast doubt on the accuracy of such estimates. One is the difficulty of determining whether a sheep, goat, or calf was actually killed by a bobcat. The other is that most of the loss data come from livestock producers, hardly an objective statistical source.

Wildlife Services stopped including financial loss figures with annual tables of reported resource losses in FY 1998. However, losses reported from 22 states to Wildlife Services in FY 2003 showed that bobcats killed 8 calves, 73 sheep, 453 lambs, 389 goats, and 864 chickens, as well as assorted ducks, geese, turkeys, rabbits, swans, pheasants, quail, two calves, and one adult horse (Wildlife Services 2005). "These loss figures represent only a fraction of the overall damage caused each year by bobcats," said Bill Clay, Deputy Administrator of Wildlife Services (personal communication), "because we only document losses from people who request our help."

Anderson (1987) pointed out that records of livestock depredation by bobcats are numerous, but their impact has generally been minor and localized. Sheep, goats, and chickens are the bobcat's most frequent domestic prey. Young reported that sheep and goat remains were found in 12% of 3,990 bobcat stomachs collected in the West from 1918 to 1922. A single bobcat was reputed to have killed 38 lambs in one night (Young 1978). Such surplus killing suggests to some that the bobcat is a bloodthirsty predator that enjoys killing. This may be true: to enjoy killing is probably necessary to survive. But like so much of the cat's behavior, it is not that simple.

Why does surplus killing occur? Hans Kruuk (1972) examined this question in foxes (*Vulpes vulpes*), spotted hyaenas (*Crocuta crocuta*), and various species of wild dogs, cats, and bears. The disadvantages to a predator of killing more than it can eat include depletion of a limited food supply in times of stress, wasted energy, and the possibility of injury during capture and killing. Conversely, clear advantages include having the opportunity to eat the carcass later when hungry, procuring food for offspring or other members of the same social group, and gaining valuable experience to be used during later kills. Under these circumstances, surplus killing is not providing extra food that is wasted. Kruuk argued that "satiation in carnivores does not inhibit further *catching* and *killing*, but it probably does inhibit *searching* and *hunting*. Thus carnivores are able to procure an 'easy prey' but normally satiation limits numbers killed" (Kruuk 1972:242). Experiments by animal behavior expert Paul Leyhausen showed that both hungry and satiated felines killed prey as long as it was presented, rather than eating prey already killed. Surplus killing occurs partly because the drive to kill outweighs the need to eat, and because domestic livestock cannot or will not escape (Leyhausen 1979). To a bobcat, making multiple kills is an efficient way to procure a lot of food in a short period of time; it is wasteful only in an artificial captive situation in which prey animals are concentrated and unable to escape, such as in a chicken coop or sheep pen.

Most states have laws that enable livestock owners to protect their animals. Depredating bobcats may be destroyed if caught in the act of attacking livestock, or they may be captured and killed after the depredation incident has been verified. As Dave Fjelline explained earlier, nonlethal preventive options are also available, such as putting a top on the chicken coop or penning the sheep at night. Traditionally, there have been two lethal approaches to bobcat depredation: kill the problem bobcat or reduce the bobcat population in areas where attacks occur. If the decision is made to kill the offending bobcat, then a variety of techniques are available (see Table 5.1).

Wildlife Services has its critics. Some wildlife advocacy organizations see the program as an anachronism, with little government oversight, that needs to be eliminated altogether. Defenders of Wildlife has urged Wildlife Services to develop formal policies acknowledging the importance of protecting native biological diversity, setting guidelines for cooperative funding from the states for predator control activities, and establishing strict standards for hiring field personnel. USDA has declined to adopt any of these recommendations. Although some advocate abolishment of the Wildlife Services program, the Humane Society of the United States (HSUS) thinks that such an action would be a mistake. HSUS believes that, without some form of federal assistance in dealing with real or perceived predator problems, ranchers, farmers, and property owners would themselves kill wildlife they believe is causing the problem and would use techniques more inhumane and nonselective than those employed by Wildlife Services. They also suggest that if the federal program were shut down, many states would simply organize their own wildlife damage control programs. HSUS's strategy has been to advocate that Wildlife Services place more emphasis on nonlethal and noninjurious wildlife damage control (HSUS 2005b). Wildlife Services counters that in FY 2002, 75% of their research funding was directed toward the development of nonlethal damage management tools and techniques (Wildlife Services 2005). NASS reports show that farmers and ranchers more frequently employ nonlethal preventive techniques such as fencing, guard dogs, lamb sheds, night penning, and herding (NASS 2000, 2004).

One of the most vocal opponents of the Wildlife Services program is the Predator Conservation Alliance (2002), a small wildlife advocacy organization based in Bozeman, Montana. Predator Conservation Alliance offered one of the most potent arguments against Wildlife Services, namely that the program consistently spends more money on predator control than livestock owners actually lose to predators. For example, in FY 2003, Wildlife Services spent $375,252 in Arizona to control predators that reportedly killed 28 cattle, 140 calves, 3 goats, 10 sheep, 49 lambs, 5 chickens, 7 ostriches, and 1 turkey (Wildlife Services 2005). That's more than $1,500 per animal, none of which were killed by bobcats. Such fiscal logic seems to defy reason, but, when confronted with this fact, Rick Wadleigh explained that Wildlife Services is required by law to provide assistance when requested. He also emphasized that without predator control livestock losses would be even higher.

Table 5.1
How to Catch and Kill a Bobcat

Steel leghold traps

Steel leghold and padded-jaw traps baited with a scent attractive to bobcats or other predators are used. Animals are usually killed with a blow to the head or shot. Steel leghold traps are banned on public lands in some states. Padded-jaw leghold traps are sometimes used by researchers to capture bobcats alive (see Figure 5.1).

Body-gripping traps

Also called Conibear traps, after the developer of the prototype, body-gripping or instant kill traps consist of two metal rectangles hinged together midway on the long side to open and close like scissors. One jaw has a trigger that can be baited. The opposite jaw has a catch that holds the trap open. When properly set, the jaws of the body-gripping trap strike the animal on the spinal column at the base of the skull for an instant kill. Body-gripping traps are banned on public lands in some states (see Figure 5.2).

Snares

Wire or light cable is looped through a locking device so that it will tighten as the animal pulls against it. When caught around the foot or leg, the bobcat is restrained until the Wildlife Services agent returns and kills it. When caught around the neck, the bobcat strangles. Snares are banned on public lands in some states.

Tracking hounds

Specially trained tracking hounds follow the bobcat's scent until the cat climbs a tree, where it is then shot.

Aerial gunning

Bobcats, coyotes, wolves, or other predators are shot from an airplane or helicopter.

Calling and shooting

Devices are used to mimic the sounds of prey or a female in heat to attract a bobcat. When the curious bobcat is within range, it is shot.

Spotlight and shooting

A spotlight is used to stun the bobcat; while it is motionless, it is shot.

Cage trap

A variety of cage traps are used by wildlife services but those most commonly used are box traps, made from wood and heavy mesh wire. Box traps are used to capture animals alive and are often baited with foods attractive to the bobcat. Trapped animals are either relocated or killed. Cage traps are sometimes used by researchers to capture bobcats alive.

M-44

A metal stake, a spring-loaded ejector, and a capsule containing a poisonous sodium cyanide mixture are used to poison coyotes, foxes, and wild dogs. When an animal bites and pulls the device, which is baited with scent, the poison is ejected into the animal's mouth. M-44s have also killed bobcats, deer, elk, black bears, raccoons, skunks, crows, ravens, and domestic dogs and cats. These devices are now rarely used.

Source: Defenders of Wildlife 1984:15–19; Virchow and Hogeland 1994.

Another organization that had ADC in its crosshairs was Wildlife Damage Review (WDR). Working out of a small office in Tucson, Arizona, this group worked to bring public scrutiny to Wildlife Services and to eliminate the predator prejudice that drives the federal program and similar state-level efforts. They worked against the entrenched myth of the western rancher. WDR agreed with the financial arguments set forth by the Predator Project for abolishing Wildlife Services. But WDR spokesperson Nancy Zierenberg (personal communication) listed another reason for shutting the program down: "There is no oversight," she explained. "ADC has no accountability. They don't have to answer to anyone. The original ADC Act of 1931 doesn't even come up for periodic review." Although the ADC budget must be approved by Congress, it usually is. WDR closed its doors in 2002.

Wildlife Services has weathered all the controversy and continues to survive, even prosper—much like the bobcat. Wildlife Services and livestock owners consider the bobcat to be a significant problem, although many wildlife biologists and predator advocates do not. A powerful Western livestock lobby and a Republican Congress have ensured, in recent years, that Wildlife Service's budget has steadily increased to its current level of $98 million (Wildlife Services 2005). Although many object to Wildlife Service's existence, in a country where the majority of people live in cities and federal budgets reach into the trillions of dollars, Wildlife Service's budget seems an insignificant blip on the political radar screen.

In 2000, Congress finally amended the Animal Damage Control Act of 1931. Specific language was removed that, according to Wildlife Services officials, reflected outdated program goals and philosophy. For example, "promulgate the best methods of eradication . . . of mountain lions, wolves, coyotes, bobcats" was changed to "conduct a program of wildlife services with respect to injurious animal species and

Table 5.2
Number of Bobcats Killed
by Wildlife Services, by Year

Fiscal year	No. killed
2003	2,503
2002	2,451
2001	2,467
2000	2,555
1999	2,350
1998	2,176
1997	1,850
1996	1,733
TOTAL	18,085

Source: Wildlife Services 2005.

Table 5.3
Number of Bobcats Taken by Wildlife Services
during Fiscal Year 2003, by Method

Method	No. killed
Cage	88
Leghold trap	1,304
Aerial gunning	290
Leg and foot snares	2
Neck snares	565
Spotlight/shooting	6
Predator calling/shooting	104
Shooting (unspecified)	49
M-44	1
Other (hunting dogs, poisons)	94
TOTAL	2,503

Source: Wildlife Services 2005

take any action the Secretary considers necessary in conducting the program. The Secretary shall administer the program in a manner consistent with all of the wildlife services authorities in effect on the day before October 28, 2000." The new language is vague and gives even broader authority to the Secretary of Agriculture. How these changes represent more modern program goals and philosophy is unclear. However, one thing is clear: from FY 1996 to FY 2003, Wildlife Services killed 18,085 bobcats, using leghold traps, neck snares, aerial gunning, and other methods (U.S. General Accounting Office 2001:52) (see Tables 5.2 and 5.3).

Wild, yet wonderfully near us, the bobcat is a valued
flagship species for many North American communities.
(Photo by Susan C. Morse)

Vermont bobcats use ledges and cliffs for
hunting, resting, escape habitat, and denning.
(Photo by Susan C. Morse)

Profile of a western bobcat showing distinctive
spots, short tail, ear tufts, and cheek ruffs.
(Photo by Susan C. Morse)

Bobats are effective predators of wetland edge
habitats. (Photo by Susan C. Morse)

Bobcat with a bird that it killed.
(Photo by Gary Koehler)

Biologist collecting measurements of a captured bobcat's foot. Biologists collect a variety of measurements including: total length from the nose to tip of tail, head, neck, and chest girth, dimensions of the foot, as well as collect samples of blood and tissue for DNA profiling and disease assessment. (Photo by Gary Koehler)

Biologists attaching a radiotelemetry collar to an anesthetized bobcat. (Photo by Gary Koehler)

Bobcat captured in a box-type live trap.
(Photo by Gary Koehler)

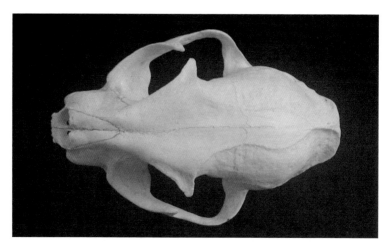

Dorsal (top) view of bobcat skull. (Photo by C. C. Haas)

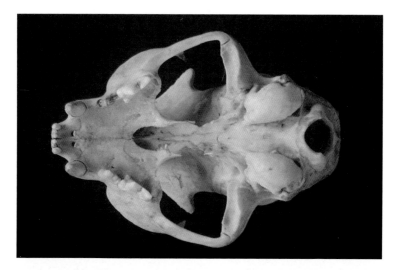

Ventral (bottom) view of bobcat skull. (Photo by C. C. Haas)

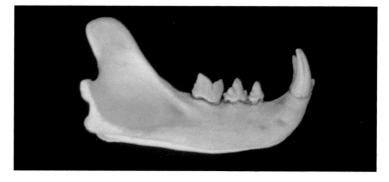

Lateral (side) view of bobcat mandible. (Photo by C. C. Haas)

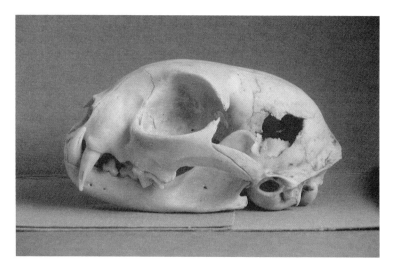

Lateral (side) view of bobcat skull with hole in cranium from puma bite.
(Photo by C. C. Haas)

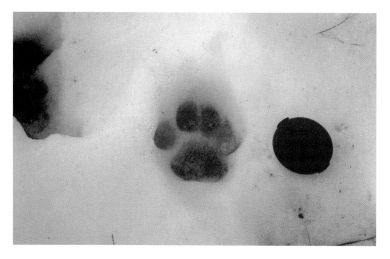

Bobcat track in snow with camera lens cap for scale.
(Photo by C. C. Haas)

An anesthetized bobcat. (National Park Service photo)

Measuring the length of an anesthetized bobcat's foot.
(National Park Service photo)

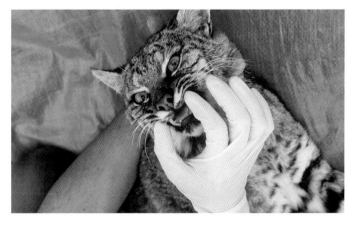

Checking an anesthetized bobcat's teeth.
(National Park Service photo)

National Park Service researcher attaching a radiotelemetry collar to a captured bobcat. (National Park Service photo)

National Park Service researcher Seth Riley draws blood from an anesthetized bobcat. (National Park Service photo)

Bobcat descending dead tree. (Photo by Lewis Kemper)

Bobcat kittens. (Photos by Lewis Kemper)

Montana bobcat grooming.
Notice the distinctive white
spots on the back of the ears.
(Photo by Lewis Kemper)

Bobcat female with kitten. (Photo by Lewis Kemper)

Bobcat kitten. (Photo by Lewis Kemper)

Montana bobcat female and her kitten. (Photo by Lewis Kemper)

Canada Lynx, the bobcat's northern cousin, in Montana.
(Photo by Lewis Kemper)

6 The Predator Puzzle

Seth Riley is attracting curious onlookers as he walks down the main road leading into the California coastal town of Bolinas. Oblivious to his audience, he listens intently to the soft electronic beeps coming from his headphones. His right arm extends over his head, rotating an H-shaped antennae. Both headphones and antennae are connected to a receiver that hangs over Seth's shoulder. The source of the signal is a small transmitter fastened around the neck of bobcat number 12. Seth captured the wild feline and attached the radio collar two years earlier.

"He's up here," Seth announces before plunging into a thicket of bushes between two buildings and up a steep hillside. I scramble up the trail behind him, trying to keep up with his long easy strides. Emerging from the vegetation near the top of the hill, we walk out onto a large level field. We are standing atop a small, flat-topped mesa. Seth slips through a barbed wire fence and moves across the field, rotating the antennae and listening to his headphones. After negotiating the fence, I walk a short distance across the field, then stop and scan the distance in front of Seth with binoculars. There is little vegetation to provide cover for the bobcat, and I'm skeptical about the reliability of the transmitter's signal. I have learned from previous experience with Seth that tracking the elusive cats, even with the help of radiotelemetry equipment, is like chasing shadows.

Lowering the binoculars, I gaze down at the buildings and houses of Bolinas to the west. To the east is Bolinas Lagoon. I turn my attention to the waterfowl and wading birds along its shore. Suddenly I glance up to see Seth running toward me.

"Did you see him?" he calls excitedly.

"See who?" I answer skeptically.

"Number 12. He's right there." Seth points to the far side of the field.

Seeing what appears to be a fence post 100 yards in the distance, I raise the binoculars. Staring back at me through the lenses is the distinctive face of an adult male bobcat. I can make out the grey-brown ruff of fur around his face and the tufts of hair at the end of each ear. Even the radio collar is visible. As he briefly turns his head, I catch a glimpse of the white spot on the back of each ear.

"I'll be damned," I whisper.

I glance over at Seth. He smiles back in vindication. I return my gaze to the bobcat, but the feline has vanished.

■

CITES

There was little public concern for the status of the bobcat, or any other furbearer, before the early 1970s. Wildlife professionals were equally disinterested. The bobcat's nocturnal and stealthy habits made it difficult to study. Its pelt rarely brought more than $5.00 between 1950 and 1970, so the bobcat was of little economic importance compared with other furbearers. With only occasional attacks on sheep or chickens, there was little incentive for state or federal wildlife agencies to conduct research or manage the bobcat (Anderson 1987; Anderson and Lovallo 2003). However, in 1973, two events converged to place the diminutive bobcat at the center of an intense political and biological controversy that would persist for the next nine years and ultimately transform the international conservation of wild felines.

The first event was passage of the Endangered Species Act (ESA) in late 1973, which prohibited the import of fur of endangered cats into the United States. With the loss of big, spotted cats as a source of pelts, commercial traders switched their attention to the smaller spotted cats, especially the Canada lynx and the bobcat (McMahan 1986; Kitchener 1991). From 1970 to 1977, the yearly harvest of bobcats jumped eightfold, from 10,854 to 83,415, while the average price per pelt rose from less than $10 to $70. The total value of pelts taken in the entire United States during the 1970–1971 season was less then $5,000. By the 1976–77 season, it was almost $6 million. Over the next ten seasons (1978–1979 to 1987–1988), furtakers killed an average of 75,742 bobcats a year (see Figure 5.3 in Chapter 5). A large male bobcat pelt could bring as much as $225 to $300 during this period. As today, the value of individual pelts varied depending on where they were taken. Pelts from the West and Northeast typically are of better quality than those from the Midwest and Southeast. Between 1970 and 2003, furtakers killed 1,484,383 bobcats, with a total value of more than $110 million (see Figure 5.3 in Chapter 5). Killing the smaller cats compounded the impact on their populations, because many more skins of bobcats than of larger cats are needed to make the same-sized garment (e.g., eight to ten bobcat pelts, compared with three leopard pelts) (Funderburk 1986; Kitchener 1991).

The second significant event was the gathering of representatives from 80 nations in Washington, D.C., to negotiate a treaty controlling international trade in wild animals and plants. Early drafts of the treaty had been produced through the joint efforts of the World Conservation Union (IUCN), the United States, Kenya, the World Wildlife Fund, the National Audubon Society, and the New York Zoological Society. The 1973 conference produced a final treaty known as the Convention on International Trade in Endangered Species of Wild Fauna and Flora (CITES), which came into force two years later in 1975. CITES was created because of global concern about the threat to many plants and animals caused by illegal trade, which amounts to billions of dollars and is second only to the illegal narcotics trade (Anderson and Lovallo 2003; CITES 2005a).

CITES divides protected species into three categories or appendices. Additions and deletions of species are voted on, primarily at the Conferences of the Parties, which are held every two to three years. The first conference was held in Berne, Switzerland, in 1976, and the most recent was in Bangkok, Thailand, in 2004. Appendix I includes species threatened with extinction. Commercial trade in these species is not allowed. Appendix II contains organisms that may become threatened with extinction unless strict regulations are enacted. Approximately 1,500 species were listed in these two appendices at the time CITES was drafted, and signatory nations have subsequently made substantial additions through the CITES's listing procedure. Appendix III is reserved for nations to list wildlife species which they protect but for which international cooperation is needed to prevent illegal trade (CITES 2005b).

CITES uses a system of permits to regulate trade in wildlife. Treaty members issue permits allowing trade only after they are satisfied that it will not pose a threat to survival of the species. CITES specifies that each signatory nation must establish a "scientific authority" to determine that export will not be detrimental to the survival of listed species. Signatory nations must also establish a "management authority" to issue export permits and to determine that listed plants or animals have been legally obtained (Rolf 1989; U.S. Fish and Wildlife Service [USFWS] 2004b).

Section 8A of the ESA implements CITES for the United States. President Gerald Ford signed Executive Order 11911 in April 1975, which established the Endangered Species Scientific Authority (ESSA) as the scientific authority and the Secretary of the Interior as the management authority for the United States.

However, Congress amended the ESA in 1979, abolishing the ESSA and designating the Secretary of the Interior as both the scientific and the management authority. The USFWS was in turn directed to carry out these responsibilities, and it does so today through its Office of Scientific Authority and Office of Management Authority (Rolf 1989; USFWS 2004b).

The primary source of controversy surrounding bobcats was a 1977 decision by CITES members to add all unprotected species of cats (except the domestic cat) to Appendix II. This was done to protect these species from uncontrolled international trade, which had previously endangered the leopard, ocelot, and cheetah, among others. Although listing in Appendix II does not prohibit international commercial trade, it requires that the scientific authority of the country of export ensure that the export of an Appendix II species "will not be detrimental to the survival of that species." Later that same year, ESSA placed a temporary ban on the export of bobcat pelts from the United States until more evidence of "no detriment" could be established. The CITES listing took place at a time when bobcat pelt prices were skyrocketing and the status of their populations was unknown (Anderson and Lovallo 2003:778).

The following year (1978), ESSA published the guidelines it would use to make the required "no detriment" evaluation. Criteria included information on population trends, size and distribution of the harvest, habitat availability, methods used to control the harvest, registration and tagging of all pelts, and annual determination of target harvest levels. Some states were unable to provide the requested data. Based on these guidelines and management commitments from most states, the scientific authority approved export in 1979 of bobcats killed in 34 states and the Navajo Nation. Export from other states was banned. This led to disputes between state and federal wildlife management authorities. Many states thought that ESSA had no right to interfere in the management of bobcats, a species most state biologists believed was widespread and abundant. However, during the 1970s, there were few reliable census data on which to base this assumption (Bean 1983).

Later in 1978, Defenders of Wildlife, a wildlife advocacy organization based in Washington, D.C., filed a lawsuit in U.S. District Court, challenging both the guidelines and the decision to authorize export. They argued that the government's authorization of unlimited bobcat exports violated the CITES requirement that export be permitted only if it would not harm the species. They won a temporary export ban in Florida, Massachusetts, New Mexico, Wisconsin, eastern Oregon, and part of Texas (Anderson 1987; Anderson and Lovallo 2003).

In late 1979, Defenders of Wildlife appealed the District Court decision on the grounds that the lower court did not address the adequacy of the government's standards for authorizing export. In February 1981, the U.S. Court of Appeals ruled that the standards for export approval were invalid under CITES. The following April, U.S. District Court Judge June L. Green issued an order prohibiting export of all bobcat pelts until reliable population estimates and harvest limits could be established (Anderson and Lovallo 2003).

Critics of the decision included state wildlife agencies, commercial fur traders, trappers, and the International Association of Fish and Wildlife Agencies (IAFWA). They argued that the state-by-state data ESSA used was sufficient to determine that export was not detrimental to the survival of the bobcat and that the USFWS regulations were adequate. They believed that the decision placed an unreasonable burden on state and federal decision makers and added unnecessarily to existing wildlife laws. The Fur Conservation Institute of America and the IAFWA even petitioned the Supreme Court to review the U.S. Court of Appeals decision in May 1981. The petition was denied later that year (Bean 1983; Anderson and Lovallo 2003).

Below the surface, the situation was further compounded by a turf war between state and federal wildlife officials. Many state wildlife agencies viewed the new regulations as an attempt by the feds to dictate to the states, and they resented the interference. In the end, the states won a partial victory.

Congress put an end to the legal wrangling over bobcats in late 1982. Although Defenders of Wildlife and other organizations testified in hearings against changing the ESA, it was amended, nullifying the Court of Appeals decision by specifying that neither the Secretary of the Interior nor the states are required to make population estimates. This negated the CITES requirement that reliable bobcat population estimates were prerequisite to the "no detriment" finding, and the Defenders of Wildlife case was dismissed (Anderson 1987; Anderson and Lovallo 2003). During the controversy and debate, there was a dramatic increase in bobcat harvest. Between 1977 and 1981, 94,000 bobcats were killed annually in the United States and Canada, with an average pelt price of $125 (Funderburk 1986; Anderson and Lovallo 2003).

In the summer of 1983, at the Conference of the Parties in Botswana, the United States was allowed to transfer the bobcat to a subsection of Appendix II. The new listing permitted management of the bobcat based on its similar appearance to other endangered felids, and not as an endangered species (Anderson 1987; Anderson and Lovallo 2003). The USFWS determined that the bobcat, with the exception of the Mexican bobcat subspecies (*Lynx rufus escuinapae*), did not qualify for CITES Appendix II based on its own conservation status. In November 1992, after a 10-year review of CITES-listed species, the United States successfully proposed downlisting the Mexican bobcat to Appendix II. Currently, the entire species is listed in Appendix II, including all subspecies

Eleven years later, in 2003, the Western Association of Fish and Wildlife Agencies and the Louisiana Department of Wildlife and Fisheries requested that the bobcat be removed from Appendix II. The USFWS investigated the consequences of removing the bobcat from the CITES appendices on the conservation of other protected small spotted cats, particularly the Canada lynx (*Lynx canadensis*), the European lynx (*Lynx lynx*), and the Iberian lynx (*Lynx pardinus*). They sought input from Canada and Mexico, and from countries where lynx species occur, to determine whether management and enforcement controls were adequate to address look-alike concerns. They also consulted with state wildlife agencies (USFWS 2004a).

October 2–14, 2004, the member nations of CITES gathered at the Thirteenth meeting of the Conference of the Parties in Bangkok, Thailand. The delegation from the United States submitted a proposal for deletion of the bobcat from Appendix II. They acknowledged that the bobcat was listed during the 4th meeting of the Conference of the Parties in 1983 due to its similarity of appearance to other spotted cats, and that other countries and observers were concerned about enforcement. They suggested that, with improvements in management and enforcement, the need for look-alike listing should decrease over time. However, they were willing to withdraw their initial proposal if an alternative proposal or draft decision were approved. The U.S. delegation then made an alternative proposal, which was that, immediately after the meeting, the CITES Animals Committee would include Felidae in its review of appendices. This review was to initially focus on the *Lynx* species complex, which included species that were listed because of similarity of appearance, such as *L. rufus*. In addition to evaluating the listings of these species against the criteria for inclusion of species in Appendices I and II, the Animals Committee was asked to assess the management and enforcement measures available to achieve effective control of trade in these species, so as to resolve the continued need for look-alike listings. The United States requested that the assessment include a review of trade information to determine whether these species are actually confused in trade or whether the look-alike problem is merely hypothetical. The Animals Committee was asked to provide a report at the 14th meeting of the Conference of the Parties on progress of the review of all Felidae, and particularly on their review of *Lynx* spp. and look-alike issues. The delegations from the Netherlands and Mexico supported this request, and after some discussion the proposal to review the *Lynx* species complex was agreed to, and the proposal to delete the bobcat from Appendix II was withdrawn (CITES 2004). The 14th meeting of the Conference of the Parties is scheduled for June 13–15, 2007, in The Hague, the Netherlands.

Counting Bobcats

The initial focus of bobcat research by state wildlife agencies in the early 1980s was on gaining more detailed information on population size, population change, and harvest. However, there is no way to accurately census bobcats in a large area because of their secretive nature, low density, and dispersed distribution. For this reason, biologists employ a variety of indirect assessments (indices) of the feline's status.

"The use of indirect indices has always been an integral part of wildlife management," explained McCord and Cardoza (1982:758). "The opinions of early wildlife managers who became very familiar with local populations were the first type of index. In the United States opinions of sportsmen and naturalists as voiced in public hearings or random surveys continue to be a source of status information." Many wildlife managers believe this type of index has proved sufficient over the years, especially when the bobcat population is large, to ensure recovery from overharvest. However, Hass (personal communication) pointed out that the problem with indirect indices is lack of validation.

Mark-recapture estimates, scent-station surveys, and track-counts have been used to study bobcats, but with mixed results (Rolley 1987; Diefenbach et al. 1994). Marking animals and recording information from recaptures or resightings is one method to obtain data for estimating certain population characteristics, but marking or tagging projects are expensive and should be conducted over a relatively long period. The technique does not work well on bobcats because of the feline's low capture probability and the low number of marked animals in most samples. Pelton (1979) proposed a more sophisticated version of the mark-recapture method, using radioisotopes injected into captured bobcats These isotopes are slowly excreted in the animal's feces. Feces are collected from throughout the study area, and the ratio of radioactive to nonradioactive feces provides an estimate of abundance. Unfortunately, this method requires that all bobcats be injected within a relatively short period and that their feces be easy to locate. Once again, the bobcat's stealthy behavior makes both these conditions difficult to meet.

Scent-station surveys, originally developed as an index to coyote abundance, are used by some wildlife agencies to monitor bobcat populations. Scent stations usually consist of a circle of sifted sand, one meter in diameter, with an attractant such as bobcat urine or a fatty acid scent at the center. The stations are spaced along a transect and checked at regular intervals for tracks or scat. The duration of the survey, length of survey lines, distance between scent stations, method of route selection, and choice of attractant and tracking surface vary with each agency, depending on research objectives and resources. Where biologists once used 50-station lines that were operated for four nights, they now use a greater number of 10-station lines operated for one night to increase survey efficiency. Unfortunately, experience with this method has shown that bobcats visit the scent stations infrequently, and some researchers do not consider the technique valid in comparing study areas (Rust 1980; Roughton and Sweeney 1982; Conner et al. 1983; Sargeant et al. 1998).

Track-transect surveys are even simpler in application than the other methods. They consist of walking predetermined lines of varying length within bobcat habitat and recording sightings of the animal, as well as tracks, scrapes, or scats. This technique is more frequently used to estimate the densities of species with more visible tracks and is not well-suited for the light-footed bobcat. However, track-counts conducted after a fresh snowfall were found to be more sensitive to bobcat population changes than were scent-station surveys (Zezulak 1981). How observations of bobcats or their tracks relate to population density is unknown and probably varies among regions (Roughton and Sweeney 1982). For instance, bobcats seem to move more when food is scarce. Both scent-station surveys and track-transect surveys have low detection rates and high variability, which make them unable to detect short-term changes in populations. Neither method can detect annual population changes of less than 50% with any degree of confidence. Despite these limitations, such techniques are able to detect long-term-trends in populations over large geographic areas, such as the apparent bobcat population decline in several western states during the 1970s (Knowlton and Tzilkowski 1979; Rolley 1987).

A method often overlooked as an indexing tool by biologists, but advocated by Anderson (1987), is the use of mail questionnaires sent to landowners asking for documentation of bobcat sightings on their land. If sighting data are compiled over several years, this low-tech approach can show regional trends. During their study of Oklahoma furbearers, Hatcher and Shaw (1981) compared two types of scent-station surveys with mail questionnaires in estimating furbearer abundance. When populations were low, the questionnaire was more accurate than the other methods.

Using mark-recapture estimates, scent-station surveys, track-count transects, or some combination of these methods, field biologists measure the density of bobcats in a small area of representative habitat and then multiply that estimate by the amount of habitat within the bobcat range to derive an estimate of total population size (extrapolation). Such estimates are expensive and take years to complete, and extrapolating population estimates in such a manner is fraught with variables that can dramatically influence total population estimates. To compensate for these problems, biologists frequently employ several techniques so that each can provide a check on the others.

Radiotelemetry provides the best estimate of absolute numbers of bobcats in an area (Anderson 1987; Anderson and Lovallo 2003), but only if almost all of the animals in the local area are captured, tagged, and suYciently tracked. Radiotelemetry was Wrst used successfully to study bobcat movements and home ranges in South Carolina (Marshall and Jenkins 1966). The number of home range studies increased dramatically between 1971 and 1985. Expectations for this new technology were high, and many wildlife biologists viewed it as a solution to the "bobcat management problem," instead of as a research tool to help answer speciWc questions. Bowing to public and political pressure, many wildlife agencies launched bobcat studies using radiotelemetry, but without clearly deWned goals or testable hypotheses to justify the research. With vague objectives to gather as much information as possible in hope of learning something new, the result was enormous duplication and little progress toward a better understanding of the species (Anderson 1987).

Radiotelemetry was the primary technique employed by states trying to obtain bobcat population size estimates during the early 1980s to comply with the requirements imposed by CITES. By combining average adult home range size, percent home range overlap, local sex ratios, and the proportion of transients in the population, field investigators were able to estimate population density within a study area. As with earlier techniques, these estimates were then extrapolated to the total area of similar habitat within the state. The accuracy of extrapolated population estimates is influenced by the presence of unmarked resident bobcats within the study area (almost a certainty when dealing with the elusive feline), but mark-recapture techniques can be used to estimate the proportion of unmarked individuals. Rolley (1987) emphasized that the validity of extrapolated estimates also depends on the similarity of the habitats to which the telemetry estimates are applied. Areas must be similar in vegetative structure and composition, as well as prey abundance and harvest pressure.

Conner and associates (1983) conducted one of the few studies comparing different censusing methods for bobcats. Their two-year study was carried out on a 2,300-acre area in northeastern Florida, where they compared scent-station indices with population abundance estimates based on trapping, radioisotope feces tagging, and radiotelemetry. They found that all of the techniques generated indices that accurately reflected changes in the population abundance of bobcats.

Recent advances hold potential for more accurately estimating bobcat populations and further penetrating the secret world of the furtive felid. These include satellite telemetry, camera trapping, and various genetic methods. Coupling conventional transmitters with Global Positioning System (GPS) technology will assist biologists in overcoming the difficulties of following animals in remote and inaccessible terrain. A GPS receiver calculates the position of the animal wearing it relative to a series of orbiting satellites. The GPS receiver can be programmed to calculate position daily, hourly, or more frequently. The data can then be stored in the receiver, relayed to another receiver, or transmitted via a low orbiting relay satellite. GPS collars and data recovery techniques cost thousands of dollars, precluding their use in most studies. However, the method has been successful in field trials with caribou, moose, polar bears, elephants, brown bears, elk, pumas, and snow leopards (Sunquist and Sunquist 2002).

Camera trapping allows scientists to collect some types of information without even handling the animal. Infrared-triggered cameras have been used to remotely record wildlife activity for more than 40 years, but the recent development of commercial camera systems have made this technique more popular with biologists. The method usually involves the use of a camera equipped with an electronic triggering device attached to a tree or post. Any animal that walks in front of the camera and triggers it through motion or heat takes a photograph of itself. Camera trapping is most frequently used to detect the presence of a species in an area, but it has been used to estimate tiger populations and densities in India (Sunquist and Sunquist 2002; Swann et al. 2004).

In addition to being the best source of information on bobcat diet, feces may soon provide scientists with additional valuable information about individual animals. Feces typically contain undigested hair, bones, and teeth of prey, but they also contain cells shed from the lining of the predator's intestine. Although the technique is still experimental, scientists may soon be able to isolate, purify, and then amplify certain DNA sequences that could allow them to recognize individual cats, determine sex, and even determine relatedness. This may allow field biologists to obtain all the information they need on a particular animal, simply by picking up feces (Sunquist and Sunquist 2002).

Hair snares or traps are hair-catching devices, such as a small square of carpet with a few tacks protruding from the pile side, which are attached to trees, logs, or other places along bobcat trails. The sites are treated with a commercially available scent lure or catnip oil to induce a passing felid to cheek-rub and thereby deposit a sample of its hair. Hair snares can be placed over a large area at low cost, but the challenge is getting the bobcat to rub against the collecting surface. Hair snares have been used to estimate Canada lynx populations (McDaniel et al. 2000), and the technique could be used to index bobcats as well. In areas where the two species overlap, DNA analysis would be necessary to distinguish the collected hairs (Foran et al. 1997). Hair snares also can be used as a form of mark-recapture technique. DNA analyses can distinguish individual bobcats that leave hair at a trap, with animals making subsequent deposits constituting the resampled population. The ratio of the individuals identified in each sample can be used to estimate population size (Foran et al. 1997; Anderson and Lovallo 2003).

Rolley (1987:677) summarized the difficulties of monitoring bobcat population changes: "The key point in estimating population changes in order to evaluate management programs is that no single existing technique has proved effective or sensitive enough for detecting changes of 10–25% within a population. A manager should consider using several techniques together so that each can provide a check on the other." As a result of these difficulties, most states (94%) use two or more methods. The most frequently used techniques are hunter/trapper surveys (31 states), harvest data such as catch per hunter/trapper and pelt sales/tagging (26 states), employee opinion (20 states), sighting reports (19 states), life table analysis (13 states), computer population model (13 states), sign/track surveys (8 states), and scent-station surveys (6 states). Techniques used by only one state each include mark-recapture, bobcats taken by predator control agents, radio-telemetry, and habitat mapping (Bluett et al. 2001).

Woolf and Hubert surveyed wildlife biologists in natural resource agencies in the 48 contiguous states by mail in 1996 to determine the status of bobcat populations and their management. The bobcat was reported to be present in every state but Delaware. Populations were reported as stable in 22 states and increasing in 20 others. No state reported bobcat numbers in decline. Once thought to be absent from major portions of six midwestern states (Illinois, Indiana, Iowa, Michigan, Missouri, and Ohio), the bobcat appears to be increasing in number and distribution. Illinois in particular has had a dramatic increase in reported sightings since 1982 (Woolf and Hubert 1998).

Table 6.1 shows a list of 43 states surveyed for this book. Of those states listed, only 10 provided a statewide bobcat population estimate. The balance (33) stated the population as unknown or data not available. Wildlife managers reported that bobcat populations are stable in 24 states and increasing in 9; the population trend was unknown or not available in 9 states. The Texas Parks and Wildlife Department listed its bobcat population as both stable and increasing. Of the 33 states that provided no population estimate, 17 listed their bobcat numbers as stable, and 8 claimed they were increasing. Only the South Dakota Department of Game Fish and Parks and the West Virginia Department of Natural Resources reported their bobcat populations as decreasing.

Harvest Management

Bobcat management has changed little over the past 30 years. Today, 38 states allow the harvest of bobcats, by trapping, hunting, or both. Nine states (Connecticut, Illinois, Indiana, Iowa, Maryland, New Hampshire, New Jersey, Ohio, and Rhode Island) protect the species with continuously closed hunting and trapping seasons (Woolf and Hubert 1998). Indiana, New Jersey, and Ohio all classify the bobcat as endangered. Harvest is controlled through some combination of season length, bag limits, quotas, or restriction on take (killing). Eight states require a special permit to kill a bobcat, and four states impose a statewide quota. Texas is the only state that allows harvest but does not protect the bobcat with either a season or a bag limit (Woolf and Hubert 1998). State reports indicate that 55% of the U.S. harvest is by trappers, and 45% is by hunters (USFWS 1982).

In Canada, seven of the eight provinces where bobcats reside allow harvest. British Columbia permits trapping and hunting. Alberta allows trapping of bobcats only in the two southern fur management zones; hunting is also allowed on a more restricted basis to protect domestic animals. Saskatchewan and Ontario both permit trapping and monitor bobcat populations through fur sales. In Manitoba, the bobcat is at the northern extent of its range and is classified as vulnerable. Trapping was stopped in 1985 but resumed in 2002. Bobcats in Quebec are found mostly in the southeastern corner of the province and along the southern shore of the St. Lawrence River. The population showed a significant decrease in the late 1980s, and trapping and hunting were halted in 1991. New Brunswick has a healthy population of bobcats in the southern part of the province, and trapping resumed in 1992 after a four-year ban. A harvest lottery system was used in 2004 and 2005. Nova Scotia boasts the highest population of bobcats in northeastern North America. Trapping and hunting are both legal in that province (International Society for Endangered Cats Canada 2001). The majority of bobcats harvested in Canada are taken by trappers for the fur market (Canadian Wildlife Service 1978).

In Mexico, bobcat hunting is regulated in five states, and shooting of suspected livestock predators is permitted on a limited basis (Nowell and Jackson 1996). No population estimates are available for *L. r. escuinapae*, but the Mexican government has stated that this subspecies is widespread and numerous, is not specialized in its habitat requirements, and is highly ecologically adaptable (USFWS

Table 6.1
Bobcat Population Estimates and Trends by State

State	Population estimate	Population trend	Year of estimate/trend	Source
Alabama	Unknown	Stable	2004	Alabama Department of Wildlife and Freshwater Fisheries
Arizona	30,000	Stable	1995	Arizona Game and Fish Department
Arkansas	N/A	Stable	2002	Arkansas Game and Fish Commission
California	70,207–74,037	Stable	2003–2004	California Dept of Fish and Game
Colorado	Unknown	Unknown	2003	Colorado Division of Wildlife
Connecticut	Unknown	Increasing	2003–2004	Connecticut Department of Environmental Protection
Florida	Unknown	Unknown	2004	Florida Fish and Wildlife Conservation Commission
Georgia	Unknown	Stable	2004	Georgia Department of Natural Resources
Idaho	Unknown	Stable	2003	Idaho Department of Fish and Game
Illinois	N/A	Increasing	2003	Illinois Dept of Natural Resources
Kansas	Unknown	Stable	2000–2001	Kansas Dept of Wildlife and Parks
Kentucky	N/A	N/A	2004	Kentucky Dept of Fish and Wildlife Resources
Louisiana	N/A	Stable	2004	Louisiana Dept of Wildlife and Fisheries
Maine	1800	Stable	1994	Maine Dept of Inland Fisheries and Wildlife
Maryland	Unknown	Stable	2004	Maryland Department of Natural Resources Wildlife and Heritage Service
Massachusetts	Unknown	Increasing	2004	Massachusetts Department of Fish and Wildlife
Michigan	Unknown	Stable	2003	Michigan Department of Natural Resources
Mississippi	N/A	N/A	N/A	Mississippi Department of Wildlife, Fisheries, and Parks
Missouri	Unknown	Unknown	Unknown	Missouri Department of Conservation
Montana	10,000	Stable	1995	Montana Department of Fish, Wildlife and Parks
Nebraska	N/A	Stable	2003–2004	Nebraska Game and Parks Commission

2005). Mexican experts add that there is no evidence of population declines in central and southern Mexico (one of the most disturbed parts of the country) during the last 25 years (USFWS 2005).

The primary justification for recreational hunting and trapping in contemporary society is based on the hypothesis that wildlife populations produce a

State	Population estimate	Population trend	Year of estimate/trend	Source
New Mexico	N/A	N/A	2003	New Mexico Department of Game and Fish
New Hampshire	700	Stable	1995	New Hampshire Fish and Game Department
Nevada	Unknown	Stable	2003	Nevada Division of Wildlife
New York	N/A	Stable	2003–2004	New York State Department of Environmental Conservation
North Carolina	Unknown	Increasing	2002/2003	North Carolina Wildlife Resources Commission
North Dakota	250	N/A	1994	Turbak 1994
Ohio	48	Increasing	2003	Ohio Division of Wildlife
Oklahoma	N/A	Increasing	2004	Oklahoma Department of Wildlife Conservation
Oregon	N/A	Stable	2004	Oregon Department of Fish and Wildlife
Pennsylvania	4000	Stable	2004	Pennsylvania Game Commission
Rhode Island	Unknown	Stable	2003-2004	Rhode Island Department of Environmental Management
South Carolina	N/A	N/A		South Carolina Department of Natural Resources
South Dakota	5,349	Decreasing	2002	Huxoll 2002
Tennessee	N/A	N/A	2004	Tennessee Wildlife Resources Agency
Texas	Unknown	Stable/ Increasing	2004	Texas Parks and Wildlife Department
Utah	N/A	Stable	1995	Utah Division of Wildlife Resources
Vermont	N/A	Increasing	N/A	Vermont Fish and Wildlife Department
Virginia	Unknown	Increasing	2000	Virginia Department of Game and Inland Fisheries
Washington	N/A	Stable	2004	Washington Department of Fish and Wildlife
West Virginia	N/A	Decreasing	2003	West Virginia Division of Natural Resources
Wisconsin	3,018	Stable	2004	Wisconsin Wildlife Surveys
Wyoming	Unknown	Stable	2003	Wyoming Game and Fish Department
Nationwide	700,000– 1.5 million		1994	U.S. Fish and Wildlife Service (Turbak 1994)

NA = Data not available.

"harvestable surplus" of individuals (Connolly 1978; Wolfe and Chapman 1987), and that removal of this surplus benefits the population as a whole by reducing competition. For example, if a portion of a mule deer herd is killed, there is less competition for forage within the remaining herd, resulting in less starvation. Therefore, the initial deaths due to hunting "compensate for" or reduce other forms of natural mortality such as starvation. Whether the surplus individuals die by starvation, predation, or hunting makes no difference; advocates of this compensatory mortality theory view hunting as a substitute form of predation (Errington 1967; Wolfe and Chapman 1987; California Department of Fish and Game [CDFG] 2001). Bolen and Robinson (1999:176) explained harvest and hunting this way: "Hunting reduces the population, but the loss also increases the growth rate. The increase in growth is the consequence of higher birth rates and lower death rates, which result from decreased competition for food and other resources (i.e., with fewer animals, there are more resources per individual). Consequently, the accelerated growth rate provides a surplus of animals beyond the number required for replacing the losses—a surplus that can be harvested." The annual surplus/compensatory mortality theory has served as the cornerstone of exploitation (hunting/harvesting) theory for most terrestrial game animals for almost 60 years (Wolfe and Chapman 1987).

The opposing hypothesis, additive mortality, holds that hunting is additive to natural mortality. That is, the harvest causes a reduction in the population rather than no change, and it is just another obstacle to survival for a given population. It has been shown that, when causes of mortality occur at different times of the year, for example, their net effect is additive, but when they affect a population concurrently, the effect is partially compensatory (Wolfe and Chapman 1987). Whether hunting and trapping are additive depends on the animal species and on the intensity of the harvest in relation to the ability of the population to compensate. Up to a certain level or threshold, hunting mortality tends to be compensatory to natural mortality. Once that threshold is exceeded, however, hunting mortality becomes additive (CDFG 2001). Harley Shaw added that environmental conditions can influence this threshold as well: "Mortality can change from additive to compensatory, depending upon positioning relative to carrying capacity. Harvesting Southwest deer at the peak of drought effects is additive; during a wet period it might be compensatory." In reality, the hypotheses of compensatory and additive mortality can be viewed as opposite ends of a spectrum, similar to reproductive strategies. Compensatory mortality would be more common among furbearers such as muskrats, squirrels, and rabbits, animals that produce large numbers of offspring, most of which die before the next reproductive period. At the other extreme are the large furbearers such as bears and mountain lions, animals that produce few offspring and are much more likely to experience additive mortality. The majority of other furbearers lie somewhere in the middle, exhibiting an intermediate response between the two extremes that varies among populations and species (Wolfe and Chapman 1987).

However, the annual surplus/compensatory mortality hypothesis has its critics. Romesburg (1981) criticized wildlife professionals for often stating the hypothesis as if it were a law, rather than a derived hypothesis that remains untested. Romesburg mathematically demonstrated that when the threshold (the population level above which an animal can be harvested) is variable, an annual predictable surplus and compensation between harvest and natural mortality are not predictable. What makes the annual surplus/compensatory mortality hypothesis so controversial is the lack of reliable methods to accurately count animal populations and the tremendous variation in mortality rates, which precludes reliable inferences. This is further complicated by the unpredictable nature of natural mortality and hunting, which vary annually (Wolfe and Chapman 1987).

Still, wildlife managers are under tremendous pressure to produce sustained yields of harvestable animals each year. Maximum sustained yield (MSY) is the largest average harvest that can be taken continuously from a population under existing conditions (Bolen and Robinson 1999). Management of harvests for MSY is coming under increasing fire from wildlife biologists (Holt and Talbot 1978). Originally developed for the commercial fishing industry, the concept was extended to terrestrial wildlife management in the 1950s. MSY, like the compensatory mortality hypothesis, assumes that removal of animals from an exploited population reduces its size but causes an increased growth rate due to decreased competition for resources. This increased growth produces a harvestable surplus of animals (i.e., more animals than are needed to maintain the population's current size). The maximum level of sustainable yield is achieved by maintaining the base population at one-half of the carrying capacity. The model is based on several overly simplistic assumptions. For example, it pertains to the exploitation of single-species populations and does not account for the impact of harvest on the interactions among species (i.e., predators, prey, competitors). Management for MSY can also produce a population with a younger age structure (as in bobcats), which results in a net decrease in reproductive rate and may lead to overharvest. Additionally, it does not take into account the noneconomic values of a species, nor the changes in carrying capacity caused by climate or succession (Wolfe and Chapman 1987).

One alternative to MSY is optimum sustained yield (OSY). OSY uses both biological and sociological criteria that are more complex to integrate. But for managers, OSY is much more flexible and can be implemented with a margin of safety, because the sustainable harvest is usually lower than the MSY and results in higher equilibrium population levels (Dixon and Swift 1981; Rolley 1987).

Bobcat studies conducted in California by Lembeck and Gould (1979) and by Zezulak and Schwab (1979) indicated that natural mortality and reproduction tend to respond to harvest in a compensatory manner. Lembeck and Gould (1979:54) concluded that the primary differences between unharvested and harvested bobcat populations are in the number of kittens surviving, the types of mortality, and the age structure of the population, not in how bobcats occupy an area. "Harvesting creates vacancies which can be occupied by young bobcats and is reflected in the age structure data. Vacancies occur irregularly in the harvested population. However, these are usually filled by yearling and two-year old transients, a group of bobcats not very noticeable in the harvested population." In Minnesota, research conducted by Fuller and coworkers (1985b) showed, at one of two study sites, that harvest mortality was significantly higher when pelt prices were high. This suggests that harvest rates are independent of density and that exploitation could become additive when excessive. Anderson and Lovallo (2003) believed that harvest is primarily additive to other forms of mortality. Adult survival rates are highest in populations that are unexploited, but the effect of harvest on population growth may not be apparent because overall population size may remain relatively constant, although the proportion of yearlings and the percentage of breeding animals increase with lower adult survival rates.

During his seven years of intensive research on bobcats in southeastern Idaho, Knick (1990) developed a population model to describe how bobcat populations respond to various harvest levels. His model indicated that harvest has little impact on population size until it exceeds 20% of the population, but even small increases in harvest above 20% lead to large population declines (see Figure 6.1). Managers have long assumed that a harvest of less than 20% does not harm the survival of bobcat populations (Rolley 1987), but dynamic factors such as environmental conditions, poaching, disease, competitors, and prey availability can combine to make 20% excessive. In moderately exploited populations, survival rates can be as high as 60%. If managers set the legal harvest at 20%, poaching, predation, disease, and accidents are likely to kill another 20%. If any of these causes of death (e.g., poaching) increases so that the level of legal harvest is exceeded,

Figure 6.1

Relationship between harvest intensity and population size, age categories, and number of occupied territories (Knick 1990).

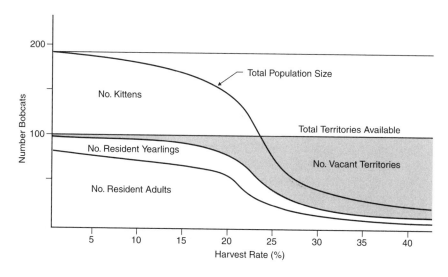

the bobcat population may decline. Moreover, to calculate 20% of the bobcat population, managers need a reasonable estimate of total population size, a number that is rarely known (Anderson and Lovallo 2003).

In states and provinces that permit harvest of bobcats, annual harvest estimates are obtained through the mandatory registration of carcasses. CITES mandates the tagging of all bobcat pelts entering the fur market. Pelt tags are usually durable plastic or metal seals of a locking design that indicate the species, state of origin, and year of harvest and have sequentially numbered figures stamped into the material. But not all harvested bobcats enter the fur market, because some are kept as trophies or taxidermic mounts. For this reason, some researchers recommend that states and provinces that use pelt registration to estimate the harvest should require all harvested bobcats be registered (Erickson 1982; Rolley 1987; Anderson and Lovallo 2003).

Wildlife managers also gather bobcat harvest data through fur dealer reports of transactions and surveys of furtakers (trappers and hunters). Because pelts are usually sold several times as they move through the fur market, wildlife managers need to be careful to distinguish between original sales and secondary sales in fur dealer reports. The reports must also account for pelts sold out of the state or province. Tallies of fur sales include only those pelts entering the fur market, so they may underestimate the total bobcat harvest during periods of low demand (Erickson 1982; Rolley 1987).

Furtaker surveys are questionnaires that are mailed to a portion of licensed trappers and hunters, who complete the surveys and return them to the wildlife agency for analysis (Erickson 1982). Rolley (1987) cautioned that the sampling method must be carefully designed, because hunters and trappers may both take bobcats in different jurisdictions and because licensing requirements may vary according to the method of take. Survey results are usually adjusted for biases that affect the accuracy of harvest estimates. Not all furtakers return the survey, and harvest effort and success frequently differ between respondents and nonrespondents (Filion 1980). Furtaker surveys can sometimes be used to estimate the number of harvested animals that are not sold or are sold out of state.

Wildlife managers have long used total annual harvest estimates of an animal as a reflection of its population levels. Although this may be valid for many game species, some biologists think it may not work for bobcats, or for other furbearers, for a variety of reasons. First, annual harvest estimates will reflect changes in population levels only if harvest pressure is relatively constant. Second, furbearer harvest levels are often directly related to pelt prices. Third, some furbearer harvest declines may occur only after repeated overharvests. And fourth, harvests may also be influenced by factors such as weather conditions during the fur harvest season (Erickson and Sampson 1978; Erickson 1982; Rolley 1987).

State agencies divide their annual game harvests into geographic zones or units. The effort exerted by each furtaker in the unit and the number of bobcats taken is a more accurate indicator of population status than is total harvest. Trends in license sales can signal changes in harvest effort. Questionnaires can be used to monitor changes in harvest effort per hunter or trapper and changes in bobcat abundance. However, an accurate measure of furtaker effort for bobcats may be difficult, because bobcats are often taken incidentally to harvest of other species (Rolley 1987).

Collected bobcat carcasses are often used to compile annual data on fecundity rates and age structure of the population. The age distribution of carcasses has also been used to infer changes in population size (Anderson and Lovallo 2003), but without additional data, age structure changes could imply an increasing, a decreasing, or a stable population (Caughley 1977). An alternative method for measuring bobcat harvest intensity involves combining the ratio of yearlings to adults with information about the prey base. If the prey base remains constant, an indication of a constant reproductive effort, then an increased yearling-to-adult ratio in a series of harvests would indicate increased harvest intensity. However, many other factors independent of prey can influence the reproduction and survival of bobcats (Knick 1990).

The most reliable way to assess changes in the bobcat population is to measure reproduction and survival. Survival rates are usually estimated from the age structure of the harvest. However, life tables require assumptions that are difficult to meet. For instance, if different age groups are more or less vulnerable to harvest (e.g., kittens are less vulnerable than adults to trapping), they may be either overrepresented or underrepresented. Additionally, life tables require knowledge of the rate of change, which is difficult to determine. Experts agree that radiotelemetry is the most accurate way to assess survival rates, but it is expensive and time-consuming and usually applies only to a small study area (Anderson and Lovallo 2003). As a result, it is infrequently used by state wildlife agencies (Bluett et al. 2001).

The California Example

California provides a good example of modern bobcat management and how changing public attitudes toward harvest are affecting policy. Until recently, bobcats could be taken with firearms (rifle, shotgun, or pistol), bow and arrow, or the use of dogs or traps. Taking is defined as hunting, pursuing, catching, capturing, or killing or attempting to hunt, pursue, catch, capture, or kill. Traps include padded-jaw leghold, conibear traps, snares, deadfalls, cage traps, and other devices designed to confine, hold, grasp, grip, clamp, or crush animals' bodies or body parts. Some hunters use a technique referred to as predator calling, which involves devices that mimic the sounds of prey or of a female in heat, to attract a bobcat. When the cat is within range, it is shot. This is legal. Specially trained tracking dogs were used to harvest almost 40% of the bobcats taken during the 1999–2000 season in California. The dogs use their sense of smell to locate a bobcat, then track and chase it, eventually "treeing" or "baying" the animal. Once in the false refuge of a tree, the bobcat is usually shot (CDFG 2001:12,17,72).

Trappers used to be able to kill bobcats (under authority of a trapping license) throughout California from November 24 through January 31 (a 69-day season). Trapping proficiency tests were required after January 1, 1983. Trappers had to demonstrate their knowledge of trapping regulations, trapping ethics, principles of wildlife management, natural history, trapping equipment, trap types, and setting of traps (CDFG 1986). However, on November 3, 1998, California voters approved Proposition 4, which made it illegal for any person "to trap for the purposes of recreation or commerce in fur any furbearing or nongame mammal with any body-gripping trap. Body-gripping traps include, but are not limited to, steel-jawed leghold traps, padded-jaw leghold traps, conibear traps and snares" (CDFG 2001:27). Hunters are still able to kill bobcats (under authority of a hunting license and bobcat hunting tags) throughout California from October 15 through February 28 (a 137-day season). Additionally, bobcats can be pursued with the aid of dogs from the day after the close of bobcat season through the day preceding the opening of the next bobcat season, except for special closures and restrictions set by the Fish and Game Commission or the Department of Fish and Game. This is known as the pursuit-only season, and houndsmen (hunters who use dogs) use this time to train their dogs and keep them fit. During this time, bobcats may be chased and treed, but not killed (CDFG 2001).

CDFG gathers various types of bobcat harvest information to monitor populations. CDFG requires annual reports from fur buyers and also requires all hunters to file reports that provide data on the number of animals taken in each county. These provide a rough estimate of the yearly harvest. The number of bobcats killed by Wildlife Services (U.S. Department of Agriculture) is also added to the total. Anyone wishing to sell or transport a bobcat fur must have it tagged by CDFG. As part of the tagging process, the hunter must provide CDFG with information on place, method of take, sex, and date. Each hunter is allowed five bobcat tags per year, and each time a bobcat is killed, a tag must be filled out and returned to CDFG (CDFG 2001).

Wildlife biologists with the CDFG have developed a mathematical bobcat population model based on population estimates and biological data (see Table 6.2.) Using the Wildlife Habitat Relationships (WHR) System, a sophisticated wildlife habitat information database, biologists found that bobcats reside in 42 of the 48 habitat types in California, consisting of 81,695,757 acres. According to CDFG's recommendations for the 2001–2002 season, "[bobcat] densities (expressed as individuals per square mile) were obtained from various sources in the wildlife literature. When California data were not available, out-of-state studies were used. The total square miles of all habitats for a particular species were divided by the density of the species to calculate low and high range population estimates. Generally, the lowest and highest densities that could be found in the literature were used. These low and high variations in population size account for the annual differences in densities due to habitat type, food availability, weather, and other factors" (CDFG 2001).

Table 6.2
**California Department of Fish and Game
Bobcat Population Model, 2001**

Parameter	
Total acres of habitat	81,695,757
Total square miles	127,650
Low density (no./sq. mi.)	0.55
High density (no./sq. mi.)	0.58
Sex ratio	0.50
Female breeding season	0.53
Litter size	2.70
Adult mortality	0.41
Juvenile mortality (estimate)	0.20

	Low/High
Total adults	70,207/74,037
Breeding females	18,605/19,620
Young at den	50,233/52,973
Population before mortality	120,441/127,010
Juvenile mortality	10,047/10,595
Adult mortality	28,785/30,355
Total mortality (including harvest)	38,832/40,950
Population after mortality	81,609/86,060
Increase if harvest compensatory	11,402/12,024
Increase if harvest additive	10,081/10,703
Trapping (10-y average)	840
Wildlife Services + 33% (1999–2000)	129
Hunting (1999–2000)	352
Annual harvest mortality	1,321

This model demonstrates that the bobcat population, beginning its annual cycle in the spring season with 70,207 adults, will produce 50,233 young during spring and summer and experience an annual mortality of 38,832 animals (37,511 from natural causes and 1,321 from harvest) during this annual cycle. There will be an increase of 11,402 bobcats to the adult population if the harvest is considered compensatory, or an increase of 10,081 if the harvest is considered additive. These increases are an expression of biotic potential only and would not be expected to occur if the bobcat population were at carrying capacity.

Source: CDFG, 2001.

Agency biologists drew heavily from the work of bobcat researchers Knick (1990) and Rolley (1983). Bobcat density estimates in the various habitats ranged from 0.55 to 0.58 per square mile. Using these data, CDFG estimated that there were between 70,207 and 74,037 adult bobcats in California, making it one of only eight states to offer a statewide bobcat population estimate (see Table 6.1) CDFG also emphasized that, since the 1982–1983 season, total annual harvest of bobcats has remained below the 14,400 statewide harvest threshold limit set in consultation with the USFWS Office of Scientific Authority and in accordance with CITES (CDFG 2001).

Knowledge of the effects of harvest on bobcat populations is incomplete. Human exploitation, both legal and illegal, seems to be the most common cause of death in bobcats (Anderson 1987; Anderson and Lovallo 2003). High harvest pressure appears to cause a shift in age distribution in exploited populations and may alter sex ratios in different age groups. Adult survival is much higher in unharvested populations than in harvested populations (Knick 1990; Chamberlain et al. 1999). Males dies more frequently than females, especially during their first several years as adults, although this may be due to a greater susceptibility of males to trapping (McCord and Cardoza 1982; Anderson and Lovallo 2003). Gilbert (1979) suggested that sex ratios may reflect the intensity of harvest. However, he warned that varying sex ratios can be the result of biased measuring techniques, and Koehler (personal communication) cautioned that one cannot assume the actual population structure is equal to the harvest sample, because different age groups are more or less susceptible to hunting and trapping. Leyhausen expressed particular concern about changes in bobcat age-class structure during heavy exploitation. He felt that there should be consideration of how such age-class changes perturb social organization, bobcat prey, and eventually other animals and plants in the ecosystem. He also pointed out that little is known about self regulating mechanisms, or even whether these exist in bobcat populations (Dyer 1979). Rolley (1987) believed that furbearer managers lack the knowledge and tools to effectively manage bobcat populations for either MSY or an OSY. He felt that population estimates lack precision and are seriously biased. He added that little information is available on the carrying capacity of various bobcat habitats. Anderson and Lovallo (2003) pointed out that harvest is somewhat independent of density, which makes bobcat populations vulnerable to overexploitation. For almost 25 years, researchers have consistently identified the need for better data on harvest impacts (McCord and Cardoza 1982; Anderson 1987; Bluett et al. 2001).

The data available on wild bobcat populations and the information on the number of bobcats harvested vary greatly from state to state. For instance, from 1977 to 1986, fewer than 40 bobcats were taken each year in Massachusetts and New Hampshire, whereas more than 12,000 were harvested annually in California. Texas holds the record for the greatest number of bobcats harvested in a single season, with 17,686 killed during 1985–1986 (Sunquist and Sunquist 2002). Harvest in the United States and Canada peaked between 1977 and 1987, averaging 94,000 pelts annually, until the stock market crash of 1987. Fur markets remained sluggish throughout the 1990s and then rebounded in the first years of the new century (see Figure 5.3 in Chapter 5). According to the International Association of Fish and Wildlife Agencies (IAWFA), 1,484,383 bobcats were harvested in the United States between 1970 and 2003, with a total fur value of more than $110 million (see Figure 5.3 in Chapter 5).

Bobcat pelt prices, bobcat harvest, and bobcat pelt exports are all increasing. In May 2005, according to the North American Fur Auction, 11,247 bobcat pelts were sold at an average price of $88.00. An exceptional pelt brought $625.00 (North American Fur Auctions 2005). The USFWS Office of Management Authority reported that 30,400 bobcat pelts valued at $4,438,021 were exported in 2003. This is

Figure 6.2

U.S. bobcat pelts exported, 1978–2003* (USFWS Office of Management Authority).

* Does not include Arizona, Arkansas, Colorado, or West Virginia.

** Does not include Kentucky, North Dakota or West Virginia.

^ Does not include Arizona, Colorado, Louisiana, Maine, Missouri, North Carolina, Tennessee, Washington, Wisconsin or Wyoming.

^^ Does not include Alabama, Arizona, Colorado, Idaho, Louisiana, Maine, Michigan, Missouri, North Carolina, North Dakota, Tennessee, Washington, Wisconsin, or Wyoming.

+ Data from World Conservation Monitoring Centre.

Note: Not all harvested pelts are exported; some are kept for domestic use. Not all tagged pelts are exported the same year they are harvested; some are retained in storage until later shipment.

a substantial increase over the 18,923 pelts, valued at $2,114,931, that were exported in 2002. Countries buying the majority of the fur include Canada (most likely for reexport), the United Kingdom, Greece, Italy, and Hong Kong (USWFS 2004c) (see Figures 6.2 and 6.3). The pelts are transformed into coats, trim, and accessories, with the white, spotted belly fur being the most valuable. Fur graders and buyers sometimes refer to bobcat pelts from northern or mountainous regions as being from lynx cats, and pelts from southern or lowland areas as being from bobcats (Obbard 1987). Currently, approximately half of the bobcats harvested in the United States are retained for domestic use (Sunquist and Sunquist 2002).

Wildlife agencies are subject to immense political pressures, not only from state, provincial, and federal legislators but from private lobbying groups, including hunters, trappers, and wildlife professionals. Frequently, sound management gives way to the demands of a special interest group (Wolfe and Chapman 1987). Because almost all wildlife managers depend on hunting license purchases as their primary source of revenue, the focus of management has been on maximizing populations for the benefit of hunters. As a result, the partnership between the hunting community and wildlife managers has a long tradition, and the influence of the hunting community on game management practices is substantial. In many cases, game populations are not managed *by* hunting, as is so often claimed; rather, populations are managed *for* hunting. Under such circumstances, politics frequently plays a bigger role in management decisions than does biology.

Anderson and Lovallo (2003) pointed out that harvest level is driven by pelt prices and accessibility. This is the most important difference between furbearer management and game management: furbearer management has a profit motive. This means that demand for furbearers can change radically with shifting fur markets. Managers must understand that demand for furbearers changes independently of furbearer population trends (Shaw 1985). In the case of bobcats, profit motive is a far greater influence than science in the management of the species.

Research and Management Needs

In his summary remarks at the Bobcat Research Conference held in Front Royal, Virginia, in 1979, Dyer expressed concern that bobcat research lacked rigor. As evidence, he pointed to a tendency to ignore study objectives, failure to clearly state hypotheses, and a failure to use all pertinent scientific literature. There was no discussion of niche/competition theory, and home range was repeatedly discussed, but not in context. He felt that many wildlife agencies had succumbed to public and political pressure by embarking on bobcat research projects using radiotelemetry without having strong scientific questions or testable hypotheses backing up the need for such work. Estimates of population density suffered from too great an extrapolation from relatively small sample sizes over large expanses, leading to a credibility problem. He believed it was necessary to consider major

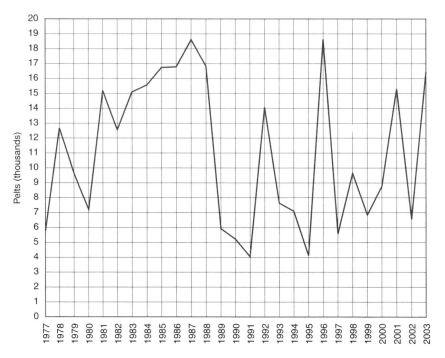

Figure 6.3
Canadian bobcat pelts exported, 1977–2003. Note that some pelts are imported to Canada from the United States and then exported to a third country. Some pelts are imported to Canada from the United States, converted into garments, and then exported to a third country. Not all harvested pelts are exported in the same year they are harvested; some are retained in storage until later shipment (World Conservation Monitoring Centre).

changes in the way bobcat research and management are conducted to satisfy both CITES and local issues. Lastly, Dyer urged a broader approach, placing bobcats in the context of community and ecosystem models as the primary driving force behind management strategies (Dyer 1979; Woolf and Nielsen 2001).

McCord and Cardoza (1982) identified the greatest research need as long-term intensive studies that include known sex and age structure, reproductive activities, home ranges, habitat use, food habits, trends in prey species, and interactions with other predators. They also suggested that the population should be harvested at different levels, to evaluate the impact of harvest on reproduction, sex and age structure, and home range establishment. Another research need identified was evaluation of the mortality rate of juveniles after dispersal and its importance in maintaining stable populations. Exploited and unexploited populations in different regions of the country need to be compared to evaluate age and sex structure, recruitment, home range establishment, and mortality. They also recommended studies of reintroduced bobcats, focusing on the best sex and age for released animals. As described in the next section, bobcats have been successfully reintroduced in New Jersey (Turbak 1994; Anderson and Lovallo 2003) and on Cumberland Island, Georgia (Diefenbach et al.1993; Anderson and Lovallo 2003).

In his critical review of bobcat literature, Anderson (1987) reiterated the need to better understand the effects of harvest on bobcat productivity, sex and age ratios, mortality rates, age of sexual maturity, dispersal rates and patterns, and social organization. He agreed there was a pressing need for an accurate, nondestructive census technique to detect changes in population numbers, one that would be applicable across a variety of habitats and climates. He also stressed how bobcat research would benefit from long-term studies that spanned decades instead of months. Other areas of inquiry included more information on bobcat physiology, especially thermal regulation, and a reexamination of taxonomy. New advances in molecular genetics may shed some light on felid relatedness and bobcat subspecies (Sunquist and Sunquist 2002).

Rolley (1987:679) suggested the need to quantify the relationship between bobcat population density and indices such as scent-station surveys and track counts. He added that such research would require the manipulation of bobcat populations through harvest. He also urged, "Although the use of techniques that have not been validated—be they population indices, aging techniques, or methods for estimating fecundity and mortality—may be a practical necessity in light of the possible consequences of no action, this leaves the furbearer manager open to making erroneous conclusions. Although skepticism is needed, managers should resist the temptation to criticize unvalidated techniques when they produce results that do not agree with their preconceived ideas. In other words, if a population index shows a decline, it may be because the population has actually declined and not just because of a problem with the technique." Rolley also warned that additional research, along with the increased administrative responsibilities resulting from CITES, will require that additional funds be provided for furbearer management programs. He suggested that additional funding should come from increased trapping license fees or a charge for issuing export tags. Another potential source of additional research revenue might be an excise tax on traps, trapping supplies, and fur products.

Conner and Leopold (1996) pointed out that research is needed to determine the relationship of forest management practices to prey abundance and bobcat habitat use. They believed that the influences of habitat structure, as affected by forest management, would be of particular importance in understanding predator-prey-habitat relationships in forests ecosystems.

In 1996, Woolf and Hubert (1998) conducted a comprehensive survey of state wildlife agencies to identify the top research and management needs for bobcats. Research needs were compiled by Bluett and associates (2001:69) in order of rank:

1. Reliable survey methods.
2. Demographics (e.g., mortality, recruitment).
3. Distribution and abundance.
4. Habitat availability and use.
5. Interactions with coyotes and other carnivores.

The top five identified management needs were the following:

1. Control harvest to better match geographic/temporal difference in abundance.
2. Monitor abundance.
3. Protect or improve habitat.
4. Improve public knowledge of and support for management techniques.
5. Evaluate effectiveness of and need for federal oversight.

Consistent with previous analyses of key research questions, the most pressing need is to develop a more precise index of abundance that is comparable across a variety of habitats and climates. Of all the wildlife biologists surveyed in the contiguous 48 states, 63% indicated a need for more reliable survey techniques and better information about the distribution, abundance, and demographics of bobcats (Woolf and Hubert 1998; Anderson and Lovallo 2003).

Despite 21 intervening years of studies, Anderson and Lovallo, in 2003, still agreed with McCord and Cardoza (1982) that bobcat management could benefit from long-term studies spanning decades instead of months. They believed that some of the conflicting results between studies might be reconciled by longer views of a population through time. Many of the generalizations about bobcat biology have been extrapolated from research on very few individuals in very few environments—something Dyer (1979) criticized. Increasing sample sizes should help biologists understand the variability and consistency of observations across a variety of temporal and spatial scales. Recent studies by Chamberlain and colleagues (2003) and by Nielsen and Woolf (2001) have shown this to be true. Of course, lack of funds is always a problem in agencies and universities.

Two other areas in need of investigation are disease and taxonomy. Understanding the impact of disease on bobcat population dynamics and behavior and monitoring the movement of disease and parasite loads through populations are likely to be important to future management. Bobcat taxonomy needs careful reconsideration. DNA analysis could reduce the number of bobcat subspecies into more biologically significant groupings (Anderson and Lovallo 2003). However, as Dave Maehr (personal communication) warned,

> Genetics can be used to lump or split species and subspecies, but species
> and subspecies were originally described based on morphology, color, and

other phenotypic characters. Genetics should be viewed as one tool among many. The issue is the potential loss of biodiversity if we believe that currently available genetic tools are sufficient to say that populations are similar or not. For example, it is now popular to consider North American pumas as a single subspecies—based solely on genetics. Does this mean that the phenotypic differences are meaningless, and that evolutionary forces were not acting differently in different parts of its range? I think not. Such thinking has the potential to lead toward biotic homogenization as we find it increasingly convenient to move animals around for the sake of management and conservation. Homogenized milk is great, but homogenized biodiversity is not.

During the Wildlife Society 2000 Conference in Nashville, Tennessee, in September 2000, a symposium was held entitled, "Current Bobcat Research and Implications for Management" (Woolf et al. 2001). Wolf and Nielsen (2001) offered an assessment of bobcat research and management over the previous two decades and a response to Dyer's (1979) criticisms at the Front Royal conference. They announced that powerful new tools such as computers, radiotelemetry, and remote sensing offer deeper insights into bobcat ecology. They felt that the quality and rigor of the papers presented during the symposium could withstand critical peer review. Recent studies reflected clear hypotheses and examined bobcats in the context of the habitats they occupied, at temporal and spatial scales not previously possible. They emphasized that both niche and competition theory were addressed through meshing of theoretical and empirical approaches. Most importantly, they believed that new research tools allow insights into bobcat-habitat relationships that hold promise for habitat-based management decisions in the future.

The researchers at the conference believed that the continental bobcat population was healthy (Woolf and Hubert 1998) and that fears for its future, expressed in the 1970s, had been unfounded. They pointed to the recent delisting of the bobcat as threatened in the State of Illinois (Bluett et al. 2001) and the Pennsylvania Game Commission's approval of the first legal harvest of bobcats in 30 years (Lovallo 2001). They expressed confidence that better data were available with which to implement science-based management. This would allow wildlife agencies to make bobcat harvest management decisions that can withstand legal challenges (Rolley et al. 2001).

Bobcat Conservation

Conner and Leopold (1996) suggested that, with the increasing popularity of ecosystem management, wildlife managers need species that can serve as reliable indicators of ecosystem health. Because bobcats as predators are intimately tied to their prey, they could be such an indicator. However, before this idea can be implemented, further research is needed to relate prey species abundance to bobcat diet, home range size, and density.

Protecting bobcat habitat is fundamental to conservation of the feline, but specific habitat prescriptions are problematic, because the species is so widely distributed and management strategies vary with habitat type. Any effort that improves the habitat for hares and rabbits, protects sufficient cover for stalking and ambush, and provides or protects den sites should improve the quality of the habitat for bobcats (Anderson and Lovallo 2003).

In Pennsylvania, Lovallo (1999) used a combination of radiotelemetry-determined locations, geographic information systems (GIS), computer simulations, and remotely sensed landcover and physiographical data to model bobcat habitat selection and predict statewide distribution. He found a general correspondence between the statewide distribution of female bobcat home ranges and reports of established populations, sightings, and captures by trappers. In Mississippi, Conner and colleagues (2001) developed similar computer models of habitat selection for bobcats. These models provide a foundation for habitat-based management and conservation strategies and can serve as a basis for development of further hypotheses concerning local- and landscape-level habitat preferences (Anderson and Lovallo 2003).

The CDFG conducted an analysis to determine what habitat changes could be expected to affect the bobcat and other furbearing mammals in the future. This impact analysis was based on the CALPLAN computer simulation model, which was developed to forecast future changes in vegetation and habitat productivity. CALPLAN compiles data on interactions between landowner management objectives, resource supply and conditions, available markets, and large-scale social, political, economic, and demographic trends. The underlying premise of the model is that these trends affect how landowners (public and private) manage land. The six most important habitats within the state for bobcat (chamise redshank chaparral, coast scrub, low sagebrush, mixed chaparral, montane chaparral, and sagebrush) were identified, and each was assigned a value for percentage increase or decrease projected over the decade 2000–2010 compared with 1990–2000. The greatest decline (4%) over the next decade was expected to occur in the coast scrub habitat type, particularly in San Diego and Santa Clara counties, areas of extensive residential development (CDFG 2001).

In British Columbia, the availability of suitable winter habitat appears to be the primary factor limiting bobcat abundance. In most regions of the province, the primary winter habitat coincides with intensively used lands in low-elevation areas where agriculture, settlement, wood fiber production, and roads are concentrated. Bobcat harvesters are advised to take all opportunities to provide input on government land. The major role of hunters and trappers in habitat management is in providing information on where bobcats occur, because forest and habitat managers rarely gather such information on their own. Areas used

148

by wintering deer usually have cover, exposure, and snow-shedding characteristics that benefit bobcats. These areas need to be identified in resource development plans. Finally, written records of harvest locations and sightings of both animals and sign are useful for documenting valuable habitat (Hatler et al. 2003).

Bobcats have been successfully reintroduced to northwestern New Jersey and on Cumberland Island, off the southeast coast of Georgia. From 1978 to 1982, wildlife officials imported 24 bobcats from Maine to New Jersey. There were some early casualties, with one male traveling almost 100 miles north before being killed in New York. Another survived only eight months before being hit by a vehicle ten miles from its release site. However, the remaining new residents seem to have settled in. They are now consistently producing young and expanding their range in the state with the densest human population in the United States. Bobcats now share one township of eight square miles with 15,000 people. In 1994, shoppers in the town of Rockaway were surprised to see a young bobcat stroll through the parking lot of their local mall (Turbak 1994; Anderson and Lovallo 2003).

Further down the East Coast, on the 20,000-acre Cumberland Island, the largest bobcat reintroduction effort ever attempted also appears to have been successful. This multiagency effort involved capturing 32 bobcats in the fall of 1988 and 1989 on the Coastal Plain of Georgia, holding them in quarantine for several weeks, and then reintroducing them to the island one to two miles offshore. While the cats were in quarantine, a prey digestibility study was conducted, and the bobcats were sexed, weighed, measured, and vaccinated. Blood samples were collected, and each bobcat was fitted with a radio transmitter. They were released in groups of two to six, about one month apart. Each bobcat was released in an area on the island that was believed to be outside the home range of previously released bobcats. Most of the new arrivals adapted to their new homes, although one female swam back to the mainland and one male ran into the Atlantic Ocean and drowned. In the spring of 1989, four dens and ten kittens were found. The bobcats on Cumberland Island have established home ranges and appear to be healthy, breeding, reproducing, and surviving. The project biologists stress the importance of continued monitoring and genetic studies to determine whether bobcats can maintain a population over the long term on Cumberland Island (Diefenbach et al.1993; Anderson and Lovallo 2003).

Because bobcats are not an endangered species and are abundant in the southeastern United States, the reintroduction effort on Cumberland Island provides an opportunity to experiment with a felid reintroduction without jeopardizing the species' existence. Future studies on Cumberland Island may allow researchers to examine the dynamics of a limited gene pool and any evolutionary bottlenecks the population may encounter. The reintroduction of bobcats to Cumberland Island provides a rare opportunity to test theoretical models of population dynamics and genetics and to empirically evaluate the effects of various management strategies on enhancing the long-term viability of an insular, or endangered, felid population (Diefenbach et al. 1993).

Human Dimensions

It is a traditional lament of wildlife biologists that wildlife management is 10% managing wildlife and 90% managing people (Fazio and Gilbert 1986). Academics and some state wildlife agencies recognize the importance of people management and have christened this specialty "human dimensions of wildlife management." Human dimensions refers to how people value wildlife, how they want wildlife to be managed, and how they affect or are affected by wildlife and wildlife management decisions. Only since the mid-1970s has human dimensions of wildlife management become an organized field of study, whereas the study of biological dimensions has been at the core of wildlife management since its beginning in the 1930s. In addition to schooling in ecology, wildlife biology, and botany, modern wildlife managers must be trained in sociology, economics, business administration, and biopolitics. Current wildlife agency education programs are beginning to extend beyond just hunter safety or trapper education programs. Many agencies are striving to expand into environmental education, protecting wildlife habitat, preserving biological diversity, and managing ecosystems instead of species. Some are reaching out to nonconsumptive constituents such as bird watchers, wildlife photographers, amateur naturalists, campers, hikers, and mainstream environmental groups (Decker et al. 2001).

Human dimensions research has shown that, along with an increasing variety of responsibilities, wildlife managers must serve an increasing variety of stakeholders. A stakeholder is any person who will affect, or be affected by, wildlife management. In the early years of wildlife management, the primary stakeholders were hunters, anglers, and trappers. Although these three groups remain important, modern stakeholders also include wildlife watchers, farmers, ranchers, businesses that cater to recreationists (gas stations, motels, restaurants, sporting goods stores, trapping equipment suppliers, guides, and outfitters), local government officials, motorists, boaters, park users, state and federal land managers, wildlife boards and commissions, and wildlife biologists and managers (Decker et al. 2001).

Not surprisingly, early research in human dimensions also showed that different stakeholders hold different values and attitudes toward wildlife, depending on individual experience and vested interest. Kellert (1980) developed a conceptual framework that identifies 11 attitudes toward wildlife. These are adapted for bobcats in Table 6.3.

Kellert (1985) has also examined how attitudes toward wildlife changed between 1900 and 1975. He found that utilitarian attitudes had declined as the need for use of wildlife for food and clothing declined. Public perceptions of wildlife changed as well; in contemporary times, people show less fear, hostility, and indifference toward wildlife. Many of these attitudes are manifest in stakeholders who influence bobcat management. An appreciation of the diversity of these attitudes, and how attitudes change over time, can help wildlife managers develop a

Table 6.3
Human Attitudes Toward Bobcats

Naturalistic

Emphasizes personal experiences people have with bobcats. Those experiences engage human curiosity and imagination and invoke feelings of adventure, exploration, discovery, and satisfaction of skill in getting close to bobcats to either hunt or observe them.

Ecologistic

Emphasizes concern for the environment as a system, and for interrelationships between bobcats and natural habitats.

Humanistic

Acknowledges the emotional connection of people to nature that fosters affection and concern. This is demonstrated by the increased protection for bobcats since the mid-1970s.

Moralistic

Pertains to the ethical responsibility that people have to conserve bobcats and to treat bobcats with respect. This has been demonstrated by the trend toward greater protection for bobcats and regulations governing their management.

Scientific

Pertains to direct study and understanding of bobcats, which foster intellectual growth about nature that can result in practical advantages to people and promote an attitude of caring for nature.

Aesthetic

Refers to the physical attraction of nature to people. Bobcats are often featured in art (e.g., photographs, paintings, sculpture) and other visual media. Bobcats invoke impressions of nature's refinement and beauty. Aesthetic perceptions of nature may have evolved in humans through our connection with animals and habitats that gave us sustenance and safety and caused people to hone survival skills.

Utilitarian

Focuses on the practical and material value. Bobcat trapping and hunting provides income to furtakers, especially when pelt prices are high. Economic benefits accrue to rural communities and specialists (e.g., taxidermists, trapping equipment companies) that provide trapping- and hunting-related services. Wild landscapes that support bobcat and prey populations provide ecosystem services, such as clean water and air, and outdoor recreation opportunities, including consumptive and nonconsumptive uses. Bobcats also contribute to the integrity of wild ecosystems through interactions with prey.

Dominionistic

Refers to the human inclination to subdue nature. This includes controlling bobcats to protect the health and safety of people and domestic animals. Hunting bobcats to either kill them or enjoy them in a nonconsumptive way (e.g., observation, photography) can demonstrate an ability to function in challenging conditions and to express strength, vigor, and boldness. This includes hunting for pure enjoyment and its competitive opportunities.

(continued)

Table 6.3
(Continued)

Negativistic

Emphasizes fear and aversion toward bobcats, and anxiety about the risk of attack—particularly to one's self and family. This may include concern over domestic and game animals that are a source of food. Such feelings may also elicit awe and respect for the animal.

Neutralistic

Represents a passive avoidance of bobcats due to indifference or lack of interest.

Symbolic

Refers the figurative significance of bobcats in modern society expressed in children's books and toys, in marketing and advertising, and as symbolic animals for schools, colleges, universities, and the professional sports industry.

Sources: Adapted from Kellert 1980; Decker et al. 2001; Kellert and Smith 2001; Cougar Management Guidelines Working Group 2005.

biologically sound and socially acceptable policy (Cougar Management Guidelines Working Group 2005).

One example of how changing stakeholder attitudes are affecting wildlife is the controversy that has plagued trapping and hunting since the turn of the century. Disagreements have been especially intense regarding furbearers such as the bobcat (Andelt et al. 1999; Manfredo et al. 1999). Advocates of trapping insist that:

1. Trapping provides wildlife managers with important information to monitor furbearer populations.
2. Trapping allows humans to use an annual crop that would otherwise be lost to other forms of death.
3. Sale of furs is important to the economies of remote communities and individuals.
4. Trapping suppresses diseases such as rabies and distemper.
5. Depredating animals can be controlled.
6. Death for a trapped animal is less traumatic than death by disease, predation, or starvation.

Those who oppose trapping offer equally enthusiastic arguments against the practice:

1. Trapping is cruel; animals caught in traps suffer pain and loss of limbs.
2. It is immoral to kill an animal for its fur.
3. Nontarget animals, including threatened, endangered, and protected species, as well as pets, are killed or injured by traps.
4. Trapping negatively affects sex and age ratios of target species.

5. Trapping may be additive rather than compensatory to populations.
6. Random trapping has no value in the control of disease or depredation.

Similar arguments are marshaled by stakeholders who are in favor of, or oppose, hunting of bobcats. Proponents of hunting argue that:

1. Fewer animals are killed by sport hunting than die each year of natural causes.
2. Most of the time hunting is compensatory, not additive.
3. Hunting offers legitimate recreational opportunities.
4. Hunting provides income to wildlife agencies through the sale of licenses, tags, and other forms of revenue.

Hunting has its share of critics as well, especially among the animal rights organizations. They maintain that:

1. Wildlife management agencies lack sufficient data on animal populations.
2. Hunting is contrary to human social values and is an unnecessary infliction of pain and death.
3. Hunting has a negative affect on sex and age ratios of target animals.
4. Hunting may be additive rather than compensatory to animal populations.
5. Hunting has no value in the control of disease or depredation.

Additionally, most bobcat hunters are houndsmen, and the use of dogs to pursue and hunt animals is controversial in itself. There are those who believe that the use of tracking dogs gives hunters an unfair advantage, causes stress to wildlife, and allows for potential abuse and injury to the dogs; they believe that both pursuit and hunting of mammals with dogs should be prohibited. Conversely, advocates contend that the use of dogs is a legitimate method of assisting in locating mammals while hunting and that pursuit-only provisions in existing regulations prevent significant negative impacts on mammal populations (Bolen and Robinson 1999; CDFG 2001).

Agency biologists are aware of the unpopularity of consumptive wildlife use among the general public. For instance, Armstrong and Rossi (2000) interviewed furbearer biologists in 48 states who indicated their state had some form of trapping license and related management within their agency. They concluded that participation in trapping has been declining, and they identified five reasons: antitrapping sentiment, lack of recruitment of new trappers, pelt prices, public image, and access to land.

Wildlife agencies have long depended on revenue from hunting and fishing licenses to operate. The common refrain was "hunting and fishing pays the bills." However, in a continuing pattern of changing attitudes toward wildlife, nonconsumptive stakeholders now spend more than consumptive stakeholders do. The USFWS reported that, in 2001, more than 34 million anglers spent $35.6 billion, or $1,046 apiece. In addition, more than 13 million hunters spent $20.6 billion, or $1,581 each. However, more than 66 million people spent $40 billion observing, feeding, and photographing wildlife in that same year (USFWS 2001). Unfortunately, much of the revenue generated from nonconsumptive users does not go to wildlife management.

With ever-expanding human populations pushing urban, residential, and agricultural development deeper into wildlife habitat, conflicts between humans and wild animals are increasing. A common tool used to assess human attitudes toward wildlife in these situations is the survey. Casey and colleagues (2005) conducted a telephone survey of local wildlife managers and a mail survey of suburban residents' knowledge of and attitude toward pumas near Tucson, Arizona. All agencies wanted more information to improve management of pumas. More than half of the individual residents surveyed responded, but their knowledge of puma biology was limited. Respondents supported management of pumas in all landscapes and opposed actions that removed protections. Local support for puma conservation was high, and investigators recommended that educational opportunities be created so that local residents could be informed about puma research and management.

The Arizona Game and Fish Department receives about 2000 telephone calls each year reporting bobcats, coyotes, mountain lions, and other wild mammals in the parks, streets, yards, and swimming pools of metropolitan Tucson. Elissa Ostergaard, urban wildlife specialist with the department, offered the following breakdown: 475 calls about bobcats, 380 calls about javelinas, 225 about coyotes, and 280 about mountain lions—at least half of which turned out to be bobcats or other small mammals (Davis 2005b).

Despite the rampant growth of urban areas and their encroachment into wildlife habitat in the United States, use of developed areas by bobcats has been rarely studied. Harrison (1998) used a mail survey to examine bobcat sightings and attitudes of homeowners toward the felid in three residential areas in New Mexico. He found that bobcats frequented residential areas and moved within the vicinity of houses, including those occurring in urban-level densities. Residents reported that more than 70% of bobcat sightings were within 25 meters of a house. Bobcats were most frequently seen in winter near areas with higher densities of houses, and most sightings were clustered near large undeveloped areas. Homeowner attitudes toward bobcats were the mostly positive. However, residents in two semirural areas were more responsive to the survey and liked the idea of having bobcats in their area more than did homeowners in an urban region.

Important biopolitical lessons were learned from the reintroduction of bobcats on Cumberland Island. The original objective of the project, as outlined in National Park Service documents and the original research proposal, was to restore biodiversity. A secondary justification of the bobcat reintroduction was to control the white-tailed deer population on the island. This was presented both in the Environmental Assessment and during two public meetings before the restoration effort took place. Within only six months after the arrival of the bobcats, the media characterized the reintroduction as a failure because the felines had done little to control deer. The researchers pointed out that it is unrealistic to expect an immediate response of a prey population to a reintroduced predator. They monitored the deer with seasonal surveys and estimated the occurrence of prey in bobcat diets by analyzing scats. This should have allowed them to infer the impact of bobcat predation on deer and other prey. Where the investigators felt they erred was in not emphasizing the original objective of restoring biodiversity They underestimated public support for a reintroduction for its own sake and therefore overemphasized the idea of the bobcat as a controlling agent. They recommended incorporating surveys of public concerns early in the planning stages of reintroduction projects. Such surveys can provide important data for an information and education program that can be used to lessen public opposition and increase public support and approval of wildlife reintroduction projects. Restoration should be justified based on a straightforward, primary objective. "In the final analysis, complete and correct information is critical to the public's understanding and support of any wildlife research or management program, including reintroduction" (Warren et al. 1990:587–588).

A few years after the reintroduction, Brooks and colleagues (1999) documented visitor attitudes toward and knowledge of reintroduced bobcats on Cumberland Island. They compared four visitor use groups—deer hunters, day-use visitors, developed-site campers, and backcountry campers—concerning their attitudes and knowledge, using a questionnaire distributed on ferries and at island campsites. With a response rate of more than 80%, deer hunters were less positive about the restored bobcats but had greater knowledge of the conservation effort than the three other user groups did. This indicated that the National Park Service, who administers the island, should design wildlife interpretive and education programs to address the differences in attitudes and knowledge among visitor user groups.

Bluett and associates (2001) lamented that there had been a fundamental shift since 1980 in social and political attitudes, not only toward wildlife, but also toward the role of wildlife managers. Decision-making based on science had given way to greater public involvement (Decker and Chase 1997). In addition to their traditional responsibilities, wildlife managers now had to contend with international treaties (Hamilton et al. 1998), citizen-sponsored ballot measures (Minnis 1998), litigation (Olson 1995), legislation (Wildlife Legislative Fund of America 1999), and public opinion (Andelt et al. 1999; Manfredo et al. 1999). In Illinois, where the bobcat was recently removed from the state list of threatened species, Woolf and Nielsen (2002:32) believed that certain stakeholders would oppose any management strategy other than continued full protection from harvest. Any proposal to hunt and trap bobcats, however restrictive, would likely be opposed in public forums and by legal action. They concluded, "Because agencies such as IDNR [Illinois Department of Natural Resources] require public support of their policies to effectively manage natural resources, whether or not a bobcat harvest is ever allowed in Illinois will be decided by public opinion rather than biological data."

Afterword: Bobcats Beyond

Dos Palmas Preserve is a 15,000-acre wildlife refuge and nature preserve in the blistering Sonoran Desert of southern California. At 130 feet below sea level in the Salt Creek Basin, the preserve's green landscape contrasts sharply with the grays and browns of the surrounding desert and mountains—the Orocopia Mountains to the north, the Chocolate Mountains to the east, and Santa Rosa Mountains (and Salton Sea) to the west and south. Underground water flowing south out of the Orocopia Mountains is dammed by a series of subterranean faults and forced to the surface as artesian springs, each ringed by a lush fan palm oases. These oases provide the green islands of life the preserve was created to protect. The endangered desert pupfish (Cyprinodon macularis) and Yuma clapper rail (Rallus longirostris yumanensis), as well as roadrunner, California yellow bat, gray fox, coyote, and bobcat, all make these oases their home. Ecologists estimate that one-third of all Sonoran Desert wildlife depend on fan palm oases for water, food, or cover.

One hot summer evening, I was exploring the preserve's largest oasis. Even late in the day the heat is oppressive, well above 110 degrees, but in the shade of the oasis it felt much cooler. After following a well-worn game trail into the core of the oasis, I crouched at the edge of a pool formed by the artesian spring. The sound of flowing water in the middle of the desert in the middle of summer is delicious. I gazed into the water as talapia fingerlings and mosquito fish darted amidst the shadows.

An intense fire had swept through the oasis five years earlier, and although most of the palms had recovered, their trunks were still charred. It was while crouched next to the oasis pool that I first noticed the thin, parallel scratch marks low on the palm trunk. Closer examination revealed another, and another. The size, shape, and depth indicated that a large bobcat had used almost every tree as a scratching post. Gazing at the claw marks on a particularly large palm, I tilted my head back and realized they went all the way up the trunk, almost 20 feet. This fellow was a very good climber.

Excited by my discovery, I left the oasis, climbed into my truck, and headed back to the refuge office. It was dusk, and the sun was setting over the Santa Rosa Mountains to the west, casting a purple glow on the Chocolate Mountains to the east. My route ran parallel to a series of cattail-lined ponds separated by narrow levees. Flocks of coots were settling down on the water for the evening, while lesser nighthawks swooped overhead, snagging bugs. As I passed one of the levees on my left, I saw something out of the corner of my eye that caught my attention.

I braked and slowly backed up the truck. Gazing to my left down one of the levees between the ponds, I could just make out a familiar shape. I turned off the engine, took out my binoculars, and settled myself into a comfortable position. With as little movement as possible, I focused the binoculars and squinted through the failing light. At the far end of the levee, about 75 yards away, the distinctive shape of a bobcat sitting in the middle of the levee came into focus. "Well, hello there," I whispered. He was looking directly back at me. I did not waver but continued to watch. The bobcat's pointed ears and cheek tufts were prominent, as was his white belly and gray-brown coat. He was a big, healthy, male and was obviously taking advantage of the refuge's abundant population of desert cottontails and jackrabbits. He broke the staring match first and glanced nervously to either side. Then he crouched and moved into some brush on the sloping bank of the levee. I held my position and patiently watched through the binoculars. Soon his head was visible in the vegetation, his gaze fixed on my truck. So the process went. The feline crossed back and forth across the levee three times, using vegetation for cover, but always closing on my position. It seems what they say about a cat's curiosity is true, although I had no fatal intention, just curiosity of my own.

Finally, the bobcat tentatively emerged from beneath a thicket of honey mesquite, 20 feet from my truck window. He stood in the open and examined the truck and me with interest. I remained absolutely still, curious how close I could lure him. He closed another five feet and sniffed the air. Then, as only cats can do, his mood abruptly shifted to nonchalant *indifference. I could almost hear him say, "I'm bored." He looked away, then marched directly to my left front tire, sniffed the tread, performed an about face, and, with a shudder of his rump, let fly with an impressive stream of urine. With a pronounced look of satisfaction, he trotted up the road and evaporated into the oasis. I wasn't sure whether to be flattered or insulted.*

The paradox of *Lynx rufus* is that it is the most exploited and most studied wild felid in the world, yet it endures throughout most of its historic range in North America and in some places actually seems to be expanding its range. Richard Mitchell, a zoologist with the U.S. Fish and Wildlife Service (USFWS), believes there are more bobcats in the United States today than during colonial times (Turbak 1994). It is an encouraging claim, but one that is impossible to verify. With no reliable method to accurately count bobcats over a large area, it is safe to assume that any bobcat census conducted during colonial times, 150 years before the existence of the science of wildlife biology, would have been even less accurate. Still, the USFWS estimates a current nationwide population of 700,000 to 1.5 million (Turbak 1994).

Koehler (1987) thought that prospects for the bobcat's future were encouraging because of increased management interest, the cat's ability to inhabit a variety of habitats, its relatively high reproductive potential, and its adaptability. He emphasized that research has shifted our perspective of the bobcat and helped us better understand its habitat and prey needs. Koehler pointed to the feline's ability to tolerate human activity and how they have expanded their range into areas where limited agricultural and timber harvest have provided favorable habitat. Finally, he believed the bobcat's new position in the management spotlight would prevent populations from being overhunted.

Rolley (1987) was more cautious and warned wildlife managers about dismissing the possibility of overkill during bobcat harvests. While under increasing scrutiny to prove that harvest is not detrimental to bobcat populations, managers must not automatically fall back on the traditional arguments that harvest cannot harm healthy wildlife populations and that, without harvest, all wildlife species would overpopulate and starve. Such arguments are oversimplifications, and managers need to understand that, in the case of the bobcat, overharvest is indeed possible under conditions of rapidly increasing demand.

Woolf and Hubert (1998:290) believed that bobcat populations were doing as well, if not better, than they had over the past 30 years. They believed that, although management efforts are not as sophisticated and precise as biologists would like and the public demands, the results have been positive:

At the range of exploitation that bobcats experienced over the last 3 decades [1970s–1990s], all evidence indicates that populations have done well. Distribution is similar to that at the beginning of the 3-decade span of interest, and populations are stable or increasing in most cases. Clearly, at the level of exploitation bobcats currently face, existing management strategies are more than adequate to afford the species protection from overexploitation, with the possible exception of a few localized cases.

But those who study the bobcat at the northern extreme of its range are not as sanguine about its future. During his study of bobcats in southern British Columbia, Clayton Apps became concerned that the best bobcat habitat coincided with the areas most heavily used by people. Much of Apps's work focused on the Rocky Mountain Trench, a semiarid valley of open ponderosa pine forests with thickets of aspen, pine, and Douglas fir and few streams or lakes. The bottom of the trench is intensively managed as Christmas tree farms, and an growing network of roads makes bobcats increasingly vulnerable to trappers and hunters. Apps (personal communication) urged that the bobcat be managed as a species of concern, because there is no *de facto* refuge for it in southern British Columbia. Even nearby Kootenay National Park has insufficient quality habitat within its borders for its bobcat population and is dependent on how land is managed outside of the park. Susan Morse (personal communication) added a voice of concern for bobcat populations in the Northern Forest of southeast Canada and northern New England. She was particularly concerned about the implications of increasing habitat fragmentation and insular bobcat populations in northern areas, where home ranges can reach 15 to 30 square miles and valley connectivity is increasingly degraded or eliminated by human development.

Most experts agree that bobcats are doing well, but loss of habitat and a fickle international fur market still pose potential threats. Although this feline still occupies much of its historical range, it has been displaced in areas of intensive agriculture and urban sprawl. Habitat loss and fragmentation still remain the greatest threat to all wildlife species. The Mexican population of bobcats (*Lynx rufus escuinipae*) is considered endangered, and although the cat is expanding its range in more northern latitudes, it is still vulnerable to habitat changes or crashes in prey populations. This is true for most populations of species at the periphery of their range, where environmental factors can greatly affect survival and reproduction.

Urban, residential, and agricultural development encroaches on bobcat habitat throughout North America. With the human population of the United States now exceeding 300 million, a concurrent demographic shift is occurring from the Northeast to the South and West, leading to rampant growth of communities in Florida, Texas, Arizona, Nevada, and California. According to the U.S. Census Bureau (2005), suburban communities surrounding Phoenix, Las Vegas, and Los Angeles made up nine of the ten fastest growing cities in 2004. All of these states and communities have resident or nearby bobcat populations. Their adaptability will be tested.

As the stress of urban living begins to take its toll, more and more people seek escape, finding temporary refuge in public lands. Many growing cities provide easy access to nearby county, state, and national parks, as well as national forests and other public lands. Annual visitation to America's national parks alone now exceeds 427 million (National Park Service 2005). Increasing numbers of hikers and backpackers penetrate forests, deserts, and remote wilderness areas—all home to the bobcat.

The U.S. Forest Service, the Bureau of Land Management, and the USFWS administer millions of acres of public lands under a policy of multiple use. This allows such activities as logging, mining, and livestock grazing, as well as recreational uses (e.g., hunting, off-road vehicles, snowmobiles). Such activities mean more roads, which further subdivide valuable wildlife habitat. Although certain types of selective logging have been shown to actually enhance bobcat habitat by creating more edge, extensive dirt road networks make bobcats more vulnerable to collisions with vehicles, hunting, and other human activities.

Paved roads are probably the most efficient wildlife slaughtering mechanisms ever devised. Each year, millions of wild animals are killed on America's highways. The California Department of Transportation estimated that automobiles kill almost 20,000 mule deer each year, a number equal to deer killed by California hunters annually (Roberts 1990). According to park researchers, more than 50,000 wild animals are run over on roads in and around Saguaro National Park in southern Arizona. The park consists of two units, on the east and west side of Tucson. Estimated annual roadkill in and around both park units is 27,000 reptiles, 17,000 amphibians, 6,000 mammals, and 1,000 birds (Davis 2005a). Studies in Illinois (Nielsen and Woolf 2002a) and in Texas (Cain et al. 2003) have shown collisions with vehicles on roads and highways to be a significant cause of death in bobcats. When combined with development, highways pose a triple threat to wildlife: as development reduces the amount of available habitat and squeezes remaining wildlife into smaller and more isolated pockets, high-speed traffic on larger and wider highways kills more and more of the remaining population (Harris and Gallagher 1989). An eight-lane interstate freeway poses a formidable and deadly obstacle to a bobcat.

"In the long run, these habitat fragmenting forces may be more degrading to North America's wildlife populations than actual loss of habitat acreage," according to Harris and Gallagher (1989:14–15), who went on to explain that habitat fragmentation results in four major consequences for wildlife:

1. "Area-sensitive" species, animals whose existence and successful reproduction depend on the size of the habitat in which they occur, disappear from the area. The bobcat, cougar, and black bear fall into this category.
2. Large species that are highly mobile and occur at low densities under the best conditions are also lost. Again, the bobcat is representative.
3. When coupled with the loss of large native carnivores, fragmented and human-altered landscapes (providing artificial sources of food and shelter) become dominated by exotic or already common species.
4. Inbreeding begins to occur in isolated populations of low density.

Preservation of large tracts of natural land as refugia certainly seems to be a logical solution, starting with our national parks, forests, and wildlife refuges. Ideal refugia need to be large (100,000 to 25,000,000 acres), roadless, and with limited, if any, industrial or agricultural exploitation. But how large is large enough? Knick (1990) examined bobcat ecology in southeastern Idaho relative to exploitation and a decline in jackrabbits, its primary prey. He found that refugia play an important role for harvested bobcat populations, which are maintained primarily by immigration. Knick developed a population model which predicted that the size of refugia needed to maintain a harvested population should be large enough to enclose three to five bobcat home ranges. The size of these home ranges of course varies according to the quality of the habitat. Based on their study of bobcat habitat use in southern Illinois, Kolowski and Woolf (2002) recommended maintaining habitats that provide thick vegetative cover, or managing existing open habitats to increase vegetative cover, particularly in winter. In areas with extensive or increasing agricultural cultivation, where bobcat use is low, the feline's persistence may depend on the presence of vegetated riparian areas, which provide resting cover, prey habitat, and potential den sites in an otherwise open landscape.

Unfortunately, even our largest national parks are losing species. Newmark (1986) surveyed the history of local extinctions of mammals in national parks of western North America and made a startling discovery. Since 14 western parks were established, 44 local extinctions have occurred among carnivores, ungulates, hares, and rabbits, the most commonly documented species. Even our largest parks are too small. This is why linkages between refugia are critical.

Connectivity is the degree to which individual animals can link populations throughout a landscape. Natural landscapes have an inherent degree of connectivity to which species have adapted over time. Habitat alteration by humans impedes connectivity for the majority of wildlife species. Tying isolated tracts of habitat together with "movement corridors" is a frequently proposed solution to the rampant habitat fragmentation currently taking place. Harris (1985) stated, "Our numerous, large wildlife sanctuaries must be made to function as a system, rather than being thought of [as] islands unto themselves. Physical interconnections of habitat must be developed and safeguarded if the wide-ranging mammals are to survive in perpetuity. In short, we need a system of wildlife conservation corridors to interconnect the many and sometimes large refuges already established."

Preserving habitat and connectivity are maxims of conservation biology. This new science focuses on how to protect and restore biological diversity (biodiversity) on Earth, at the habitat, species, and genetic levels. Some argue that conservation biology is not a new science but a combination of applied ecology and wildlife management, more a management tool than a science (Conservation Biology 2003). Some conservation biologists emphasize that a third maxim is the presence of carnivores within core areas or refugia. As the consummate carnivore, cats sit at the apex of the food chain. As such, they are indicators of the overall well-being, or integrity, of the environment: healthy populations of cats mean healthy populations of prey and a healthy environment (Hummel 1990; Sweanor 1990; Conner and Leopold 1996). This is why the ability to monitor bobcat populations is so important.

However, wildlife agencies rarely engage in long-term monitoring of any species, certainly not bobcats. With burgeoning responsibilities to manage more species and habitats, and the need to comply with the documentation and constraints required by the National Environmental Policy Act (NEPA), the Endangered Species Act (ESA), and other legislation, wildlife officials now spend more time at their desks than outdoors. They are buried under a mountain of environmental impact statements, environmental assessments, and wildlife management plans. When research is conducted, wildlife professionals tend to use a high-tech approach, employing sophisticated equipment and techniques such as Global Positioning Systems (GPS), remote cameras, satellite telemetry, and computer modeling, along with esoteric statistical analyses of data. Shaw (1999:193) suggested a different approach: "Instead of speculations derived from short-term intensive study and subsequent prediction, what we need, in many cases, is long-term monitoring of sign [tracks, scrapes, scat]. Natural systems are too large and too complex to be studied exclusively through intensive, high-tech research, and their management ultimately must rely upon more subjective judgments based on long observation and experience—long tuning to the background. I believe this is where well-trained amateurs could play a role in resource management."

Two examples of organizations employing this low-tech approach to wildlife monitoring can be found on opposite sides of the United States. Susan Morse is founder and program director of Keeping Track, Inc., a nonprofit organization based in Vermont that trains and assists community volunteers in establishing wildlife habitat monitoring programs in their towns. She teaches people how to detect, identify, interpret, and record the track and sign of certain target species, such as the bobcat. She also educates people about habitat fragmentation and degradation, how to identify habitat types, and how to apply the principles of habitat selection by target species in designing and monitoring study areas, or transects. Communities are responsible for running their own programs, with support and assistance from Keeping Track. Their cumulative data are then used to aid local and regional planners in making informed decisions about wildlife habitat protection (Keeping Track 2005).

As an example of Keeping Track's success, volunteers from the town of Charlotte, Vermont, using Keeping Track's methods and training, discovered and documented an important wildlife travel corridor through this formerly agricultural town that is rapidly becoming a suburb of the larger city of Burlington. The corridor represents one of few remaining paths for wildlife access to the rich lowlands of the Champlain Valley. At that time, the Charlotte Planning Commission encouraged homebuilding within or near the woods, so as not to impinge on the pastoral aspect of the remaining fields. Track and survey data collected by the Charlotte Keeping Track group showed that a new house was to be located in the middle

of the wildlife travel corridor. The group brought this information to town officials and were able to demonstrate existence of the travel corridor through Keeping Track's proven track and sign survey techniques. This led to moving the site
for the new house to the edge of the fields, thus protecting the interests of wildlife
and establishing a precedent for wildlife habitat stewardship in this community.
Morse believes this helped the community become more aware of the needs of
wildlife and feel connected to the land.

The Sky Island Alliance is an organization working to preserve and restore
the native biological diversity in the southwestern United States and northwestern Mexico. The term *sky islands* refers to isolated mountain ranges that are separated from each other by valleys of grassland or desert. The valleys of this basin
and range country act as barriers to the movement of woodland and forest species, much as saltwater seas isolate plants and animals on oceanic islands. These
mountain islands are among the most diverse ecosystems in North America, due
to their great topographic complexity and unique location where several major
desert and biotic provinces converge. Sky Island Alliance operates an extensive
wildlife monitoring program using trained volunteers. Working within a scientific protocol developed by Keeping Track and modified by the Sky Island Alliance's
staff and science committee, volunteers monitor the movements of mammals such
as black bears, mountain lions, and bobcats between mountain ranges by looking
for and recording their tracks. "The importance of biological connectivity is mag-
nified here in the Sky Island Region," said Matt Skroch, executive director for Sky
Island Alliance. "Because of the relatively small mountain ranges separated by wide
valleys, populations of large mammals such as the black bear and mountain lion
depend on the ability to move from range to range in response to environmental
fluctuations, food availability, and mate-searching. These populations are fluid—
isolation decreases the stability of local populations." In addition to collecting data
not possible to obtain without volunteer help, Skroch and his staff hope that volunteers will develop a better understanding and deeper appreciation for the Sky
Islands region. "People can learn about the area, feel a part of it, become inter-
ested in it and dedicated to its protection," said Janice Przybyl, the wildlife monitoring program coordinator (Sky Island Alliance 2005).

Track counts are not necessarily better than agency models, investigations
using telemetry, or the use of remote cameras, but they provide a continuous and
long-term source of data that are obtained at low cost and, most importantly,
provide an opportunity for volunteer citizen-scientists to be involved in wildlife
management. Such citizen involvement is a vital element of human dimensions
of wildlife management (Decker et al. 2001).

Advancements in science and technology have equipped wildlife researchers
with better tools and methods to study wild animals (Sunquist and Sunquist 2002).
The bobcat will continue to give up its secrets under the penetrating gaze of per-
sistent biologists. In their recommendations for future research, bobcat investigators consistently list the necessity for determining the impact of harvest on

populations, the need for more precise (and nonlethal) censusing techniques, and the importance of more long-term studies. The social organization of the bobcat needs to be better understood, as does it physiology, and additional funding sources are needed. However, the future of the bobcat—in fact, all wildlife—depends not on just what we learn, but on how that knowledge is applied.

Science is critical to understanding of the bobcat, but it has always played a secondary role in its management. This is because furbearer harvests are fundamentally driven by the opportunity for profit. Demand for furbearers changes dramatically with shifting fur markets, independently of furbearer population trends (Shaw 1985). In the case of the bobcat, economics has been a far greater influence than science in the management of the species. It was economics that initiated the massive exploitation of bobcats in the mid-1970s, and it was economics that dramatically reduced harvest with the stock market crash of 1987. Economics and politics ignited the controversy over bobcat management in 1975, and economics and politics ended it in 1982. Economics and politics led to the flurry of bobcat research and its subsequent decline over the same period.

American economics and politics are deeply rooted in a culture that embraces an anthropocentric Manifest Destiny—a view that the world's plants, animals, minerals, and so on, exist for the express purpose of benefitting humans. This belief system presumes that treating these things simply as resources to be exploited not only is acceptable but is the right and proper course of action (Nebel and Wright 1996). It is an ethos based on profit, natural resource consumption, land development, and an ardent belief that humans are exempt from the laws of nature. Biologists can appeal to reason all they want, but ours is not a reasonable culture. In such an environment, scientists find themselves at the mercy of two of the most skilled predators in existence—the politician and businessman. Too many wildlife biologists have watched in helpless frustration as their science-based recommendations are either ignored or manipulated by politicians and businessmen with economic agendas who sit on local planning boards, state wildlife commissions, and federal agencies. Too often science has been sacrificed at the altar of economic and political expediency (Wolfe and Chapman 1987).

There is, of course, another view. The world is not infinite. Continued exploitation is not sustainable. The continued well-being of humans depends on the conservation of wild plants and animals and the protection of air and water resources (Nebel and Wright 1996). Nature and humans are one. Whether we like it or not, we are in the game. Our relationship with wildlife should be based on knowledge, respect, tolerance, and a willingness to share the land. Those with vested interests in the previous perspective dismiss this view as naive and misanthropic. Others believe that the older world view is selfish, short-sighted, and cynical.

Lying between these two paradigms is the bobcat—the bobcat as commodity to be exploited and the bobcat as a member of a community to which humans belong. Wildlife managers believe that the two views are compatible and in fact already coexist. Others, especially antitrapping and antihunting groups, do not believe we can have it both ways. Wildlife managers insist that the requirements of the Convention on International Trade in Endangered Species of Wild Flora and Fauna (CITES) and controlled harvest through a combination of season length, bag limits, quotas, and restrictions on take (killing) provide adequate safeguards to ensure the survival of bobcats as a species in perpetuity. Skeptics want to know how it is possible to continue to kill tens of thousands of bobcats each year, when the feline is impossible to accurately census, the impacts of harvest are poorly understood, and, most importantly, bobcat harvest is subject to market forces that operate independent of bobcat population dynamics and outside wildlife managers' control. At their core, trapping and hunting are philosophical issues; like economics and politics, they are rooted deeply in our culture. Reconciliation of such dilemmas will require a completely new approach. British philosopher and writer Mary Midgely understood this: "All around us, we can see people trying to solve by logical argument, or by the gathering of information, problems that can only be dealt with by a change of heart—a change of attitude, a new policy and direction (Midgley 1990:48)."

Recent developments in the status and management of bobcats elicit contrasting interpretations. Consider the following:

1. In 1999, Illinois delisted bobcats as a threatened species (Bluett et al. 2001).
2. In 2000, the Pennsylvania Game Commission approved the first legal harvest of bobcats in 30 years (Lovallo 2001).
3. In 2002, bobcat trapping resumed in Manitoba after being halted in 1985 (International Society for Endangered Cats Canada 2001; Province of Manitoba 2004).
4. In 2003, Iowa's Natural Resources Commission removed the bobcat from its threatened species list (Iowa Department of Natural Resources Wildlife 2003).
5. At the request of the National Trappers Association, the USFWS has announced its intention to delist the Mexican bobcat (*L. r. escuinipae*) as an endangered species (USFWS 2005).
6. In 2003, the Western Association of Fish and Wildlife Agencies and the Louisiana Department of Wildlife and Fisheries requested that the bobcat be removed from Appendix II of CITES, and the United States made the request at the CITES Conference of Parties in 2004 (CITES 2004).
7. Bobcat pelt prices are increasing (North American Fur Auctions 2005).
8. Bobcat harvest is increasing (see Figure 5.3 in Chapter 5).

Wildlife managers and some biologists are quick to cite these developments as evidence of successful management. Critics are less sanguine. They believe that decreasing habitat and protection, combined with increasing pelt prices and harvest, holds ominous potential for the bobcats' future. Perhaps predicting conflicts to come, the Humane Society of the United States (HSUS) recently filed comments with the USFWS requesting that the Mexican bobcat remain protected under the ESA (HSUS 2005a).

Whatever the future holds for *L. rufus*, it is too important to be left in the hands of businessmen, politicians, or wildlife managers. An informed, caring, and engaged public is critical to the conservation of bobcats and all wildlife. Get out in the bobcat's habitat and consider how they make a living. Learn all you can about the animals. Consult the bibliography in this book, or contact your state wildlife department. Contact the agencies responsible for wildlife and natural resource management and learn what they are doing to conserve bobcats, other carnivores, and their habitats. Urge your legislators to stop or modify development in bobcat habitat and to support funding for purchase and enhancement of critical habitat for bobcats, cougars, deer, and other wildlife. Attend wildlife commission meetings and let them know what you think. Encourage local land use planners to consider wildlife in their decisions. Likewise, let the federal land management agencies (Bureau of Land Management, U.S. Forest Service, and USFWS) know that you consider wildlife conservation important. Make sure that government appointees to wildlife management commissions or boards have a thorough understanding of biology and ecology (Logan and Sweanor 2001). Insist that managers of state wildlife agencies be able to explain and justify bobcat harvest levels and any bobcat depredation control actions. Volunteer your time with state wildlife agencies or nonprofit organizations such as Keeping Track, Inc., or Sky Island Alliance. Consider making a donation on behalf of wildlife. Famed conservationist Aldo Leopold once learned that a colleague had dismissed public participation in forest management by insisting that such things be left to experts. Leopold responded thus: "I suspect there are two categories of judgement that *cannot* be delegated to experts, which every man *must* judge for himself, and on which the intuitive conclusion of the non-expert is perhaps as likely to be correct as that of the professional. One of these is what is right. The other is what is beautiful" (Meine 1988:361).

Our relationship with predators has always been ambivalent. Native cultures deified the bobcat but killed it for food and other uses. Early trappers named streams and canyons after the cat but killed it for its pelt. Early settlers saw the bobcat as a competitor vying for the abundant game of the New World and as a threat to domestic livestock. Modern biologists hold them up as a model of resilience and adaptability.

Some feel that concern for the bobcat's future is premature, because federal wildlife officials have not declared the diminutive feline an endangered species. The ESA of 1973 was designated to identify and protect plant and animal species that have become sufficiently depleted to warrant special protection of their populations and habitats. The Act, as amended, specifically affords protection to three biological categories: species, subspecies, and populations. That is why the Mexican bobcat is listed as endangered while other subspecies are not. However, to infer from this that there is no cause for concern is to assume that endangered status is some biological tripwire that indicates when action should be taken. This assumption overestimates our ability to make such a designation with accuracy and in time to implement protective measures. Sadly, the popular aphorism, "Endangered means there is still time," is frequently untrue. In the case of predators, past evidence indicates that such a designation is simply a prelude to the oblivion of extinction. Indeed, the bobcat is not an endangered species, and we are in a position now to ensure that it never is.

The bobcat has evolved for millions of years to do one thing: kill. That is neither good nor bad; it simply is. Where the feline gets into trouble is when we insist on holding it to a *human* standard of behavior. But the bobcat does not live in our world. *L. rufus* moves through a landscape of sights, sounds, and odors that it explores with extended senses so far superior to ours that it creates a reality humans can barely fathom. This is what makes cats appear so otherworldly, so mysterious—and we love a mystery. It drives both the biologist's research and the layperson's imagination.

We fold the bobcat into our mythology, admire its independence, praise its dignity, and hold it up as a symbol of wildness. We catch its limbs in steel-jawed traps and peel its skin, in the name of commerce. Our schools and sports teams enshrine it as their mascot, a symbol of ferocity, tenacity, and pugnacity. We chase it with dogs and shoot it out of trees, in the name of sport. We glimpse this feline wraith during a hike in the woods and count ourselves lucky. We extol its skill as the ultimate hunter. We capture it, inject it with drugs, hang radio transmitters around its neck, and follow it relentlessly, in the name of science. We work for its conservation, and we slaughter it by the millions. We curse, venerate, envy, respect, persecute, even worship it. Through it all, one thing remains certain: the bobcat will never enter the room, sit down across the table, and negotiate its relationship with us. It is indifferent to our efforts, wishes, or intentions. It is too busy being a bobcat—hunting, killing, eating, sunning on a ledge, feeding its young. The bobcat goes its own way, on its own terms.

Bibliography

Albone, E.S., and S.G. Shirley. 1984. Mammalian seriochemistry. John Wiley, Chichester, United Kingdom.

Allen, J.A. 1903. A new deer and a new lynx from the state of Sinaloa, Mexico. Bulletin of the American Museum of Natural History 19:614.

Altman, C.D., Jr. 1997. Food habits of bobcats (*Felis rufus*) in the Trans-Pecos and Edwards Plateau regions of Texas. Thesis, Sul Ross State University, Alpine, Texas, USA. (Abstract)

Andelt, W.F., R.L. Phillips, R.H. Schmidt, and R.B. Gill. 1999. Trapping furbearers: an overview of the biological and social issues surrounding a public controversy. Wildlife Society Bulletin 27:53–64.

Anderson, A.J., E.C. Greiner, C.T. Atkinson, and M.E. Roelke. 1992. Sarcocysts in the Florida bobcat (*Felis rufus floridanus*). Journal of Wildlife Diseases 28:116–120.

Anderson, E.M. 1987. A critical review and annotated bibliography of literature on bobcat. Special Report Number 62, Colorado Division of Wildlife, Terrestrial Wildlife Research, Denver, Colorado, USA.

———. 1988. Effects of male removal on spatial distribution of bobcats. Journal of Mammalogy 69:637–641.

———. 1990. Bobcat diurnal loafing sites in southeastern Colorado (USA). Journal of Wildlife Management 54:600–602.

———, and M.J. Lovallo. 2003. Bobcat and lynx. Pages 759–786 *in* G.A. Feldhamer, B.C. Thompson, and J.A. Chapman, editors. Wild mammals of North America: biology, management, and conservation. The Johns Hopkins University Press, Baltimore, Maryland, USA.

Apps, C.D. 1995a. East Kootenay bobcat research project, annual progress report 1994–1995. British Columbia Environment, Wildlife Branch, Cranbrook, British Columbia, Canada.

———. 1995b. East Kootenay bobcat research. Report to the British Columbia Trappers Association. (Unpublished)

———, and S. Herrero. 1994. GIS based habitat suitability assessment for bobcats in southeast British Columbia. Faculty of Environmental Design, University of Calgary, Alberta, Canada.

Armstrong, J.B., and A.N. Rossi. 2000. Status of avocational trapping based on the perspectives of state furbearer biologists. Wildlife Society Bulletin 28:825–832.

Aubry, K.B., G.M. Koehler, and J.R. Squires. 2000. Ecology of Canadian lynx in southern boreal forests. Pages 393–396 *in* L.F. Ruggiero, K.B. Aubry, S.W. Buskirk, G.M. Koehler, C.J. Krebs, K.S. McKelvey, and J.R. Squires, editors. Ecology and conservation of lynx in the United States. University of Colorado Press, Boulder, Colorado, USA.

Bailey, J.A. 1984. Principles of wildlife management. John Wiley and Sons, New York, New York, USA.

Bailey, T.N. 1971. Immobilization of bobcats, coyotes, and badgers with phencyclidine hydrochloride. Journal of Wildlife Management 35:847–849.

———. 1974. Social organization in a bobcat population. Journal of Wildlife Management 38:435–446.

———. 1979. Den ecology, population parameters and diet of eastern Idaho bobcats. Pages 62–69 *in* L. Blum and P.C. Escherich, editors. Proceedings of the 1979 bobcat research conference: current research on biology and management of *Lynx rufus*. Scientific and Technical Series 6. National Wildlife Federation, Washington, D.C., USA.

———. 1981. Factors of bobcat social organization and some management implications. Pages 984–1000 *in* J.A. Chapman and D. Pursley, editors. Proceedings of the Worldwide Furbearer Conference, Frostburg, Maryland, USA.

———. 1984a. Bobcat and lynx: habitat and physique. Page 51 *in* D. MacDonald, editor. The encyclopedia of mammals. Facts on File Publications, New York, New York, USA.

———. 1984b. North America's secretive cats. Pages 54–55 *in* D. MacDonald, editor. The encyclopedia of mammals. Facts on File Publications, New York, New York, USA.

Baker, L.A., R.J. Warren, D.R. Diefenbach, W.E. James, and M.J. Conroy. 2001. Prey selection by reintroduced bobcat (*Lynx rufus*) on Cumberland Island, Georgia. The American Midland Naturalist 145:80–93.

Batcheller, G.R., T.A. Decker, D.A. Hamilton, and J.F. Organ. 2000. A vision for the future of furbearer management in the United States. Wildlife Society Bulletin 28:833–840.

Beale, D.M., and A.D. Smith. 1973. Mortality of pronghorn antelope fawns in western Utah. Journal of Wildlife Management 37:343–352.

Bean, M.J. 1983. The evolution of national wildlife law. Second edition. Praeger Publishers, New York, New York, USA.

Beasom, S.L., and R.A. Moore. 1977. Bobcat food habit response to a change in prey abundance. The Southwest Naturalist 21:451–457.

Beeler, I.E. 1985. Reproductive characteristics of captive and wild bobcats (*Felis rufus*) in Mississippi. Thesis, Mississippi State University, Mississippi State, Mississippi, USA.

Bell, J.F., and J.R. Reilly. 1981. Tularemia. Pages 213–231 *in* J.W. Davis, L.H. Karstad, and D.O. Trainer, editors. Infectious diseases of wild mammals. Second edition. Iowa State University Press, Ames, Iowa, USA.

Belluomini, L.A. 1978. Estimated hunter take of bobcat in California during 1977. California Department of Fish and Game Report on Federal Aid for Wildlife Restoration Project W-54-R-10, Job IV-1.6, Progress Report.

Beltran, J.F., and M. Delibes. 1993. Physical characteristics of Iberian lynxes. Journal of Mammalogy 74:852–862.

———, and M.E. Tewes. 1995. Immobilization of ocelots and bobcats with ketamine hydrochloride and xylazine hydrochloride. Journal of Wildlife Diseases 31:43–48.

Benson, J.F., M.J. Chamberlain, and B.D. Leopold. 2004. Land tenure and occupation of vacant home ranges by bobcats (*Lynx rufus*). Journal of Mammalogy 85:983–988.

Berg, W.E. 1979. Ecology of bobcats in northern Minnesota. Pages 55–61 *in* L. Blum and P.C. Escherich, editors. Proceedings of the 1979 bobcat research conference: current research on biology and management of *Lynx rufus*. Scientific and Technical Series 6. National Wildlife Federation, Washington, D.C., USA.

Bergan, J.F. 1990. Kleptoparasitism of a river otter, *Lutra canadensis*, by a bobcat, *Felis rufus*, in South Carolina (USA). Brimleyana 0(16):63–65. (Abstract)

Best, M.S. 1988. A scent station–trapping technique for developing furbearer population indices in east Texas. Thesis, Stephen F. Austin State University, Nacogdoches, Texas, USA.

Blackwell, B.H., G.T. Frost, J.T. Flinders, and H.A. Barber. 1991. Radio harness system for bobcat kittens. Great Basin Naturalist 51:343–347.

Blankenship, T.L. 2000. Ecological response of bobcats to fluctuating prey populations on the Welder Wildlife Foundation Refuge. Dissertation, Texas A&M University, College Station, Texas, USA. (Abstract)

———, and W.G. Swank. 1979. Population dynamic aspects of the bobcat in Texas. Pages 116–122 *in* L. Blum and P.C. Escherich, editors. Proceedings of the 1979 bobcat research conference: current research on biology and management of *Lynx rufus*. Scientific and Technical Series 6. National Wildlife Federation, Washington, D.C., USA.

Blouin, E.F., A.A. Kocan, B.L. Glenn, K.M. Kocan, and J.A. Hair. 1984. Transmission of *Cytauxzoon felis* Kier, 1979 from bobcats, *Felis rufus* (Schreber), to domestic cats by *Dermacentor variabilis* (Say). Journal of Wildlife Diseases 20:241–242.

Bluett, R.D., G.F. Hubert, and A. Woolf. 2001. Perspectives on bobcat management in Illinois. Pages 67–73 *in* A. Woolf, C.K. Nielsen, and R.D. Bluett, editors. Proceedings of a symposium on current bobcat research and implications for management. The Wildlife Society 2000 Conference, Nashville, Tennessee, USA.

———, M.E. Tewes, and B.C. Thompson. 1989. Geographic distribution of commercial bobcat harvest in Texas (USA) 1978–1986. Texas Journal of Science 41:379–394. (Abstract)

Blum, L.G., and P.C. Escherich, editors. 1979. Proceedings of the 1979 bobcat research conference: current research on biology and management of *Lynx rufus*. Scientific and Technical Series 6. National Wildlife Federation, Washington, D.C., USA.

Bolen, E.G, and W.L. Robinson. 1999. Wildlife ecology and management. Fourth edition. Prentice-Hall, Upper Saddle River, New Jersey, USA.

Boyce, M.S. 1979. Seasonality and patterns of natural selection for life histories. American Naturalist 114:569–583.

Boyle, K.A., and T.T. Fendley. 1987. Habitat suitability index models: bobcat. U.S. Fish and Wildlife Service Biological Report 82(10):147.

Bradley, L.C., and D.B. Fagre. 1988. Coyote and bobcat responses to integrated ranch management practices in south Texas. Journal of Range Management 41:322–327.

Brady, J.R. 1979. Pages 101–103 *in* L. Blum and P.C. Escherich, editors. Preliminary results of bobcat scent station transects in Florida. Proceedings of the 1979 bobcat research conference: current research on biology and management of *Lynx rufus*. Scientific and Technical Series 6. National Wildlife Federation, Washington, D.C., USA.

Brainerd, S.M. 1985. Reproductive ecology of bobcats and lynx in western Montana. Thesis, University of Montana, Missoula, Montana, USA.

Brand, C.J., and L.B. Keith. 1979. Lynx demography during a snowshoe hare decline in Alberta. Journal of Wildlife Management 43:827–849.

Brittell, J.D., S.J. Sweeney, and S.T. Knick. 1979. Washington bobcats: diet, population dynamics, and movement. Pages 107–110 *in* L. Blum and P.C. Escherich, editors. Proceedings of the 1979 bobcat research conference: current research on biology and management of *Lynx rufus*. Scientific and Technical Series 6. National Wildlife Federation, Washington, D.C., USA.

Brooks, J.J., R.J. Warren, M.G. Nelms, and M.A. Tarrant. 1999. Visitor attitudes toward and knowledge of restored bobcats on Cumberland Island National Seashore, Georgia. Wildlife Society Bulletin 27:1089–1097.

Buie, D.E., T.T. Fendley, and H. McNab. 1979. Fall and winter home ranges of adult bobcats on the Savannah River Plant, South Carolina. Pages 42–46 *in* L. Blum and P.C. Escherich, editors. Proceedings of the 1979 bobcat research conference: current research on biology and management of *Lynx rufus*. Scientific and Technical Series 6. National Wildlife Federation, Washington, D.C., USA.

Burridge, M.J., W.J. Bigler, K.J. Forrester, and J.M. Hennemann. 1979. Serologic survey for *Tosoplasma gondii* in wild animals in Florida. Journal of the American Veterinary Medical Association 175:964–967.

Burton, A.M., S.N. Perez, and C.C. Tovar. 2003. Bobcat ranging behavior in relation to small mammal abundance in Colima Volcano, Mexico. Anales del Instituto de Biologia, Universidad Nacional Autonoma de Mexico, Serie Zoologia 74(1):67–82.

Buskirk, S.W., L.F. Ruggiero, and C.J. Krebs. 2000. Habitat fragmentation and interspecific competition: implications for lynx conservation. Pages 83–100 *in* L.F. Ruggiero, K.B. Aubry, S.W. Buskirk, G.M. Koehler, C.J. Krebs, K.S. McKelvey, and J.R. Squires, editors. Ecology and conservation of lynx in the United States. University Press of Colorado, Boulder, Colorado, USA.

Buttrey, G.W. 1979. Food habits and distribution of the bobcat (*Lyns rufus*) on the Catoosa Wildlife Management Area. Pages 87–91 *in* L. Blum and P.C. Escherich, editors. Proceedings of the 1979 bobcat research conference: current research on biology and management of *Lynx rufus*. Scientific and Technical Series 6. National Wildlife Federation, Washington, D.C., USA.

Cain, S.A., chairman. 1972. Predator control–1971. Institute for Environmental Quality. University of Michigan, Ann Arbor, Michigan, USA.

Cain, A.T. 1999. Bobcat use of highway crossing structures and habitat use near a highway expansion in southern Texas (*Lynx rufus*). Thesis, Texas A&M University, Kingsville, Texas, USA. (Abstract)

———, V.R. Tuovila, D.G. Hewitt, and M.E. Tewes. 2003. Effects of a highway and mitigation project on bobcats in southern Texas. Biological Conservation 114:189–197.

Canadian Wildlife Service. 1978. CITES report no. 1: annual report for Canada. Canadian Wildlife Service, Ottawa, Ontario, Canada.

Carey, A.B., and R.G. McLean. 1978. Rabies antibody prevalence and virus tissue tropism in wild carnivores in Virginia. Journal of Wildlife Diseases 14:487–491.

Casey, A.L., P.R. Krausman, W.W. Shaw, and H.G. Shaw. 2005. Knowledge of and attitudes toward mountain lions: a public survey of residents adjacent to Saguaro National Park, Arizona. Human Dimensions of Wildlife 10:29–38.

Cat in a Quandary. 1979. National Wildlife 17(August):44–47.

Caughley, G. 1970. Eruption of ungulate populations, with emphasis on Himalayan thar in New Zealand. Ecology 51:53–72.

———. 1977. Analysis of vertebrate populations. John Wiley and Sons, New York, New York, USA.

———, and A.R.E. Sinclair. 1994. Wildlife ecology and management. Blackwell Scientific Publications, Boston, Massachusetts, USA.

[CDFG] California Department of Fish and Game. 1986. Get set to trap: a California trapper education guide. Wildlife Management Division, Sacramento, California, USA.

———. 2001. Furbearing and nongame mammal hunting and trapping: draft environmental document. State of California, The Resources Agency, Department of Fish and Game, Sacramento, California, USA.

Chamberlain, M.J. 1999. Ecological relationships among bobcats, coyotes, gray fox, and raccoons and their interactions with wild turkey hens. Dissertation, Mississippi State University, Mississippi State, Mississippi, USA. (Abstract)

———, L.M. Conner, B.D. Leopold, and K.J. Sullivan. 1998. Diel activity patterns of adult bobcats in central Mississippi. Proceeding of the Annual Conference of the Southeastern Association of Fish and Wildlife Agencies 52:191–196.

———, and B.D. Leopold. 1999. Dietary patterns of sympatric bobcats and coyotes in central Mississippi. Proceedings of the annual conference of the Southeastern Association of Fish and Wildlife Agencies 52:204–218.

———, and ———. 2001. Spatio-temporal relationships among adult bobcats in central Mississippi. Pages 45–50 *in* A. Woolf, C.K. Nielsen, and R.D. Bluett, editors. 2001. Proceedings of a symposium on current bobcat research and implications for management. The Wildlife Society 2000 Conference, Nashville, Tennessee, USA.

———, ———, L.W. Burger, B.W. Plowman, and L.M. Conner. 1999. Survival and cause-specific mortality of adult bobcats in central Mississippi. Journal of Wildlife Management 63:613–620.

———, ———, and L.M. Conner. 2003. Space use, movements and habitat selection of adult bobcats (*Lynx rufus*) in central Mississippi. American Midland Naturalist 149:395–405.

Chapman, J.A., and G.A. Feldhamer, editors. 1982. Wild mammals of North America: biology, management, and economics. The Johns Hopkins University Press, Baltimore, Maryland, USA.

Cherfas, J. 1987. How to thrill your cat this Christmas. New Science 116:42–45.

Chilelli, M. 1988. Modeling the population dynamics of Maine's white-tailed deer. Dissertation, University of Maine, Orono, Maine, USA. (Abstract)

[CITES] Convention on International Trade in Endangered Species of Wild Flora and Fauna. 2004. Thirteenth Meeting of the Conference of Parties, Bangkok (Thailand), 2–14 October 2004, Proposals for amendment of Appendices I and II. Available at http://www.cites.org/eng/cop/13/prop/index.shtml. Accessed 05 March 2006.

———. 2005a. What is CITES? Available at http://www.cites.org/eng/disc/what.shtml. Accessed 05 March 2006.

———. 2005b. How CITES works. Available at http://www.cites.org/eng/disc/how.shtml. Accessed 05 March 2006.

Conley, R.H., and J.H. Jenkins. 1969. An evaluation of several techniques for determining the age of bobcat (*Lynx rufus*) in the southeast. Proceedings of the annual conference of the Southeastern Association of Fish and Wildlife Agencies 23:104–109.

Conner, L.M. 1991. Bobcat home range, habitat use, and core use areas in east-central Mississippi. Thesis, Mississippi State University, Mississippi State, Mississippi, USA. (Abstract)

———. 1995. Space use patterns and habitat utilization by bobcats in managed forests of Mississippi. Dissertation, Mississippi State University, Mississippi State, Mississippi, USA. (Abstract)

———, and B.D. Leopold. 1996. Bobcat habitat use at multiple spatial scales. Proceedings of the annual conference of the Southeastern Association of Fish and Wildlife Agencies 50:622–631.

———, and ———. 1998. A multivariate habitat model for female bobcats: a GIS approach. Proceedings of the annual conference of the Southeastern Association of Fish and Wildlife Agencies 52:232–243.

———, ———, and M.J. Chamberlain. 2001. Multivariate habitat models for bobcats in southern forested landscapes. Pages 51–55 *in* A. Woolf, C.K. Nielsen, and R.D. Bluett, editors. 2001. Proceedings of a symposium on current bobcat research and implications for management. The Wildlife Society 2000 Conference, Nashville, Tennessee, USA.

———, B. Plowman, B.D. Leopold, and C. Lovell. 1999. Influence of time-in-residence on home range and habitat use of bobcats. Journal of Wildlife Management 63:261–269.

Conner, M.C., R.F. Labisky, and D.R. Progulske, Jr. 1983. Scent-station indices as measures of population abundance for bobcats, racoons, gray foxes, and opossums. Wildlife Society Bulletin 11:146–152.

Connolly, G.E. 1978. Predators and predator control. Pages 369–394 *in* J.L. Schmidt and D.L. Gilbert, editors. Big game in North America: ecology and management. Wildlife Management Institute, Stackpole Books, Mechanicsburg, Pennsylvania, USA.

Conover, M.R. 2001. Effect of hunting and trapping on wildlife damage. Wildlife Society Bulletin 29:521–532.

Conservation Biology. 2003. Frequently Asked Questions About Conservation Biology and Biodiversity. Available at http://www.conbio.org/Resources/Education/faq.cfm. Accessed 05 March 2006.

Cook, R.S., M. White, D.O. Trainer, and W.C. Glazener. 1971. Mortality of young white-tailed deer fawns in south Texas. Journal of Wildlife Management 35:47–56.

Cooperrider, A.Y., R.J. Boyd, and H.R. Stuart, editors. 1986. Inventory and monitoring of wildlife habitat. U.S. Department of the Interior, Bureau of Land Management Service Center, Denver, Colorado, USA.

Cougar Management Guidelines Working Group. 2005. Cougar management guidelines. First edition. WildFutures, Bainbridge Island, Washington, USA.

Cronon, W. 1983. Changes in the land: indians, colonists, and the ecology of New England. Hill and Wang, New York, New York, USA.

Crowe, D.M. 1972. The presence of annuli in bobcat tooth cementum layers. Journal of Wildlife Management 36:1330–1332.

———. 1975a. Aspects of ageing, growth, and reproduction of bobcats from Wyoming. Journal of Mammalogy 56:177–198.

———. 1975b. A model for exploited bobcat populations in Wyoming. Journal of Wildlife Management 39:408–415.

———, and D. Strickland. 1975. Population structures of some mammalian predators in southeastern Wyoming. Journal of Wildlife Management 39:449–450.

Cumbie, P.M. 1975. Mercury in hair of bobcats and raccoons. Journal of Wildlife Management 39:419–425.

Czech, B. 2000. Economic growth as the limiting factor for wildlife conservation. Wildlife Society Bulletin 28:4–15.

Dasmann, R.F. 1981. Wildlife biology. Second edition, John Wiley and Sons, New York, New York, USA.

Davis, T. 2005a. "Roadkill: huge toll on park-area highways." Arizona Daily Star, 16 May 2005, page A1.

———. 2005b. "Wild critters abound in Tucson." Arizona Daily Star, 28 August 2005, page A10.

Davis, W.S. 1981. Aging, reproduction, and winter food habits of bobcat (*Lynx rufus*) and river otter (*Lutra canadensis*) in Mississippi. Thesis, Mississippi State University, Mississippi State, Mississippi, USA.

Decker, D.J., T.L. Brown, and W.F. Siemer, editors. 2001. Human dimensions of wildlife management in North America. The Wildlife Society, Bethesda, Maryland, USA.

———, and L.C. Chase. 1997. Human dimensions of living with wildlife: a management challenge for the 21st century. Wildlife Society Bulletin 25:788–795.

Defenders of Wildlife. 1984. Changing U.S. trapping policy: a handbook for activists. Defenders of Wildlife, Washington, D.C., USA.

Delibes, M., M.C. Blazquez, R. Rodriquez-Estrella, and S.C. Zapata. 1997. Seasonal food habits of bobcats (*Lynx rufus*) in subtropical Baja California Sur, Mexico. Canadian Journal of Zoology 74:478–483.

DeStefano, S. 1987. The lynx. Pages 411–421 *in* Audubon Wildlife Report 1987. National Audubon Society, New York, New York, USA.

DeVos, A. 1953. Bobcat preying on porcupine. Journal of Mammalogy 34:129–130.

Dibello, F.J., S.M. Arthur, and W.B. Krohn. 1990. Food habits of sympatric coyotes,

Canis latrans, red foxes, *Vulpes vulpes*, and bobcats, *Lynx rufus*, in Maine (USA). Canadian Field-Naturalist 104:403–408. (Abstract)

Diefenbach, D.R. 1992. The reintroduction of bobcats to Cumberland Island, Georgia: validation of the scent-station survey technique and analysis of population viability. Dissertation, University of Georgia, Athens, Georgia, USA. (Abstract)

———, L.A. Baker, W.E. James, R.J. Warren, and M.J. Conroy. 1993. Reintroducing bobcats to Cumberland Island, Georgia. Restoration Ecology (December):241–247.

———, M.J. Conroy, R.J. Warren, W.E. James, L.A. Baker, and T. Hon. 1994. A test of the scent-station survey technique for bobcats. Journal of Wildlife Management 58:10–17.

———, M.J. Lovallo, L.A. Hansen, R.J. Warren, and M.J. Conroy. 2001. Changes in spacing patterns with increasing population density of an insular reintroduced bobcat population. Page 80 *in* A. Woolf, C.K. Nielsen, and R.D. Bluett, editors. 2001. Proceedings of a symposium on current bobcat research and implications for management. The Wildlife Society 2000 Conference, Nashville, Tennessee, USA. (Abstract)

Dill, H.H. 1947. Bobcat preys on deer. Journal of Mammalogy 28:63.

Disney, M., and L.K. Spiegel. 1992. Sources and rates of San Joaquin kit fox mortality in western Kern County, California. Transactions of the Western Section of the Wildlife Society, 28:73–82.

Dixon, J. 1925. Food predilections of predatory and fur-bearing mammals. Journal of Mammalogy 6:34–46.

Dixon, K.R. 1930. Symposium on predatory animal control: food habits of California bobcats. Journal of Mammalogy 11:375–376.

———. 1982. Mountain lion. Pages 711–727 *in* J.A. Chapman and G.A. Feldhamer, editors. Wild mammals of North America. Johns Hopkins University Press, Baltimore, Maryland, USA.

———, and M.C. Swift. 1981. The optimal harvesting concept in furbearer management. Pages 1524–1551 *in* J.A. Chapman and D. Pursley, editors. Proceedings of the Worldwide Furbearer Conference, Frostburg, Maryland, USA.

Dobson, F.S., and Wigginton, J.D. 1996. Environmental influences on the sexual dimorphism in body size of western bobcats. Oecologia 108:610–616.

Donegan, P.B. 1994. Foraging behavior of free-ranging bobcats: a consideration of optimality theory. Thesis, San Francisco State University, San Francisco, California, USA.

Duke, K.L. 1949. Some notes on the histology of the ovary of the bobcat (*Lynx*) with special reference to corporea lutea. Anatomical Record 103:111–132.

———. 1954. Reproduction in the bobcat *Lynx rufus*. Anatomical Record 120:816–817.

Dyer, M.I. 1979. Conference summary: current status of North American bobcat programs. Pages 134–137 *in* L. Blum and P.C. Escherich, editors. Proceedings of the 1979 bobcat research conference: current research on biology and management of *Lynx rufus*. Scientific and Technical Series 6. National Wildlife Federation, Washington, D.C., USA.

Earle, R.D., D.M. Lunning, V.R. Tuovila, and and J.A. Shivik. 2003.Evaluating injury mitigation and performance of #3 Victor Soft Catch traps to restrain bobcats. Wildlife Society Bulletin 31:617–629.

Eaton, R.L. 1976. Why some felids copulate so much. Pages 73–94 *in* R.L. Eaton, editor. The world's cats. Volume 3. Carnivore Research Institute, University of Washington, Seattle, Washington, USA.

Edwards, D.A., Jr. 1996. Ecological relationships among bobcats, coyotes, and gray foxes in central Mississippi. Thesis, Mississippi State University, Mississippi State, Mississippi, USA. (Abstract)

Elman, R. 1980. The great bobcat controversy. Outdoor Life 165(May):24–26.

Elton, C., and M. Nicholson. 1942. The ten-year cycle in numbers of lynx in Canada. Journal of Animal Ecology 11:215–244.

Emmons, R.W., L.L. Leonard, F. DeGenaro, Jr., E.S. Protas, P.L. Bazeley, S.T. Giamonna, and K. Sturckow. 1973. A case of human rabies with prolonged survival. Intervirology 1:60–72.

Epple, G., J.R. Mason, D.L. Nolte, and D.L. Campbell. 1993. Effects of predator odors on feeding in the mountain beaver (*Aplodontia rufa*). Journal of Mammalogy 74:715–722.

Epstein, M.B., G.A. Feldhamer, and R.L. Joyner. 1983. Predation on white-tailed deer fawns by bobcats, foxes, and alligators: predator assessment. Proceedings of the annual conference of the Southeast Association of Fish and Wildlife Agencies 37:161–172.

Erickson, A.W. 1955. An ecological study of the bobcat in Michigan. Thesis, Michigan State University, East Lansing, Michigan, USA.

Erickson, D.W. 1981. Furbearing harvest mechanics: An examination of variables influencing fur harvests in Missouri. Pages 1469–1491 *in* J.A. Chapman and D. Pursley, editors. Proceedings of the Worldwide Furbearer Conference, Frostburg, Maryland, USA.

———. 1982. Estimating and using furbearer harvest information. Pages 53–65 *in* G.C. Sanderson, editor. Midwest furbearer management. Proceedings of the Symposium of the 43rd Midwest Fish and Wildlife Conference, Wichita, Kansas, USA.

———, and F.W. Sampson. 1978. Impact of market dynamics on Missouri's furbearer harvest system. Proceedings of the annual conference of the Southeast Association of Fish and Wildlife Agencies 32:17–29.

Errington, P.L. 1967. Of predation and life. Iowa State University, Ames, Iowa, USA.

Estes, R.D. 1972. The role of the vomeronasal organ in mammalian reproduction. Mammalia 36:315–341.

Ewer, R.F. 1973. The carnivores. Cornell University Press, Ithaca, New York, New York, USA.

Fascione, N., H. Ridgley, and M. Selden. 2000. Proceedings of the Defenders of Wildlife's Carnivores 2000: A conference on carnivore conservation in the 21st century, Denver, Colorado. Defenders of Wildlife, Washington, D.C., USA.

Fazio, J.R., and D.L. Gilbert. 1986. Public relations and communications for natural resource managers. Second edition. Kendal/Hunt, Dubuque, Iowa, USA.

Fedriani, J.M., T.K Fuller, R.M Sauvajoet, and E.C. York. 2000. Competition and intraguild predation among three sympatric carnivores. Oecologia 125:258–270.

Feldhamer, G.A., B.C. Thompson, and J.A. Chapman, editors. 2003. Wild mammals of North America: biology, management, and conservation. The Johns Hopkins University Press, Baltimore, Maryland, USA.

Fendley, T.T., and D.E. Buie. 1986. Seasonal home range and movement patterns of the bobcats on the Savannah River Plant. Pages 237–259 *in* S.D. Miller and D.D. Everett, editors. Cats of the world: biology, conservation, and management. National Wildlife Federation, Washington, D.C., USA.

Filion, F.L. 1980. Human surveys in wildlife management. Pages 441–453 *in* S.D. Schemnitz, editor. Wildlife management techniques manual. Fourth edition. The Wildlife Society, Washington, D.C., USA.

Fischer, C.V. 1998. Habitat use by free-ranging felids in an agroecosystem (*Lynx rufus*, *Leopardus pardalis*), in Texas. Thesis, Texas A&M University, Kingsville, Texas, USA. (Abstract)

Foote, L.E. 1945. Sex ratio and weights of Vermont bobcats in autumn and winter. Journal of Wildlife Management 9:326–327.

Foran, D.R., S.C. Minta, and K.S. Heinemeyer. 1977. DNA-based analysis of hair to identify species and individuals for population research and monitoring. Wildlife Society Bulletin 25:840–847.

Fox, J.S. 1983. Relationship of diseases and parasites to the distribution and abundance of bobcats in New York. Dissertation, State University of New York College of Environmental Science and Forestry, Syracuse, New York, USA. (Abstract)

Fox, L.B. 1990. Ecology and population biology of the bobcat, *Felis rufus* in New York. Dissertation. State University of New York, College of Environmental Science and Forestry, Syracuse, New York, USA. (Abstract)

Franti, C.E., G.E. Connolly, H.P. Riemann, D.E. Behymer, R. Ruppanner, C.M. Willadsen, and W. Longhurst. 1975. A survey for *Toxoplasma gondii* antibodies in deer and other wildlife on a sheep range. Journal of the American Veterinary Medical Association 167:565–568.

Fredrickson, L.F., and L.A. Rice. 1979. Bobcat management survey study in South Dakota, 1977–1979. Pages 32–36 *in* L. Blum and P.C. Escherich, editors. Proceedings of the1979 bobcat research conference: current research on biology and management of *Lynx rufus*. Scientific and Technical Series 6. National Wildlife Federation, Washington, D.C., USA.

Friedrich, P.D., G.E. Burgoyne, T.M. Cooley, S.M. Schmitt. 1984. Use of lower canine teeth in determining the sex of bobcats in Michigan. Page 15 *in* J.A. Litvaitis and J.A. Bissonette, editors. Eastern bobcat workshop. Maine Cooperative Research Unit, Orono, Maine, USA.

Frisbie, C.J. 1987. Navajo medicine bundles or jish: acquisition, transmission, and disposition in the past and present. University of New Mexico Press, Albuquerque, New Mexico, USA.

Frisina, M.R., and K.L. Alt. 1992. Identification of Montana's furbearing mammals. Montana Outdoors, Montana Department of Fish, Wildlife and Parks.

Fritts, S.H., and J.A. Sealander. 1978a. Reproductive biology and population characteristics of bobcats (*Lynx rufus*) in Arkansas. Journal of Mammalogy 59:347–353.

———. 1978b. Diets of bobcats in Arkansas with special reference to age and sex differences. Journal of Wildlife Management 42:533–539.

Frost, G.C., J.T. Flinders, and S.R. Woodard. 1992. RAPD DNA analysis and population biology of a Utah bobcat population. Utah Bobcat Recruitment and Prey Base Analysis, Pittman-Robertson Federal Aid Program, Project Number W-140-

R, U.S. Fish and Wildlife Service, Utah Division of Wildlife Resources, Brigham Young University, U.S. Forest Service and Bureau of Land Management.

Fuller, T.K., W.E. Berg, and D.W. Kuehn. 1985a. Bobcat home range size and daytime cover-type use in northcentral Minnesota. Journal of Mammalogy 66:568–571.

———, ———, and ———. 1985b. Survival rates and mortality factors of adult bobcats in north-central Minnesota. Journal of Wildlife Management 49:292–296.

———, K.D. Kerr, and P.D. Karns. 1985c. Hematology and serum chemistry of bobcats in northcentral Minnesota. Journal of Wildlife Diseases 21:29–32.

———, S.L. Berendzen, T.A. Decker, and J.E. Cardoza. 1995. Survival and cause-specific mortality rates of adult bobcats (*Lynx rufus*). The American Midland Naturalist, 134:404–408.

Funderburk, S. 1986. International trade in U.S. and Canadian bobcats, 1977–1981. Pages 489–501 *in* S.D. Miller and D.D. Everett, editors. Cats of the world: biology, conservation, and management. National Wildlife Federation, Washington, D.C, USA.

Fur Information Council of America. 2005. Frequently Asked Questions. Available at http://www.fur.org/poen_faqs.cfm. Accessed 05 March 2006.

Gaona, P., P. Ferreras, and M. Delibes.1998. Dynamics and viability of a meta-population of the endangered Iberian lynx (*Lynx pardinus*). Ecological Monograph 68:349–370.

Garcia-Perea, R. 1996. Patterns of postnatal development in skulls of lynxes, genus *Lynx* (Mammalia: Carnvora). Journal of Morphology 229:241–254.

Garner, G.W., and J.A. Morrison. 1980. Observations of interspecific behavior between predators and white-tailed deer in southwestern Oklahoma. Journal of Mammalogy 61:126–130.

Gashwiler, J.S., W.L. Robinette, and O.W. Morris. 1960. Foods of bobcats in Utah and eastern Nevada. Journal of Wildlife Management 24:226–229.

———, ———, and ———. 1961. Breeding habits of bobcats in Utah. Journal of Mammalogy 42:76–84.

Gates, W.H. 1937. Spotted skunks and bobcats. Journal of Mammalogy 18:240.

Genest, F.B., P. Morisset, and R.P. Patenaude. 1987. Chromosomes du Lynx roux, *Lynx rufus*. Canadian Journal of Zoology 65:3192–3196.

Gentile, J.R. 1987. The evolution of antitrapping sentiment in the United States: a review and commentary. Wildlife Society Bulletin 15:490–503.

Gerstell, R. 1985. The steel trap in North America. Stackpole Books, Harrisburg, Pennsylvania, USA.

Giddings, B.J., G.L. Risdahl, and L.R. Irby. 1991. Bobcat habitat use in southeastern Montana (USA) during periods of high and low lagomorph abundance. Prairie Naturalist 22:249–258. (Abstract)

Gilbert, F.F. and D.G. Dodds. 1987. The philosophy and practice of wildlife management. Robert E. Krieger Publishing Company, Malabar, Florida, USA.

Gilbert, J.H. 2000. Impacts of reestablished fishers on bobcat populations in Wisconsin. Dissertation, University of Wisconsin, Madison, Wisconsin, USA. (Abstract)

———, and L.B. Keith. 2001. Impacts of reintroduced fishers on Wisconsin's bobcat populations. Pages 18–31 *in* A. Woolf, C.K. Nielsen, and R.D. Bluett, editors. 2001. Proceedings of a symposium on current bobcat research and implications for management. The Wildlife Society 2000 Conference, Nashville, Tennessee, USA.

Gilbert, J.R. 1979. Techniques and problems of population modeling and analysis of age distribution. Pages 130–133 *in* L. Blum and P.C. Escherich, editors. Proceedings of the 1979 bobcat research conference: current research on biology and management of *Lynx rufus*. Scientific and Technical Series 6. National Wildlife Federation, Washington, D.C., USA.

Giles, R.H., Jr. 1978. Wildlife management. W.H. Freeman and Company, San Francisco, California, USA.

Gill, R.B. 1985. Wildlife research: an endangered species. Wildlife Society Bulletin, 13:580–587.

Gittleman, J.L., editor. 1989. Carnivore behavior, ecology, and evolution. Cornell University Press, Ithaca, New York, USA.

Glenn, B.L., A.A. Kocan, and E.F. Blouin. 1983. Cytauxzoonosis in bobcats. Journal of the American Veterinary Medical Association 183:1155–1158.

———, R.E. Rolley, and A.A. Kocan. 1982. Cytauxzoon-like piroplasms in erythrocytes of wild-trapped bobcats in Oklahoma. Journal of the American Veterinary Medical Association 181:1251–1253.

Golden, H.N. 1999. An expert-system model for lynx management in Alaska. Pages 205–231 *in* G. Proulx, editor. Mammal trapping. Alpha Wildlife Research & Management Ltd., Sherwood Park, Alberta, Canada.

Golley, F.B., G.A. Petrides, E.L. Rauber, and J.H. Jenkins. 1965. Food intake and assimilation by bobcats under laboratory conditions. Journal of Wildlife Management 29:442–447.

Goodwin, G.G. 1963. A new subspecies of bobcat (*Lynx rufus*) from Oaxaca, Mexico. American Museum Novitates 2139:1–7.

Gould, G.I., Jr. 1977a. Estimated hunter take of bobcats in California during 1976. California Department of Fish and Game Report on Federal Aid for Wildlife Restoration Project W-54-R, Job IV-1.0.

———. 1977b. The status of the bobcat in northeastern California. California Department of Fish and Game Report on Federal Aid for Wildlife Restoration Project W-54-R.

———. 1978. Bobcat study and survey. California Department of Fish and Game Report on Federal Aid for Wildlife Restoration Project W-54-R-10, Job IV-1.6.

———. 1979. Techniques used in assessing bobcat populations and harvests in California. Pages 40–41 *in* L. Blum and P.C. Escherich, editors. Proceedings of the 1979 bobcat research conference: current research on biology and management of *Lynx rufus*. Scientific and Technical Series 6. National Wildlife Federation, Washington, D.C., USA.

———. 1980a. Bobcat study, San Diego County, California. California Department of Fish and Game Report on Federal Aid for Wildlife Restoration Project E-W-3, Job IV-1.7.

———. 1980b. Bobcat study and survey. California Department of Fish and Game Report on Federal Aid for Wildlife Restoration Project W-54-R-11, Job IV-1.6.

———. 1981a. Age and sex structure of bobcats in California. California Department of Fish and Game Report on Federal Aid for Wildlife Restoration Project W-54-R-12, Job IV-7.

———. 1981b. Information requested by the Office of Scientific Authority, U.S. Fish and Wildlife Service for approval of the international export of bobcats from

California during the 1980–1981 season. California Department of Fish and Game Report on Federal Aid for Wildlife Restoration Project W-54-R-12, Jobs IV-6 and IV-7.

———. 1982. Information requested by the Office of Scientific Authority, U.S. Fish and Wildlife Service for approval of the international export of bobcats from California during the 1982–1983 season. California Department of Fish and Game Report on Federal Aid for Wildlife Restoration Project W-54-R-14, Jobs IV-6 and IV-7.

———. 1990. Bobcat harvest assessment. 1988–1989. California Department of Fish and Game, Technical Report 1990-1, Nongame Bird and Mammal Section Report.

Grenfell, W.E., Jr. 1992. Bobcat harvest assessment, 1990–1991. California Department of Fish and Game, Nongame Bird and Mammal Section Report 1990–1991.

Griffith, M.A., D.E. Buie, T.T. Fendley, and D.A. Shipes. 1981. Preliminary observations of subadult bobcat movement behavior. Proceedings of the annual conference of the Southeastern Association of Fish and Wildlife Agencies 34:563–571.

———, and T.T. Fendley. 1986a. Influence of density on the movement behavior and home range size of adult bobcats on the Savannah River plant. Pages 261–275 *in* S.D. Miller and D.D. Everett, editors. Cats of the world: biology, conservation, and management. National Wildlife Federation, Washington, D.C.

———, and ———. 1986b. Pre and post dispersal movement behavior of subadult bobcats on the Savannah River Plant. Pages 277–289 *in* S.D. Miller and D.D. Everett, editors. Cats of the world: biology, conservation, and management. National Wildlife Federation, Washington, D.C.

Gruell, G.E., and N.J. Papez. 1963. Movements of mule deer in northeastern Nevada. Journal of Wildlife Management 27:414–422.

Guenther, D.D. 1980. Home range, social organization, and movement patterns of the bobcat, *Lynx rufus*, from spring to fall in south-central Florida. Thesis, University of South Florida, Tampa, Florida, USA.

Guggisberg, C.A.W. 1975. Wild cats of the world. Taplinger Publishing Co., New York, New York, USA.

Guthery, F.S., and S.L. Beasom. 1978. Effectiveness and selectivity of neck snares in predator control. Journal of Wildlife Management 42:457–459.

Guthrie, W.J. 1990. Selected zoonoses of wild mammals in Terrell County, Texas. Thesis, Sul Ross State University, Alpine, Texas, USA. (Abstract)

Hair, J.D., D. Hazel, R.A. Lancia, S.D. Miller, and D.K. Woodward. 1979. Progress report: status, population dynamics, and habitat preference of the bobcat in North Carolina. Page 125 *in* L. Blum and P.C. Escherich, editors. Proceedings of the 1979 bobcat research conference: current research on biology and management of *Lynx rufus*. Scientific and Technical Series 6. National Wildlife Federation, Washington, D.C., USA.

Hall, E.R. 1981. The mammals of North America. Second edition, 2 volumes. John Wiley and Sons, New York, New York, USA.

———, and J.D. Newsom. 1978. Summer home ranges and movement patterns of the bobcat in bottomland hardwoods of southern Louisiana. Proceedings of the annual conference of the Southeastern Association of Fish and Wildlife Agencies. 30:427–436.

Hamilton, D.A. 1982. Ecology of the bobcat in Missouri. Thesis, University of Missouri, Columbia, Missouri, USA.

————, G. Linscombe, N.R. Jotham, H. Noseworthy, and J.L. Stone. 1998. The European Union's wild fur regulation: a battle of politics, cultures, animal rights, international trade and North America's wildlife policy. Transactions of the North American Wildlife and Natural Resources Conference 63:572–588.

Hamilton, W.J., and R.P. Hunter. 1939. Fall and winter food habits of Vermont bobcats. Journal of Wildlife Management 3:99–103.

Hansen, K. 1992. Cougar: the American lion. Northland Publishing, Flagstaff, Arizona, USA.

Hanson, W.R. 1956. Aggressive behavior of mule deer toward bobcat. Journal of Mammalogy 37:458.

Harris, L.D., and P.B. Gallagher. 1989. New initiatives for wildlife conservation: the need for movement corridors. Pages 11–34 *in* Gay Mackintosh, editor. Preserving communities and corridors. Defenders of Wildlife, Washington, D.C., USA.

Harrison, R.L. 1998. Bobcats in residential areas: distribution and homeowner attitudes. The Southwestern Naturalist 43:469–475.

Harveson, P.M. 1996. Using GIS to analyze habitat selection by ocelot and bobcat populations in southern Texas (*Felis pardalis*, *Felis rufus*). Thesis, Texas A&M University, Kingsville, Texas, USA. (Abstract)

Hass, C.C. 1989. Bighorn lamb mortality: predation, inbreeding, and population effects. Canadian Journal of Zoology 67:699–705.

————. 2001. Southern Arizona mammal tracks. (Set of five cards used for field identification of mammal tracks)

Hatcher, R.T., and J.H. Shaw. 1981. A comparison of three indices to furbearer populations. Wildlife Society Bulletin 9:153–156.

Hatler, D.F., K.G. Poole, and A.M. Beale. 2003. British Columbia furbearer management guidelines: Bobcat (*Lynx rufus*). Available at http://www.env.gov.bc.ca/fw/documents/bobcat.pdf. Accessed 05 March 2006.

Heilbrun, R.D., D.M. Lunning, V.R. Tuovila, and J.A. Shivik. 2003. Using automatically triggered cameras to individually identify bobcats. Wildlife Society Bulletin 31:748–755.

Heisey, D.M., and T.K. Fuller. 1985. Evaluation of survival and cause specific mortality rates using telemetry data. Journal of Wildlife Management 49:668–674.

Heller, S.P., and T.T. Fendley. 1986. Bobcat habitat on the Savannah River Plant, South Carolina. Pages 415–423 *in* S.D. Miller and D.D. Everett, editors. Cats of the world: biology, conservation, and management. National Wildlife Federation, Washington, D.C., USA.

Hemmer, H. 1976. Gestation period and postnatal development in felids. Pages 143–165 *in* R.L. Eaton, editor. The world's cats. Volume 3. Carnivore Research Institute, University of Washington, Seattle, Washington, USA.

————. 1979. Gestation period and postnatal development in felids. Carnivore 2:90–100.

Henderson, C.L. 1979. Bobcat (*Lynx rufus*) distribution, management, and harvest in Minnesota, 1977–1979. Pages 27–31 *in* L. Blum and P.C. Escherich, editors. Proceedings of the 1979 bobcat research conference: current research on biology and management of *Lynx rufus*. Scientific and Technical Series 6. National Wildlife Federation, Washington, D.C., USA.

Henke, S.E., and F.C. Bryant. 1999. Effects of coyote removal on the faunal community in western Texas. Journal of Wildlife Management 63:1066–1081.

Hill, J.O., E.J. Pavlik, G.L. Smith, III, G.M. Burghardt, and P.B. Coulson. 1976. Species characteristic response to catnip by undomesticated felids. Journal of Chemical Ecology 2:239–253.

Hill, W.W. 1938. The agricultural and hunting methods of the Navaho Indians. Yale University Publications in Anthropology, New Haven, Connecticut, USA. Pages 168–170.

Hilton, H. 1979. Bobcat management in Maine. Pages 107–110 *in* L. Blum and P.C. Escherich, editors. Proceedings of the 1979 bobcat research conference: current research on biology and management of *Lynx rufus*. Scientific and Technical Series 6. National Wildlife Federation, Washington, D.C., USA.

———, and N.P. Kutscha. 1978. Distinguishing characteristics of the hairs of eastern coyote, domestic dog, red fox and bobcat in Maine. The American Midland Naturalist, 100:223–227.

Hiltz, M., and L.D. Roy. 2001. Use of anaesthetized animals to test humaneness of killing traps. Wildlife Society Bulletin 29:606–611.

Holt, S.J., and L.M. Talbot. 1978. New principles for the conservation of wild living resources. Wildlife Monographs 59.

Hon, T. 1979. Relative abundance of bobcats in Georgia: survey techniques and preliminary results. Pages 104–106 *in* L. Blum and P.C. Escherich, editors. Proceedings of the 1979 bobcat research conference: current research on biology and management of *Lynx rufus*. Scientific and Technical Series 6. National Wildlife Federation, Washington, D.C., USA.

Honacki, J.H., K.E. Kinman, and J.W. Koeppl., editors. 1982. Mammal species of the world: a taxonomic and geographic reference. Allen Press, Inc., and Association of Systematics Collections, Lawrence, Kansas, USA.

Hoppe, R.T. 1979. Population dynamics of the Michigan bobcat (*Lynx rufus*) with reference to age structure and reproduction. Pages 111–115 *in* L. Blum and P.C. Escherich, editors. Proceedings of the 1979 bobcat research conference: current research on biology and management of *Lynx rufus*. Scientific and Technical Series 6. National Wildlife Federation, Washington, D.C., USA.

Horne, J.S. 1998. Habitat partitioning of sympatric ocelot and bobcat in southern Texas (*Leopardus pardalis*, *Lynx rufus*). Thesis, Texas A&M University, Kingsville, Texas, USA. (Abstract)

Hornocker, M., and T. Bailey. 1986. Natural regulation in three species of felids. Pages 211–220 *in* S.D. Miller and D.D. Everett, editors. Cats of the world: biology, conservation, and management. National Wildlife Federation, Washington, D.C.

Houston, D.C. 1988. Digestive efficiency and hunting behaviour in cats, dogs and vultures. Journal of Zoology (London) 216:603–605.

[HSUS] Humane Society of the United States. 2005a. The HSUS Files Comments to Protect Endangered Mexican Bobcat. Available at http://www.hsus.org/press_and_publications/press_releases/the_hsus_files_comments_to_protect_endangered_mexican_bobcat.html. Accessed 05 March 2006.

———. 2005b. Lethal predator control courtesy of Wildlife Services. Available at http://www.hsus.org/wildlife/issues_facing_wildlife/lethal_predator_control_courtesy_of_wildlife_services/. Accessed 05 March 2006.

Hubel, D.H. 1959. Single unit activity in striate cortex of unrestrained cats. Journal of Physiology 147:226–238.

Hughes, A. 1976. A supplement to the cat schematic eye. Vision Research 16:149–154.

Hummel, M. 1990. A conservation strategy for large carnivores in Canada. World
  Wildlife Fund, Toronto, Canada.
————, and S. Pettigrew. 1991. Wild hunters: predators in peril. Key Porter Books,
  Toronto, Ontario, Canada.
Huxoll, C. 2002. South Dakota game report no. 2003-11. 2002 annual report, county
  wildlife assessments with a summary of the 1991–2002 assessments. Planning
  Section/Wildlife Administration, Wildlife Division, South Dakota Department of
  Game, Fish and Parks, Pierre, South Dakota, USA.
[IAFWA] International Association of Fish and Wildlife Agencies. 1997. Improving
  animal welfare in U.S. trapping programs: process recommendations and
  summaries of existing data. IAFWA Fur Resources Technical Subcommittee and
  Trapping Work Group, Washington, D.C., USA.
International Society for Endangered Cats Canada. 2001. Canadian cats: provincial
  status. Available at http://www.wildcatconservation.org/cats/canadian.shtml.
  Accessed 05 March 2006.
Iowa Department of Natural Resources Wildlife. 2003. Bobcats Make a Comeback—
  Iowa DNR Lists Bobcats as Protected. Available at http://www.iowadnr.com/
  wildlife/files/bobcat.html. Accessed 05 March 2006.
[IUCN/SSC] The World Conservation Union/Species Survival Commission. 2006. Cat
  Specialist Group, Project 104: distribution and status of the bobcat and puma in
  the Mexican Sierras. Available at http://lynx.uio.no/lynx/catsportal/cats-project-
  database/20_cat-projectdb/home/index_en.htm. Accessed 10 May 2006.
————. 2004. The IUCN Red List of Threatened Species: *Lynx lynx*. Available at http://
  www.iucnredlist.org/search/details.php?species=12519. Accessed 05 March 2006.
Jackson, D.H. 1986. Ecology of bobcats in east-central Colorado (*Lynx rufus, Felis rufus*).
  Dissertation, Colorado State University, Fort Collins, Colorado, USA. (Abstract)
————, L.S. Jackson, and W.K. Seitz.1985. An expandable drop-off transmitter harness
  for young bobcats. Journal of Wildlife Management 49:46–49.
Jackson, D.L., E.A. Gluesing, and H.A. Jacobson. 1988. Dental eruption in bobcats.
  Journal of Wildlife Management 52:515–517.
James, W.E. 1992. Bobcat movements and habitat use on Cumberland Island, Georgia
  during two years of controlled population increases. Thesis, University of
  Georgia, Athens, Georgia, USA.
Janczewski, D.N. 1993. Phylogenetic relationships of the great cats based on mitochon-
  drial DNA sequence analysis. Dissertation, University of Maryland, College Park,
  Maryland, USA. (Abstract)
Jenkins, J.H., E.E. Provost, T.T. Fendley, J.R. Monroe, I.L. Brisbin, Jr., and M.S.
  Lenarz. 1979. Techniques and problems with a consecutive twenty-five year
  furbearer trapline census. Pages 1–7 *in* L. Blum and P.C. Escherich, editors.
  Proceedings of the 1979 bobcat research conference: current research on biology
  and management of *Lynx rufus*. Scientific and Technical Series 6. National
  Wildlife Federation, Washington, D.C., USA.
Johnson, C. 1977. Southwest mammals: Navajo beliefs and legends. San Juan School
  District Media Center, Blanding, Utah. Page 26.
Johnson, M.K., and D.R. Aldred. 1982. Mammalian prey digestibility by bobcats.
  Journal of Wildlife Management 46:530.
————, D.R. Aldred, E.W. Clinite, and M.J. Kutilek. 1979. Biochemical identification

of bobcat scats. Pages 92–96 *in* L. Blum and P.C. Escherich, editors. Proceedings of the 1979 bobcat research conference: current research on biology and management of *Lynx rufus*. Scientific and Technical Series 6. National Wildlife Federation, Washington, D.C., USA.

———, R.C. Belden, and D.R. Aldred. 1984. Differentiating mountain lion *Felis concolor* and bobcat *Felis rufus* scats. Journal of Wildlife Management 48:239–244.

Johnson, N.F. 1979. Efforts to understand Kansas' bobcat populations. Pages 37–39 *in* L. Blum and P.C. Escherich, editors. Proceedings of the 1979 bobcat research conference: current research on biology and management of *Lynx rufus*. Scientific and Technical Series 6. National Wildlife Federation, Washington, D.C., USA.

———, B.A. Brown, and J.C. Bosomworth. 1981. Age and sex characteristics of bobcat canines and their use in population assessment. Wildlife Society Bulletin 9:203–206.

———, and D.J. Halloran. 1985. Reproductive activity of Kansas bobcats. Journal of Wildlife Management 49:42–46.

Johnson, R.E., C.B. Male, S.B. Linhart, and R.M. Engeman. 1986. Electronic measurement of closure speed for steel foothold traps. Wildlife Society Bulletin 14:223–225.

Jones, J.H., and N.S. Smith. 1979. Bobcat density and prey selection in central Arizona. Journal of Wildlife Management 43:666–672.

Jones, J.K., Jr, D.C. Carter, and H.H. Genoways. 1975. Revised checklist of North American mammals north of Mexico. Occasional Papers, the Museum, Texas Tech University 28: 1–14.

Jones, M.L. 1982. Longevity of captive mammals. Zoologische Garten 52:113–128.

Jorgensen, S.E., and L.D. Mech, editors.1971. Proceedings of a symposium on the native cats of North America: their status and management. U.S. Bureau of Sport Fisheries and Wildlife, Region 3, Twin Cities, Minnesota, USA.

Kamler, J.F., P.S. Gipson, and T.R. Snyder. 2000. Dispersal characteristics of young bobcats from northeastern Kansas. The Southwestern Naturalist 13:543–546.

Karpowitz, J.F., and J.T. Flinders. 1979. Bobcat research in Utah—a progress report. Pages 70–73 *in* L. Blum and P.C. Escherich, editors. Proceedings of the 1979 bobcat research conference: current research on biology and management of *Lynx rufus*. Scientific and Technical Series 6. National Wildlife Federation, Washington, D.C., USA.

Kaufman, J.H. 1962. Ecology and social behavior of the coati, *Nasua narica,* on Barro Colorado Island, Panama. University of California Publications in Zoology 60:95–222.

Kautz, M., B. Devan, and B. Sharick. 2001. Utility of bobcat observation reports for documenting presence of bobcats. Pages 56–60 *in* A. Woolf, C.K. Nielsen, and R.D. Bluett, editors. 2001. Proceedings of a symposium on current bobcat research and implications for management. The Wildlife Society 2000 Conference, Nashville, Tennessee, USA.

Keeping Track. 2005. Keeping Track Wildlife Conservation Education Tracking. Available at http://www.keepingtrack.org. Accessed 05 March 2006.

Kellert, S.R. 1980. Contemporary values of wildlife in American society. Pages 31–60 *in* W.W. Shaw and E.H. Zube, editors. Wildlife values. U.S. Forest Service, Fort Collins, Colorado, USA.

———. 1985. Social and perceptual factors in endangered species management. Journal of Wildlife Management 49:528–536.

———, and C.P. Smith. 2001. Human values toward large mammals. Pages 30–63, *in* S. Demarias and P. Krausman, editors. Ecology and management of large mammals in North America. Prentice-Hall, Upper Saddle River, New Jersey, USA.

Kelson, K.R. 1946. Notes on the comparative osteology of the bobcat and house cat. Journal of Mammalogy 27:255–264.

Kenward, R. 1987. Wildlife radio tagging: equipment, field techniques and data analysis. Academic Press, London, England.

Kerby, G. 1984. The 28 species of small cats. Pages 52–53 *in* D. MacDonald, editor. The Encyclopedia of Mammals. Facts on File Publications, New York, New York, USA.

Kier, A.B., J.E. Wagner, and L.G. Morehouse. 1982a. Experimental transmission of *Cytauxzoon felis* from bobcats (*Lynx rufus*) to domestic cats (*Felis domesticus*). American Journal of Veterinary Research 43:97–101.

———, S.R. Wightman, and J.E. Wagner. 1982b. Interspecies transmission of *Cytauxzoon felis.* American Journal of Veterinary Research 43:101–105.

Kight, J. 1962. An ecological study of the bobcat *Lynx rufus* (Schreber), in west-central South Carolina. Thesis, University of Georgia, Athens, Georgia, USA.

Kiltie, R.A. 1991. How cats work. Pages 54–67 *in* J. Seidensticker and S. Lumpkin, editors. Great cats: majestic creatures of the wild. Rodale Press, Emmaus, Pennsylvania, USA.

Kinley, T.A. 1992. Ecology and management of bobcats (*Lynx rufus*) in the East Kootenay District of British Columbia. Thesis, University of Calgary, Calgary, Alberta, Canada.

Kitchener, A. 1991. The natural history of the wild cats. Cornell University Press, Ithaca, New York, USA.

Kitchings, J.T., and J.D. Story. 1979. Home range and diet of bobcats in eastern Tennessee. Pages 47–52 *in* L. Blum and P.C. Escherich, editors. Proceedings of the 1979 bobcat research conference: current research on biology and management of *Lynx rufus.* Scientific and Technical Series 6. National Wildlife Federation, Washington, D.C., USA.

———, and ———. 1984. Movement and dispersal of bobcats in east Tennessee. Journal of Wildlife Management 48:957–961.

Kleiman, D.G., and J.F. Eisenberg. 1973. Comparison of canid and felid social systems from an evolutionary perspective. Animal Behavior 21:637–659.

Klepinger, K.E., W.A. Creed, and J.E. Ashbrenner. 1979. Monitoring bobcat harvest and population in Wisconsin. Pages 23–26 *in* L. Blum and P.C. Escherich, editors. Proceedings of the 1979 bobcat research conference: current research on biology and management of *Lynx rufus.* Scientific and Technical Series 6. National Wildlife Federation, Washington, D.C., USA.

Kluckhohn, C., W.W, Hill, and L.W. Kluckholn. 1971. Navaho material culture. Belknap Press of Harvard University, Cambridge, Massachusetts, USA.

Knick, S.T. 1987. Ecology of bobcats in southeastern Idaho. Dissertation, University of Montana, Missoula, Montana, USA. (Abstract)

———. 1990. Ecology of bobcats relative to exploitation and a prey decline in southeastern Idaho. Wildlife Monographs 108:1–42.

———, and T.N. Bailey. 1986. Long distance movements by two bobcats from southeastern Idaho. The American Midland Naturalist 116:222–223.

————, J.D. Brittell, and S.J. Sweeney. 1985. Population characteristics of bobcats in Washington State. Journal of Wildlife Management 49:721–728.

————, E.C. Hellgren, and U.S. Seal. 1993. Hematologic, biochemical, and endocrine characteristics of bobcats during a prey decline in southeastern Idaho. Canadian Journal of Zoology 71:1448–1453. (Abstract)

————, S.J. Sweeney, J.R. Alldredge, and J.D. Brittell. 1984. Autumn and winter food habits of bobcats in Washington state. Great Basin Naturalist 44:70–74.

Knowles, P.R. 1985. Home range size and habitat selection of bobcats, *Lynx rufus*, in north-central Montana. The Canadian Field-Naturalist 99:6–12.

Knowlton, F.F., and W.M. Tzilkowski. 1979. Trends in bobcat visitations to scent-station lines in western United States, 1972–1978. Pages 8–12 *in* L. Blum and P.C. Escherich, editors. Proceedings of the 1979 bobcat research conference: current research on biology and management of *Lynx rufus*. Scientific and Technical Series 6. National Wildlife Federation, Washington, D.C., USA.

Kocan, A.A., E.F. Blouin, and B.L. Glenn. 1985. Hematologic and serum chemical values for free-ranging bobcats, *Felis rufus* (Schreber), with reference to animals with natural infections of *Cytauxzoon felis* Kier, 1979. Journal of Wildlife Diseases 21:190–192.

Koehler, G.M. 1987. The bobcat. Pages 399–409 *in* Audubon Wildlife Report 1987. National Audubon Society, New York, New York, USA.

————. 1988a. Bobcat bill of fare. Natural History 97:48–57.

————. 1988b. Demography of a low productivity bobcat population (Idaho). Dissertation, University of Idaho, Moscow, Idaho, USA. (Abstract)

————, and K.B. Aubry. 1994. Lynx. Pages 74–98 *in* L.F. Ruggiero, K.B. Aubry, S.W. Buskirk, L.J. Lyons and W.J. Zielinski, editors. The scientific basis for conserving forest carnivores: American martin, fisher lynx, and wolverine in the Western United States. General Technical Report RM-254, U.S. Forest Service.

————, and M.G. Hornocker. 1989. Influences of seasons on bobcats in Idaho. Journal of Wildlife Management 53:197–202.

————, and ————. 1991. Seasonal resource use among mountain lions, bobcats, and coyotes. Journal of Mammalogy 72:391–396.

Kolowski, J.M., and A Woolf. 2002. Microhabitat use by bobcats in southern Illinois. Journal of Wildlife Management 66:822–832.

Krebs, J.W., M. Smith, C.E. Rupprecht, and J.E. Childs. 1999. Rabies among non-reservoir, carnivorous mammals in the United States, 1960–1997. American Journal of Tropical Medicine and Hygiene 61:172–173.

Kruuk, H. 1972. Surplus killing in carnivores. Journal of Zoology 166:233–244.

Kurten, B. 1965. The Pleistocene Felidae of Florida. Bulletin of the Florida State Museum 9:215–273.

Labelle, P., M. Igor, D. Martineau, S. Beaudin, N. Blanchette, R. Lafond, and S. St-Onge. 2000. Seroprevalence of leptospirosis in lynx and bobcats from Quebec. Canadian Veterinary Journal 41:319.

Labisky, R.F. 1998. Behaviors of bobcats preying on white-tailed deer in the Everglades. The American Midland Naturalist 139:275–281.

Lancia, R.A., D.K. Woodward, and S.D. Miller. 1986. Summer movement patterns and habitat use by bobcats on Croatan National Forest, North Carolina. Pages 425–436 *in* S.D. Miller and D.D. Everett, editors. Cats of the world: biology, conservation, and management. National Wildlife Federation, Washington, D.C.

Lariviere, S., and L.R. Walton. 1997. *Lynx rufus*. Mammalian Species No. 563. American Society of Mammalogists. Pages 1–8.

Lawhead, D.N. 1984. Bobcat *Lynx rufus* home range, density and habitat preferences in south-central Arizona. Southwestern Naturalist 29:105–113.

Laycock, G. 1979. You'll never see a bobcat. Audubon 81(July):56–63.

Leach, H.R., and W.H. Frazier. 1953. A study on the possible extent or predation on heavy concentrations of valley quail with special references to the bobcat. California Fish and Game 39:527–538.

Lembeck, M. 1978. Bobcat study, San Diego County, California. California Department of Fish and Game Report on Federal Aid for Wildlife Restoration Project E-W-2, Study IV-1–7.

———. 1986. Long term behavior and population dynamics of an unharvested bobcat population in San Diego County. Pages 305–310 *in* S.D. Miller and D.D. Everett, editors. Cats of the world: biology, conservation, and management. National Wildlife Federation, Washington, D.C., USA.

———, and G.I. Gould, Jr. 1979. Dynamics of harvested and unharvested bobcat populations in California. Pages 53–54 *in* L. Blum and P.C. Escherich, editors. Proceedings of the 1979 bobcat research conference: current research on biology and management of *Lynx rufus*. Scientific and Technical Series 6. National Wildlife Federation, Washington, D.C., USA.

Leone, C.A., and A.L. Wiens. 1956. Comparative serology of carnivores. Journal of Mammalogy 37:11–23.

Leopold, A. 1933. Game management. Charles Scribner's Sons, New York, New York, USA.

Leopold, A.S. 1959. Wildlife of Mexico: the game birds and mammals. University of California Press, Berkeley, California, USA.

Leopold, B.D., and P.R. Krausman. 1986. Diets of 3 predators in Big Bend National Park, Texas. Journal of Wildlife Management 50:290–295.

Leyhausen, P. 1979. Cat behavior: the predatory and social behavior of domestic and wild cats. Garland STPM Press, New York, New York, USA.

Linscombe, R.G. 1988. Efficiency of padded foothold traps for capturing terrestrial furbearers. Wildlife Society Bulletin 16:307–309.

Litvaitis, J.A. 1984. Bobcat movements in relation to prey density. Dissertation, University of Maine, Orono, Maine, USA. (Abstract)

———. 1993. Response of early successional vertebrates to historic changes in land use. Conservation Biology 7:866–873.

———, and J.A. Bissonette, editors. 1984. Eastern bobcat workshop. Maine Cooperative Wildlife Research Unit, University of Maine, Orono, Maine, USA. (Abstract)

———, A.G. Clark, and J.H. Hunt. 1986a. Prey selection and fat deposits of bobcats (*Felis rufus*) during autumn and winter in Maine. Journal of Mammalogy 67:389–392.

———, and D.J. Harrison. 1989. Bobcat-coyote niche relationships during a period of coyote population increase. Canadian Journal of Zoology 67:1180–1188.

———, J.T. Major, and J.A. Sherburne. 1986b. A status report: bobcat movements in relation to snowshoe hare density. Page 375 *in* S.D. Miller and D.D. Everett, editors. Cats of the world: biology, conservation, and management. National Wildlife Federation, Washington, D.C. (Abstract)

———, ———, and ———. 1987. Influence of season and human-induced mortality on spatial organization of bobcats (*Felis rufus*) in Maine. Journal of Mammalogy 68:100–106.

———, J.A. Sherburne, and J.A. Bissonette. 1986c. Bobcat habitat use and home range size in relation to prey density. Journal of Wildlife Management 50:110–117.

———, ———, M. O'Donoghue, and D. May. 1982. Cannibalism by a free-ranging bobcat, *Lynx rufus*. Canadian Field-Naturalist 96:476–477.

———, C.L. Stevens, and W.W. Mautz. 1984. Age, sex, and weight of bobcats in relation to winter diet. Journal of Wildlife Management 48:632–635.

Logan, K.A., and L.L. Sweanor. 2001. Desert puma: evolutionary ecology and conservation of an enduring carnivore. Island Press, Washington, D.C., USA.

Lopez-Gonzalez, C.A., A. Gonzalez-Romero, and J.W. Laundre. 1998. Range extension of the bobcat (*Lynx rufus*) in Jalisco, Mexico. The Southwestern Naturalist 43:103–105.

Lovallo, M.J. 1999. Multivariate models of bobcat habitat selection for Pennsylvania landscapes (*Lynx rufus*). Dissertation, Pennsylvania State University, University Park, Pennsylvania, USA. (Abstract)

———. 2001. Status and management of bobcats in Pennsylvania. Pages 74–79 *in* A. Woolf, C.K. Nielsen, and R.D. Bluett, editors. 2001. Proceedings of a symposium on current bobcat research and implications for management. The Wildlife Society 2000 Conference, Nashville, Tennessee, USA.

Lovallo, M.J., and E.M. Anderson. 1995. Range shift by a female bobcat (*Lynx rufus*) after removal of neighboring female. The American Midland Naturalist 134:409–412.

———, and ———. 1996a. Bobcat (*Lynx rufus*) home range size and habitat use in northwest Wisconsin. The American Midland Naturalist 135:241–252.

———, and ———. 1996b. Bobcat movements and home ranges relative to roads in Wisconsin. Wildlife Society Bulletin 24:71–76.

———, J.H. Gilbert, and T.M. Gehring. 1993. Bobcat (*Felis rufus*) dens in an abandoned beaver (*Castor canadensis*) lodge. Canadian Field-Naturalist 107:108–109. (Abstract)

———, G.L. Storm, D.S. Klute, and W.M. Tzilkowski. 2001. Multivariate models of bobcats habitat suitability in Pennsylvania. Pages 4–17 *in* A. Woolf, C.K. Nielsen, and R.D. Bluett, editors. 2001. Proceedings of a symposium on current bobcat research and implications for management. The Wildlife Society 2000 Conference, Nashville, Tennessee, USA.

Lovell, C.D. 1996. Bobcat, coyote, and gray fox micro-habitat use and interspecies relationships in a managed forest in central Mississippi. Thesis, Mississippi State University, Mississippi State, Mississippi, USA. (Abstract)

———, B.D. Leopold, and C. C. Shropshire. 1998. Trends in Mississippi predator populations, 1980–1995. Wildlife Society Bulletin 26:552–556.

Lyren, L.M. 2001. Movement patterns of coyotes and bobcats relative to roads and underpasses in the Chino Hills area of southern California. Thesis, California State Polytechnic University, Pomona, California, USA.

MacDonald, D., editor. 1984. The encyclopedia of mammals. Facts on File Publications, New York, New York, USA.

Maehr, D.S. 1997. Comparative ecology of the bobcat, black bear and Florida panther in south Florida. Bulletin of the Florida Museum of National History 40:1–177

————, and J.R. Brady. 1986. Food habits of bobcats in Florida. Journal of Mammalogy 67:133– 138.

————, E.D. Land, D.B. Shindle, O.L. Bass, and T.S. Hoctor. 2002. Florida panther dispersal and conservation. Biological Conservation 106:187–197.

————, M.A. Orlando, and J.J. Cox. 2005. Pages 293–314 *in* J.C. Ray, K.H. Redford, R.S. Steneck, and J. Berger, editors. Large carnivores and the conservation of biodiversity. Island Press, Washington, DC, USA.

Mahan, C.J. 1979. Age determination of bobcats (*Lynx rufus*) by means of canine pulp cavity ratios. Pages 126–129 *in* L. Blum and P.C. Escherich, editors. Proceedings of the 1979 bobcat research conference: current research on biology and management of *Lynx rufus*. Scientific and Technical Series 6. National Wildlife Federation, Washington, D.C., USA.

Major, J.T. 1983. Ecology and interspecific relationships of coyotes, bobcats, and red foxes in western Maine (radiotelemetry). Dissertation, University of Maine, Orono, Maine, USA. (Abstract)

————, and J.A. Sherburne. 1987. Interspecific relationships of coyotes, bobcats, and red foxes in western Maine. Journal of Wildlife Management 51:606–616.

————, ————, J.A. Litvaitis, and D.J. Harrison. 1986. Resource use and interspecific relationships between bobcats and other large mammalian predators in Maine. Page 291 *in* S.D. Miller and D.D. Everett, editors. Cats of the world: biology, conservation, and management. National Wildlife Federation, Washington, D.C., USA. (Abstract)

Major, M., M. K. Johnson, W.S. Davis, and T.F. Kellogg. 1980. Identifying scats by recovery of bile acids. Journal of Wildlife Management 44:290–293.

Makar, P.W. 1980. Bobcat and coyote food habits and habitat use in Rocky Mountain National Park. Thesis, Colorado State University, Fort Collins, Colorado, USA.

Manfredo, M.J., C.L. Pierce, D. Fulton, J. Pate, and B.R. Gill. 1999. Public acceptance of wildlife trapping in Colorado. Wildlife Society Bulletin 27:499–508.

Mangrum, J.W. 1994. Evaluation of four attractants as indices of relative abundance of wildlife with emphasis on bobcats (*Felis rufus*). Thesis, Mississippi State University, Mississippi State, Mississippi, USA. (Abstract)

Marchiondo, A.A., D.W. Duszynski, and G.O. Maupin. 1976. Prevalence of antibodies to *Toxoplasma gondii* in wild and domestic animals of New Mexico, Arizona, and Colorado. Journal of Wildlife Diseases 12:226–232.

Marshall, A.D., and J.H. Jenkins. 1966. Movements and home ranges of bobcats as determined by radio-tracking in the upper coastal plain of west-central South Carolina. Proceedings of the Annual Conference of the Southeast Game and Fish Commission 20:206–214.

Marston, M.A. 1942. Winter relations of bobcats to white-tailed deer in Maine. Journal of Wildlife Management 6:328–337.

Martin, C. 1978. Keepers of the game: Indian–animal relationships and the fur trade. University of California Press, Berkeley, California, USA.

Maser, C., and D.E. Toweill. 1984. Bacula of mountain lion, *Felis concolor*, and Bobcat, *F. rufus*. Journal of Mammalogy 65:496–497.

Matlack, C.R., and A.J. Evans. 1992. Diet and condition of bobcats, *Lynx rufus*, in Nova Scotia during autumn and winter. Canadian Journal of Zoology 70:1114–1119.

Matson, J.O. 1977. Records of mammals from Zacatecas, Mexico. Journal of Mammalogy 58:110.

Matson, J.R. 1948. Cat kills deer. Journal of Mammalogy 29:69–70.

Matson, G., and J. Matson. 1993. Progress Report no.13. Matson's Laboratory, Milltown, Montana, USA.

Matthews, O.P. 1986. Who owns wildlife? Wildlife Society Bulletin 14:459–465.

Matthiessen, P. 1987. Wildlife in America. Viking Penguin, New York, New York, USA.

Mattina, M.J.I., J.J. Pignatello, and R.K. Swihart. 1991. Identification of volatile components of bobcat (*Lynx rufus*) urine. Journal of Chemical Ecology 17:451–462. (Abstract)

Mautz, W.W., and P.J. Pekins. 1989. Metabolic rate of bobcats as influenced by seasonal temperatures. Journal of Wildlife Management 53:202–205.

McCord, C.M. 1974a. Selection of winter habitat by bobcats (*Lynx rufus*) on the Quabbin Reservation, Massachusetts. Journal of Mammalogy 55:428–437.

———. 1974b. Courtship behavior in free-ranging bobcats. Pages 76–87 *in* R.L. Eaton, editor. The world's cats. Volume 2. World Wildlife Safari, Winston, Oregon, USA.

———, and J.E. Cardoza. 1982. Bobcat and lynx. Pages 728–766 *in* J.A. Chapman and G.A. Feldhammer, editors. Wild mammals of North America. The Johns Hopkins University Press, Baltimore, Maryland, USA.

McDaniel, G.W., K.S. McKelvey, J.R. Squires, and L.F. Ruggiero. 2000. Efficacy of lures and hair snares to detect lynx. Wildlife Society Bulletin 28:119–123.

McGee, Jr., H.F. 1987. The use of furbearers by native North Americans after 1500. Pages 13–20 *in* M. Novak, J.A. Baker, M.E. Obbard, and B. Malloch, editors. Wild furbearer management and conservation in North America. Ontario Ministry of Natural Resources, Toronto, Ontario, Canada.

McKinney, T.D., and M.R. Dunbar. 1976. Weight of adrenal glands in the bobcat (*Lynx rufus*). Journal of Mammalogy 57:378–380.

McLaughlin, G.S., M. Obstbaum, D.J. Forrester, M.E. Roelke, and J.R. Brady. 1993. Hookworms of bobcats (*Felis rufus*) from Florida. Journal of the Helminthological Society of Washington 60:10–13. (Abstract)

McLean, D.D. 1934. Predatory animal studies. California Fish and Game 20:30–36.

McMahan, L.R. 1986. The international cat trade. Pages 461–487 *in* S.D. Miller and D.D. Everett, editors. Cats of the world: biology, conservation, and management. National Wildlife Federation, Washington, D.C., USA.

Mehrer, C.F. 1975. Some aspects in reproduction in captive mountain lions (*Felis concolor*), bobcats (*Lynx rufus*), and lynx (*Lynx canadensis*). Dissertation, University of North Dakota, Grand Forks, North Dakota, USA.

Meine, C. 1988. Aldo Leopold: his life and work. The University of Wisconsin Press, Madison, Wisconsin, USA.

Mellen, J. 1991. Cat behavior. Pages 68–75 *in* J. Seidensticker and S. Lumpkin, editors. Great cats: majestic creatures of the wild. Rodale Press, Emmaus, Pennsylvania, USA.

Middleton, H. 1986. The forest's shadow. Southern Living 21(March):56–59.

Midgley, M. 1990. Why smartness is not enough. Pages 39–52 *in* M.E. Clark and S.A. Wawrytko, editors. Rethinking the curriculum: toward an integrated, interdisciplinary college education. Contributions to the Study of Education, Number 40. Greenwood Press, Westport, Connecticutt, USA.

Miller, D.L. 1995. Feasibility of embryo transfer using the bobcat (*Felis rufus*). Dissertation, Mississippi State University, Mississippi State, Mississippi, USA. (Abstract)

Miller, N.L., J.K. Frenkel, and J.P. Dubey. 1972. Oral infections with Toxoplasma cysts and oocusts in felines, other mammals, and in birds. Journal of Parasitology 58:928–937.

Miller, S.D. 1980. The ecology of the bobcat in south Alabama. Dissertation, Auburn University, Auburn, Alabama, USA. (Abstract)

———. 1991. Bobcats and lynxes. Pages 148–155 *in* J. Seidensticker and S. Lumpkin, editors. Great cats: majestic creatures of the wild. Rodale Press, Emmaus, Pennsylvania, USA.

———, and D.D. Everett, editors. 1986. Cats of the world: biology, conservation, and management. National Wildlife Federation, Washington, D.C., USA.

———, and D.W. Speake. 1979. Progress report: demography and home range of the bobcat in south Alabama. Pages 123–124 *in* L. Blum and P.C. Escherich, editors. Proceedings of the 1979 bobcat research conference: current research on biology and management of *Lynx rufus*. Scientific and Technical Series 6. National Wildlife Federation, Washington, D.C., USA.

Mills, J.K. 1984. Food habits of bobcats, *Lynx rufus*, in Nova Scotia. The Canadian Field Naturalist 98:50–51.

Minnis, D.L. 1998. Wildlife policy-making by the electorate: an overview of citizen-sponsored ballot measures on hunting and trapping. Wildlife Society Bulletin 26:75–83.

Mitchell, R.L., and S.L. Beasom. 1974. Hookworms in south Texas coyotes and bobcats. Journal of Wildlife Management 38:455–458.

Montana Fish, Wildlife and Parks. 2003. State furbearer program newsletter. Available at http://fwp.mt.gov/hunting/trapping/default.html. Accessed 10 May 2006.

Morse, S.C. 1992. Wildlife habitat inventory, East Jericho, Vermont. Morse & Morse Forestry and Wildlife Consultants, Jericho, Vermont, USA.

———. 1994. Good forestry is good for wildlife. Morse & Morse Forestry and Wildlife Consultants, Jericho, Vermont, USA.

———. 1995. Lewis Creek wildlife habitat study, phase II. Morse & Morse Forestry and Wildlife Consultants, Jericho, Vermont, USA.

Moses, S. 1983. On the track of the cat. Sports Illustrated 58(January):94–108.

Murphy, K.M., T. Potter, J. Halfpenney, K. Gunther, T. Jones, and P. Lundberg. 2004. The presence and distribution of Canada lynx (*Lynx canadensis*) in Yellowstone National Park, Wyoming: final report. Yellowstone National Park, Wyoming, USA. (Unpublished)

Murray, C.A., W.D. Webster, and K.W. Markham. 1992. Seasonal variation in the diet of bobcats in eastern North Carolina. Journal of the Elisha Mitchell Scientific Society 108:25–28. (Abstract)

Myers, N. 1971. The spotted cats and the fur trade. Pages 276–326 *in* R.L. Eaton, editor. The world's cats. Volume 1. Lion Country Safari, Laguna Hills, California, USA.

Nash, R.F. 1989. The rights of nature: a history of environmental ethics. The University of Wisconsin Press, Madison, Wisconsin, USA.

[NASS] National Agricultural Statistics Service. 2000. U.S. Cattle and Calves Predator Loss, 2000. Available at http://usda.mannlib.cornell.edu/reports/nassr/livestock/pct-bbpl/ctpro501.txt. Accessed 05 March 2006.

————. 2004. Sheep and Goats Death Loss, 2004. Available at http://usda.mannlib .cornell.edu/reports/nassr/livestock/pgg-bbsg/predan05.txt. Accessed 05 March 2006.

National Park Service. 2005. National Park Service visitation report, January-December 2004. Available at http://www2.nature.nps.gov/NPstats/dspSystem.cfm. Accessed 10 May 2006.

[NWRC] National Wildlife Research Center. 2004. U.S. Department of Agriculture, Animal and Plant Health Inspection Service, Wildlife Services, National Wildlife Research Center. Available at http://aphis.usda.gov/ws/nwrc/. Accessed 05 March 2006.

Neale, J.C.C. 1996. Comparative resource use by sympatric bobcats and coyotes: food habits, habitat use, activity and spatial relationships. Thesis, University of California at Berkeley, Berkeley, California, USA.

————, B.N. Sacks, M.M. Jaeger, and D. McCullough. 1998. A comparison of bobcat and coyote predation on lambs in north-central California. Journal of Wildlife Management 62:700–706.

Nebel, B.J., and R.T. Wright. 1996. Environmental science: the way the world works. Fifth edition. Simon & Schuster, Upper Saddle River, New Jersey, USA.

Neff, N.A. 1991. The cats and how they came to be. Pages 14–23 *in* J. Seidensticker and S. Lumpkin, editors. Great cats: majestic creatures of the wild. Rodale Press. Emmaus. Pennsylvania, USA.

Nelms, N.G., L.A. Hansen, R.J. Warren, J.J. Brooks, and D.R. Diefenbach. 2001. Deer herd trends, bobcat food habits, and vegetation change over 18 years on Cumberland Island, Georgia, before and after bobcat reintroduction. Page 80 *in* A. Woolf, C.K. Nielsen, and R.D. Bluett, editors. 2001. Proceedings of a symposium on current bobcat research and implications for management. The Wildlife Society 2000 Conference, Nashville, Tennessee, USA. (Abstract)

Newell, D. 1985. Treedogs. Field & Stream 90(July):77.

Newhouse, S. 1893. The trapper's guide for capturing fearbearing animals and curing their skins. Oneida Community, Kenwood, New York, USA.

Newmark, W.D. 1986. Species-area relationship and its determinants for mammals in western North America national parks. Biological Journal of the Linnean Society 28:83–98.

Nielsen, C.K., and A. Woolf. 2001a. Bobcat habitat use relative to human dwellings in southern Illinois. Pages 40–44 *in* A. Woolf, C.K. Nielsen, and R.D. Bluett, editors. 2001. Proceedings of a symposium on current bobcat research and implications for management. The Wildlife Society 2000 Conference, Nashville, Tennessee, USA.

————, and ————. 2001b. Spatial organization of bobcats (*Lynx rufus*) in southern Illinois. American Midland Naturalist 146:43–52.

————, and ————. 2002a. Habitat-relative abundance relationship for bobcats in southern Illinois. Wildlife Society Bulletin 30:222–230.

————, and ————. 2002b. Survival of unexploited bobcats in southern Illinois. Journal of Wildlife Management 66:833–838.

North American Fur Auctions. 2005. Wild fur sales results: May 2005. Available at http://nafa.ca/auction/results/MAY-05-WF-US.pdf. Accessed 05 March 2006.

North Dakota Game and Fish Department. 2004. 2003–2004 bobcat harvest season

summarized 062304. Available at http://www.state.nd.us/gnf/news/2004/0406
.html. Accessed 05 March 2006.

Novak, M. 1987. Traps and trap research. Pages 941–969 *in* M. Novak, J.A. Baker,
M.E. Obbard, and B. Malloch, editors. Wild furbearer management and conserva-
tion in North America. Ontario Ministry of Natural Resources, Toronto, Ontario,
Canada.

———, J.A. Baker, M.E. Obbard, and B. Malloch, editors. 1987. Wild furbearer
management and conservation in North America. Ontario Ministry of Natural
Resources, Toronto, Ontario, Canada.

Nowak, R.M. 1991. Walker's mammals of the world. Volumes 1 and 2. Fifth edition.
Johns Hopkins University Press, Baltimore, Maryland, USA.

Nowak, R.N., and J.L. Paradiso. 1983. Walker's mammals of the world. 4th edition,
Volume II. The Johns Hopkins University Press, Baltimore, Maryland, USA.

Nowell, K. and P. Jackson, editors. 1996. Wild cats: status survey and action plan.
World Conservation Union (IUCN): Gland, Switzerland. Pages 140–144.

Nunley, G.L. 1978. Present and historical bobcat population trends in New Mexico and
the west. Proceedings of the Vertebrate Pest Conference 8:77–84.

Obbard, M.E. 1987. Fur grading and pelt identification. Pages 717–826 *in* M. Novak,
J.A. Baker, M.E. Obbard, and B. Malloch, editors. Wild furbearer management
and conservation in North America. Ontario Ministry of Natural Resources,
Toronto, Ontario, Canada.

———, J.G. Jones, R. Newman, A. Booth, A.J. Satterthwaite, and G. Linscombe. 1987.
Furbearer harvests in North America. Pages 1007–1034 *in* M. Novak, J.A. Baker,
M.E. Obbard, and B. Malloch, editors. Wild furbearer management and conserva-
tion in North America. Ontario Ministry of Natural Resources, Toronto, Ontario,
Canada.

O'Brien, S.J. 1991. Molecular evolution of cats. Page 18 *in* J. Seidensticker and S.
Lumpkin, editors. Great cats: majestic creatures of the wild. Rodale Press.
Emmaus, Pennsylvania, USA.

Ohio Department of Natural Resources. 2005. Wildlife Biologists Verify 14 Bobcat
Sightings in Ohio during 2004. Available at http://www.dnr.ohio.gov/news/feb05/
0215bobcats.htm. Accessed 05 March 2006.

Olson, J. 1995. Bobcats and the Wisconsin Supreme Court. Page 83 *in* C. Brown, editor.
Proceedings of the 1995 joint fur resources workshop. West Virginia Division of
Natural Resources, Charleston, West Virginia, USA.

Ommundsen, P.D. 1991. The morphological differences between lynx and bobcat
skulls. Northwest Science 65:248–250. (Abstract)

Orihel, T.C., and A.L. Ash. 1964. Occurrence of *Dirofilaria striata* in the bobcat (*Lynx
rufus*) in Louisiana with observations of its larval development. Journal of
Parasitology 50:590–591.

Parker, G.R., J.W. Maxwell, L.D. Morton, and G.E.J. Smith. 1983. The ecology of the
lynx (*Lynx canadensis*) on Cape Breton Island. Canadian Journal of Zoology
61:770–786.

———, and G.E.J. Smith. 1983. Sex- and age-specific reproductive and physical
parameters of the bobcat (*Lynx rufus*) on Cape Breton Island, Nova Scotia.
Canadian Journal of Zoology 61:1771–1782.

Pavlik, S. 2000. Na'azheel: "the ones who hunt"—the role of small carnivores in

Navajo culture. Paper presented at the Defenders of Wildlife Conference, Denver, Colorado, November 14, 2000.

Pecon-Slattery, J., and S.J. O'Brien. 1998. Patterns of Y and X chromosome DNA sequence divergence during the Felidae radiation. Genetics 148:1245–1255.

Peek, J.M. 1986. A review of wildlife management. Prentice-Hall, New York, New York, USA.

Pelton, M.R. 1979. Potential use of radioisotopes for determining densities of bobcats. Pages 97–100 *in* L. Blum and P.C. Escherich, editors. Proceedings of the 1979 bobcat research conference: current research on biology and management of *Lynx rufus.* Scientific and Technical Series 6. National Wildlife Federation, Washington, D.C., USA.

Pence, D.B., and S. Eason. 1980. Comparison of the helminth faunas of two sympatric top carnivores from the rolling plains of Texas. Journal of Parasitology 66:115–120.

———, F.D. Matthews, III, and L.A. Windberg. 1982. Notoedric mange in the bobcat, *Felis rufus,* from south Texas. Journal of Wildlife Diseases 18:47–50.

———, H.P. Samoil, and J.E. Stone. 1978. Spirocercid stomach worms (Nematoda: Spirocercidae) from wild felids in North America. Canadian Journal of Zoology 56:1032–1042.

———, and J.E. Stone. 1977. Lungworms (Nematoma: Pneumospiruridae) from west Texas carnivores. Journal of Parasitology 63:979–991.

Peters, G. 1991. Vocal communication in cats. Pages 76–77 *in* J. Seidensticker and S. Lumpkin, editors. Great cats: majestic creatures of the wild. Rodale Press, Emmaus, Pennsylvania, USA.

Petraborg, W.H., and V.E. Gunvalson. 1962. Observations on bobcat mortality and bobcat predation on deer. Journal of Mammalogy 43:430–431.

Pfeiffer, E.W. 1956a. Bobcat as a laboratory animal for courses in zoology. Journal of Mammalogy 37:548–549.

———. 1956b. Electrocardiogram of the bobcat. Journal of Mammalogy 37:549.

Plowman, B.W. 1997. Bobcat interactions and core area dynamics in central Mississippi. Thesis, Mississippi State University, Mississippi State, USA. (Abstract).

Poland, J.D., A.M. Barnes, and J.J. Herman. 1973. Human bubonic plague from exposure to a naturally infected wild carnivore. American Journal of Epidemiology 97:332–337.

Pollack, E.M. 1950. Breeding habits of the bobcat in northeastern United States. Journal of Mammalogy 31:327–330.

———. 1951a. Food habits of the bobcat in the New England states. Journal of Wildlife Management 15:209–213.

———. 1951b. Observations on New England bobcats. Journal of Mammalogy 32:356–358.

Povey, R.C., and E.W. Davis. 1977. Panleucopenia and respiratory virus infection in wild felids. Pages 120–128 *in* R.L. Eaton, editor. The world's cats. Volume 3. Carnivore Research Institute, University of Washington, Seattle, Washington, USA.

Powers, J.G., W.W. Mautz, and P.J. Pekins. 1989. Nutrient and energy assimilation of prey by bobcats. Journal of Wildlife Management 53:1004–1008.

Predator Conservation Alliance. 2002. Wildlife "Services"? A presentation and analysis of the USDA Wildlife Services Program's expenditures and kill figures for fiscal year 2000. Available at http://www.predatorconservation.org/about_us/research/wildlifeservicesreport2002.html. Accessed 05 March 2006.

Progulske, D.R. 1955. Game animals utilized as food by the bobcat in the southern Appalachians. Journal of Wildlife Management 19:249–253.

Province of Manitoba. 2004. Manitoba Trapping Guide 2004/2005. Available at http://www.gov.mb.ca/conservation/wildlife/trapping/index.html. Accessed 05 March 2006.

Provost, E.E., C.A. Nelson, and A.D. Marshall. 1973. Population dynamics and behavior in the bobcat. Pages 42–67 *in* R.L. Eaton, editor. The world's cats. Volume 1. Lion Country Safari, Laguna Hills, California.

Quinn, N.W.S. 1987. Dynamics of an exploited Canada lynx population in Ontario. Journal of Wildlife Management 51:297–305.

———, and G. Parker. 1987. Lynx. Pages 682–694 *in* M. Novak, J.A. Baker, M.E. Obbard, and B. Malloch, editors. Wild furbearer management and conservation in North America. Ontario Ministry of Natural Resources, Toronto, Ontario, Canada.

Ragsdale, L.L. 1993. Den characteristics, activity patters, and habitat use of reintro-duced female bobcats on Cumberland Island, Georgia. Thesis, University of Georgia, Athens, Georgia, USA.

Ray, A.J. 1987. The fur trade in North America: an overview from a historical geo-graphical perspective. Pages 21–30 *in* M. Novak, J.A. Baker, M.E. Obbard, and B. Malloch, editors. Wild furbearer management and conservation in North America. Ontario Ministry of Natural Resources, Toronto, Ontario, Canada.

Read, J.A. 1981. Geographic variation in the bobcat (*Felis rufus*) in the south-central United States. Thesis, Texas A & M University, College Station, Texas, USA. (Abstract)

Regan, T.W., and D.S. Maehr. 1990. Melanistic bobcats in Florida. Florida Field Naturalist 18(4):84–87.

Revised Checklist of North American Mammals, publ. by Texas Technological University, Lubbock, 1975

Rezendes. P. 1999. Tracking and the art of seeing. HarperCollins Publishers, New York, New York, USA.

Riemann, H.P., J.A. Howarth, R. Ruppanner, C.E. Franti, and D.E. Behymer. 1975. Toxoplasma antibodies among bobcats and other carnivores of northern California. Journal of Wildlife Diseases 11:272–276.

———, R.A. Thompson, D.E. Behymer, R. Ruppanner, and C.E. Franti. 1978. Toxo-plasmosis and Q fever antibodies among wild carnivores in California. Journal of Wildlife Management 42:198–202.

Riley, S.P.D. 1999. Spatial organization, food habits and disease ecology of bobcats (*Lynx rufus*) and gray foxes (*Urocyon cinereoargenteus*) in national park areas in urban and rural Marin County, California (Golden Gate National Recreation Area). Dissertation, University of California, Davis, California, USA. (Abstract)

———. 2001. Spatial and resource overlap of bobcats and gray foxes in urban and rural zones of a national park. Pages 32–39 *in* A. Woolf, C.K. Nielsen, and R.D. Bluett, editors. 2001. Proceedings of a symposium on current bobcat research and implications for management. The Wildlife Society 2000 Conference, Nashville, Tennessee, USA.

———, R.M. Sauvajoet, T.K. Fuller, E.C. York, D.A. Kamradt, C. Bromley, and R.K. Wayne. 2003. Effects of urbanization and habitat fragmentation on bobcats and coyotes in southern California. Conservation Biology 17:566–576.

Roberts, R, 1990. "There is no turning back: instincts of deer herd lead them across roads, where they lose escape skills." Los Angeles Times, 31 October 1990.

Robinson, W.B. 1961. Population changes of carnivores in some coyote control areas. Journal of Mammalogy 42:510–515.

———, and E.F. Grand. 1958. Comparative movements of bobcats and coyotes as disclosed by tagging. Journal of Wildlife Management 22:117–122.

Rolf, D.J. 1989. The Endangered Species Act: a guide to its protections and implementation. Stanford Environmental Law Society, Stanford Law School, Stanford, California, USA.

Rolley. R.E. 1983. Behavior and population dynamics of bobcats in Oklahoma. Dissertation, Oklahoma State University, Stillwater, Oklahoma, USA. (Abstract)

———. 1985. Dynamics of a harvested bobcat population in Oklahoma. Journal of Wildlife Management 49:283–292.

———. 1987. Bobcat. Pages 671–681 *in* M. Novak, J.A. Baker, M.E. Obbard, and B. Malloch, editors. Wild furbearer management and conservation in North America. Ontario Ministry of Natural Resources, Toronto, Ontario, Canada.

———, B.E. Kohn, and J.F. Olson. 2001. Evolution of Wisconsin's bobcat harvest management program. Pages 61–66 *in* A. Woolf, C.K. Nielsen, and R.D. Bluett, editors. 2001. Proceedings of a symposium on current bobcat research and implications for management. The Wildlife Society 2000 Conference, Nashville, Tennessee, USA.

———, and W.D. Warde.1985. Bobcat habitat use in southeastern Oklahoma. Journal of Wildlife Management 49:913–920.

Rollings, C.T. 1945. Habits, foods and parasites of the bobcat in Minnesota. Journal of Wildlife Management 9:131–145.

Romesburg, H.C. 1981. Wildlife science: gaining reliable knowledge. Journal of Wildlife Management 45:293–313.

Rosenzweig, M.L. 1966. Community structure in sympatric Carnivora. Journal of Mammalogy 47:602–612.

Roughton, R.D., and M.W. Sweeney. 1982. Refinements in scent-station methodology for assessing trends in carnivore populations. Journal of Wildlife Management 46:217–229.

Rust, W.D. 1980. Scent-station transects as a means of indexing bobcat population fluctuations. Thesis, Tennessee Technological University, Cookville, Tennessee, USA.

Ryden, H. 1981a. Following the shadowy trail of the cat that walks by itself. Smithsonian (June):37–46.

———. 1981b. Bobcat year. Viking Press, New York, New York, USA.

Samson, F.B. 1979. Multivariate analysis of cranial characteristics among bobcats, with a preliminary discussion of the number of subspecies. Pages 80–86 *in* L. Blum and P.C. Escherich, editors. Proceedings of the 1979 bobcat research conference: current research on biology and management of *Lynx rufus*. Scientific and Technical Series 6. National Wildlife Federation, Washington, D.C., USA.

Sandell, M. 1989. The mating tactics and spacing patterns of solitary carnivores. Pages 164–182 *in* J.L. Gittleman, editor. 1989. Carnivore behavior, ecology, and evolution. Cornell University Press, Ithaca, New York, USA.

Sargeant, G.A., D.H. Johnson, and W.E. Berg. 1998. Interpreting carnivore scent-station surveys. Journal of Wildlife Management 62:1235–1245.

Schmidt, J.L., and D.L. Gilbert, editors. 1978. Big game of North America, ecology and management. Wildlife Management Institute, Stackpole Books, Harrisburg, Pennsylvania, USA.

Schnell, J.H. 1968. The limiting effects of natural predation on experimental cotton rat populations. Journal of Wildlife Management 32:698–711.

Schwartz, M.K., K.L. Pilgrim, K.S. McKelvey, E.L. Lindquist, J.J. Claar, S. Loch, and L.F. Ruggiero. 2004. Hybridization between Canada lynx and bobcats: genetic results and management implications. Conservation Genetics 5:349–355.

Scott, P.P. 1968. The special feature of nutrition in cats, with observation on wild Felidae nutrition in the London zoo. Symposia of the London Zoological Society 21:21–36.

———. 1976. Diet and other factors affecting the development of young felids. Pages 166–179 *in* R.L. Eaton, editor. The world's cats. Volume 3, No. 2. Carnivore Research Institute, University of Washington, Seattle, Washington, USA.

Seidensticker, J., and S. Lumpkin, editors. 1991. Great cats: majestic creatures of the wild. Rodale Press, Emmaus, Pennsylvania, USA.

Shaw, H.G. 1989. Soul among lions. Johnson Books, Boulder, Colorado, USA.

———. 1999. Sign. Pages 187–197 *in* S. Ewing and E. Grossman, editors. Shadowcat: encountering the American mountain lion. Sasquatch Books, Seattle, Washington, USA.

Shaw, J.H. 1985. Introduction to wildlife management. McGraw-Hill Book Company, New York, New York, USA.

Sikes, R.S., and M.L. Kennedy. 1992. Morphologic variation of the bobcat (*Felis rufus*) in the eastern United States and its association with selected environmental variables. American Midland Naturalist 128:313–324.

———, and ———. 1993. Geographic variation in sexual dimorphism of the bobcat (*Felis rufus*) in the eastern United States. Southwestern Naturalist 38:336–344. (Abstract)

Sky Island Alliance. 2005. Sky Island Alliance homepage, wildlife monitoring program, and what are the sky islands? Available at http://www.skyislandalliance.org. Accessed 05 March 2006.

Small, R.L. 1971. Interspecific competition among three species of Carnivora on the Spider Ranch, Yavapai County, Arizona. Thesis, University of Arizona, Tucson, Arizona, USA.

Smith, D.S. 1984. Habitat use, home range, and movements of bobcats in western Montana. Thesis, University of Montana, Missoula, Montana, USA.

Smith, K.E., J.R. Fischer, and J.P. Dubey. 1995. Toxoplasmosis in a bobcat (*Felis rufus*). Journal of Wildlife Diseases 31:555–557.

Snyder, D.E., A.N. Hamir, V.F. Nettles, and C.E. Rupprecht. 1991. Lesions associated with pulmonary parasites in bobcats (*Felis rufus*) from Arkansas. Journal of Wildlife Diseases 27:170–174.

Stock Market Crash. 2005. Black Monday: the stock market crash of 1987. Available at http://www.stock-market-crash.net/1987.htm. Accessed 05 March 2006.

Stone, J.E., and D.B. Pence. 1977. Ectoparasites of the bobcat from west Texas. The Journal of Parasitology 63:463.

Stys, E.D., and B.D. Leopold. 1993. Reproductive biology and kitten growth of captive bobcats in Mississippi. Proceeding of the Southeastern Association of Fish and Wildlife Agencies 47:80–89.

Sullivan, K.J. 1995. Diel activity and movement patterns of adult bobcats in central Mississippi (*Felis rufus*). Thesis, Mississippi State University, Mississippi State, Mississippi, USA. (Abstract)

Sunquist, F.C. 1987. The nature of cats. Pages 47–50 *in* Kingdom of cats. National Wildlife Federation, Washington, D.C., USA.

———. 1991. The living cats. Pages 28–53 *in* J. Seidensticker and S. Lumpkin, editors. Great cats: majestic creatures of the wild. Rodale Press, Emmaus, Pennsylvania, USA.

———, and M. Sunquist. 2000. New look at cats! International Wildlife (March/April):12–22.

Sunquist, M., and F.C. Sunquist. 2002. Wild cats of the world. University of Chicago Press, Chicago, Illinois, USA.

Swann, D.E., C.C. Hass, D.C. Dalton, and S.A. Wolf. 2004. Infrared-triggered cameras for detecting wildlife: an evaluation and review. Wildlife Society Bulletin 32:1–9.

Sweanor, L.L. 1990. Mountain lion social organization in a desert environment. Thesis, University of Idaho, Moscow, Idaho, USA.

Sweeney, S.J. 1978. Diet, reproduction, and population structure of the bobcat in western Washington. Thesis, University of Washington, Seattle, Washington, USA.

———, and R.J. Poelker.1977. Survey of the native cats of Washington: a contribution towards an annotated bibliography on the bobcat (*Lynx rufus*) and the Canada lynx (*Lynx canadensis*). Washington Game Department, Job Completion Report, W-84-R-4, Job 1.

Swihart, K.R., J.J. Pignatello, and M.J.I. Mattina. 1991. Aversive responses of white-tailed deer, *Odocoileus virginianus*, to predator urines. Journal of Chemical Ecology 17:767–778. (Abstract)

Tansley, K. 1965. Vision in vertebrates. Chapman & Hall, London, Great Britain.

Thornton, D.H., M.E. Sunquist, and M.B. Main. 2004. Ecological separation within sympatric populations of coyotes and bobcats in south-central Florida. Journal of Mammalogy 85:973–982.

Tiekotter, K.L. 1985. Helminth species diversity and biology in the bobcat, *Lynx rufus* (Scherber), from Nebraska. Journal of Parasitology 71:227–234.

Tigas, L.A., D.H. Van Vuren, and R.M. Sauvajoet. 2002. Behavioral responses of bobcats and coyotes to habitat fragmentation and corridors in an urban environment. Biological Conservation 108:299–306.

Tinker, B. 1986. Mexican wilderness and wildlife. University of Texas Press, Austin, Texas, USA.

Toweill, D.E. 1979. Bobcat populations: a review of available literature. Information Report Series, Wildlife No. 79-2. Oregon Department of Fish and Wildlife, Research and Development Section, Portland, Oregon, USA.

———. 1980. Sex and age structure in Oregon bobcat populations. Information Report Series, Wildlife No. 80-1. Oregon Department of Fish and Wildlife, Research and Development Section, Portland, Oregon, USA.

———. 1986. Resource partitioning by bobcats and coyotes in a coniferous forest. Dissertation, Oregon State University, Corvallis, Oregon, USA.

————, and R.G. Anthony.1984. Ecology of an exploited bobcat population in western Oregon, Job Nos. 3-6, Project no. W-80-R-1, Oregon Wildlife Research. Oregon Cooperative Wildlife Research Unit, Oregon Department of Fish and Wildlife, Portland, Oregon, USA.

Trevor, J.T., R.W. Seabloom, and S.H. Allen. 1989. Food habits in relation to sex and age of bobcats from southwestern North Dakota (USA). Prairie Naturalist 21:163–168. (Abstract)

Tumlison, R. 1987. *Felis lynx.* Mammalian species No. 269. American Society of Mammalogists. Pages 1–8.

————, and V.R. McDaniel. 1984a. Morphology, replacement mechanisms, and functional conservation in dental replacement patterns of the bobcat (*Felis rufus*). Journal of Mammalogy 65:111–117.

————, and ————. 1984b. A description of the baculum of the bobcat (*Felis rufus*), with comments on its development and taxonomic implications. Canadian Journal of Zoology 62:1172–1176.

Tuovila, V.R. 1999. Bobcat movements and survival near United States Highway 281 in southern Texas (*Lynx rufus*). Thesis, Texas A&M University, Kingsville, Texas, USA. (Abstract)

Turbak, G. 1985. A tale of two cats. International Wildlife 15(March/April):4–11.

————. 1987. Bobcat. Pages 46–51 *in* Kingdom of cats. National Wildlife Federation, Washington, D.C., USA.

————. 1994. Bounce-back bobcat. Wildlife Conservation 97(November/December):22–31.

————, and A. Carey. 1986. America's great cats. Northland Publishing, Flagstaff, Arizona, USA.

U.S. Census Bureau. 2005. Population clocks. Available at http://www.census.gov/. Accessed 05 March 2006.

[USDA] U.S. Department of Agriculture. 1997. Animal damage control program: final environmental impact statement (EIS). Volumes 1–3. Animal and Plant Health Inspection Service, U.S. Department of Agriculture, Washington, D.C., USA.

[USFWS] U.S. Fish and Wildlife Service. 1982. Proposal to remove the bobcat from appendix II of the Convention on International Trade in Endangered Species of Wild Fauna and Flora. Federal Register 47(6):1241–1246.

————. 2000. Determination of threatened status for the contiguous U.S. distinct population segment of the Canada lynx: final rule. Federal Register 65(58):16051–16086.

————. 2002. 2001 National survey of fishing, hunting, and wildlife-associated recreation: preliminary findings. U.S. Department of the Interior, Washington, D.C., USA.

————. 2003a. Scientists confirm hybridization of Canada lynx with bobcats in Minnesota. News release, June 03, 2003. Available at http://mountain-prairie .fws.gov/pressrel/archives.htm. Accessed 10 May 2006.

————. 2003b. DNA tests confirm hybridization of Canada lynx with bobcats in Maine. Media release, August 27, 2003. Available at http://northeast.fws.gov/ lynxhybr.html. Accessed 05 March 2006.

————. 2004a. CITES Thirteenth Conference of the Parties (COP13): Announcement of Species Proposals, Proposed Resolutions, Proposed Decisions, and Agenda Items Being Considered by the United States. II. Recommendations for Species

Proposals for the United States to Consider Submitting at COP13. B. Species proposals for which the United States is still undecided, pending additional information and consultations. Mammals. 8. Bobcat (*Lynx rufus*)—Proposal for removal from Appendix II. Available at http://international.fws.gov/cop%2013/Jan12%20Species%20Proposals.htm. Accessed 05 March 2006.

———. 2004b. The Endangered Species Act of 1973. Available at http://www.fws.gov/endangered/esa.html. Accessed 05 March 2006.

———. 2004c. U.S. bobcat exports. CITES annual field defect reports: wildlife description defect, 1978–2003. Office of Management Authority, Washington, D.C., USA.

———. 2005. 12-month petition finding and proposed rule to delist the Mexican bobcat (*Lynx rufus escuinipae*). Federal Register 70(96): 28895–28900.

U.S. General Accounting Office. 2001. Wildlife Services Program. Information on activities to manage wildlife damage. GAO-02-138. Washington, D.C., USA.

Utah Division of Wildlife Resources. 2003 (July 18). Cougar, prairie dogs and bobcats focus of upcoming public meetings. Available at http://www.wildlife.utah.gov/news/03-07/meetings.html. Accessed 05 March 2006.

Vandomelen, E.D. 1992. Nutrition, prey, assimilation, and bioenergetics of captive bobcats. Thesis, Mississippi State University, Mississippi State, Mississippi, USA. (Abstract)

Virchow, D., and D. Hogeland. 1994. Bobcats. Pages C-35–C-43 *in* S.E. Hygnstrom, S.M. Timm, and G.E. Larson, editors. Prevention and control of wildlife damage. Cooperative Extension Division, Institute of Agriculture and Natural Resources, University of Nebraska, Lincoln, Nebraska, USA.

Vogt, J.E. 1979. Michigan's bobcat harvest. Pages 17–22 *in* L. Blum and P.C. Escherich, editors. Proceedings of the 1979 bobcat research conference: current research on biology and management of *Lynx rufus*. Scientific and Technical Series 6. National Wildlife Federation, Washington, D.C., USA.

Warren, R.J., M.J. Conroy, W.E. James, L.A. Baker, and D.R. Diefenbach. 1990. Reintroduction of bobcats on Cumberland Island, Georgia: a biopolitical lesson. Pages 580–589 *in* Transactions of the 55th North American Wildlife and Natural Resources Conference, Denver, Colorado, USA. 16–21 March.

Wassmer, D.A., D.D. Guenther, and J.N. Layne. 1988. Ecology of the bobcat in south-central Florida. Bulletin of the Florida State Museum of Biological Sciences 33:159–228.

Watson, T.G., V.F. Nettles, and W.R. Davidson. 1981. Endoparasites and selected infectious agents in bobcats (*Felis rufus*) from West Virginia and Georgia. Journal of Wildlife Diseases 17:547–554.

Weaver, R.A., and J.L. Mensch. 1970. Observed interaction between desert bighorn sheep, *Ovis canadensis*, and reported predator species. California Fish and Game 56:206–207.

Wehinger, K.A., M.E. Roelke, and E.C. Greiner. 1995. Ixodid ticks from panthers and bobcats in Florida. Journal of Wildlife Diseases 31:480–485.

Werdelin, L. 1981. The evolution of lynxes. Annales Zoologici Fennici 18:37–71.

Whittle, R.K. 1979. Age in relation to winter food habits and helminth parasites of the bobcat (*Lynx rufus*, Schreber) in Oklahoma. Thesis, Oklahoma State University, Stillwater, Oklahoma, USA.

Wigginton, J.D., and F.S. Dobson. 1999. Environmental influences on geographic variation in body size of western bobcats. Canadian Journal of Zoology 77:802–813.

Wildlife Legislative Fund of America. 1999. Anti-trapping amendment dropped from Interior appropriations bill. WLFA Update 18(9):1.

Wildlife Services. 2005. U.S. Department of Agriculture, Animal and Plant Health Inspection Service, Wildlife Services. Available at http://www.aphis.usda.gov/ws/index.html. Accessed 05 March 2006.

Wildlife Services. 2006a. U.S. Department of Agriculture, Animal and Plant Health Inspection Service, Wildlife Services. Available at http://www. aphis.usda.gov/ws/tables/03.tables.html, Table 10T, Number of Animals Killed and Methods Used by the WS Program, FY2003. Accessed 10 May 2006.

Wildlife Services. 2006b. U.S. Department of Agriculture, Animal and Plant Health Inspection Service, Wildlife Services. Available at http://www.aphis.usda.gov/ws/tables/03.tables.html, Table 1, Wildlife Services FY2003, Federal and Cooperative Funding by Resource Category. Accessed 10 May 2006.

Wildlife Services. 2006c. U.S. Department of Agriculture, Animal and Plant Health Inspection Service, Wildlife Services. Available at http://www. aphis.usda.gov/ws/tables/03.tables.html, Table 3, Resource Losses Reported to the WS Program, FY2003. Accessed 10 May 2006.

Wildlife Services. 2006d. U.S. Department of Agriculture, Animal and Plant Health Inspection Service, Wildlife Services. Available at http://www.aphis.usda.gov/ws/introreportsindex.html, Wildlife Services Develops Nonlethal Methods (pdf). Accessed 10 May 2006.

Williams, B.K. 1997. Logic and science in wildlife biology. Journal of Wildlife Management 61:1007–1015.

Williams, R.D. 1990. Bobcat electrocutions on powerlines. California Fish and Game 76:187– 189.

Williams, T. 1984. The fur still flies. Audubon 86(January):28–32.

———. 1989. The bobcat. Country Journal 16(March/April):86–90.

Wilson, D.E., and D.M. Reeder, editors. 1993. Mammal species of the world: a taxonomic and geographic reference. Smithsonian Institution Press in association with the American Society of Mammalogists, Washington, D.C., USA.

Winegarner, C.E., and M.S. Winegarner. 1982. Reproductive history of a bobcat. Journal of Mammalogy 63:680–682.

Witmer, G.W., and D.S. DeCalesta. 1986. Resource use by unexploited sympatric bobcats and coyotes in Oregon. Canadian Journal of Zoology 64:2333–2338.

Witter, J.F. 1981. Brucellosis. Pages 280–287 *in* J.W. Davis, L.H. Karstad, and D.O. Trainer, editors. Infectious diseases of wild mammals. Second edition. Iowa State University Press, Ames, Iowa, USA.

Wolfe, M.L., and J.A. Chapman. 1987. Principles of furbearer management. Pages 101–112 *in* M. Novak, J.A. Baker, M.E. Obbard, and B. Malloch, editors. Wild furbearer conservation and management in North America. Ontario Ministry of Natural Resources, Toronto, Ontario, Canada.

Woolf, A. 1999. Status of the bobcat in Illinois: final report, Federal Aid Project W-126-R-4. Illinois Department of Natural Resources. Carbondale, Illinois, USA.

————, and G.F. Hubert, Jr. 1998. Status and management of bobcats in the United States over three decades: 1970s–1990s. Wildlife Society Bulletin 26:287–293.

————, and C.K. Nielsen. 2001. Bobcat research and management: have we met the challenge? Pages 1–3 *in* A. Woolf, C.K. Nielsen, and R.D. Bluett, editors. Proceedings of a symposium on current bobcat research and implications for management. The Wildlife Society 2000 Conference, Nashville, Tennessee, USA.

————, and ————. 2002. The bobcat in Illinois. Southern Illinois University, Carbondale, Illinois, USA.

————, ————, and R.D. Bluett, editors. 2001. Proceedings of a symposium on current bobcat research and implications for management. The Wildlife Society 2000 Conference, Nashville, Tennessee, USA.

————, ————, T. Weber, and T. J. Gibbs-Kieninger. 2002. Statewide modeling of bobcat, *Lynx rufus*, habitat in Illinois, USA. Biological Conservation 104:191–198.

Wozencraft, W.C. 1993. Order Carnivora. Pages 279–348 *in* D.E. Wilson and D.M. Reeder, editors. Mammal species of the world: a taxonomic and geographic reference. Smithsonian Institiution Press in association with the American Society of Mammalogists, Washington, D.C., USA and London, England.

Wright, J.V. 1987. Archaeological evidence for the use of furbearers in North America. Pages 3–12 *in* M. Novak, J.A. Baker, M.E. Obbard, and B. Malloch, editors. Wild furbearer management and conservation in North America. Ontario Ministry of Natural Resources, Toronto, Ontario, Canada.

Wyman, L.C., and F.L. Bailey. 1943. Navajo upward-reaching way: objective, rationale, and sanction. University of New Mexico Bulletin, Albuquerque, New Mexico, USA.

Young, S.P. 1978. The bobcat of North America. University of Nebraska Press. Lincoln, Nebraska, USA.

Zezulak, D.S. 1980a. Bobcat biology in a Mojave Desert community: report on Federal Aid for Wildlife Restoration Project W-54-R-12, Job IV-4. California Department of Fish and Game, Sacramento, California, USA.

————. 1980b. Northeastern California bobcat study: report on Federal Aid for Wildlife Restoration Project W-54-R-12, Job IV-3. California Department of Fish and Game, Sacramento, California, USA.

Zezulak, D.S. 1981. Northeastern California bobcat study (Federal Aid Wildlife Restoration Project W-54-R-R, Job IV-3) California Department of Fish and Game, Sacramento, California, USA.

————. 1998. Spatial, temporal, and population characteristics of two bobcat, *Lynx rufus* (Carnivora: Felidae), populations in California (ranging behavior, population distribution, sex ratio). Dissertation, University of California, Davis, California, USA. (Abstract)

————, and R.G. Schwab. 1979. A comparison of density, home range and utilization of bobcat populations on Lava Beds and Joshua Tree National Monuments, California. Pages 74–79 *in* L. Blum and P.C. Escherich, editors. Proceedings of the 1979 bobcat research conference: current research on biology and management of *Lynx rufus*. Scientific and Technical Series 6. National Wildlife Federation, Washington, D.C., USA.

Index